ALSO BY JEFFREY TOOBIN

Opening Arguments: A Young Lawyer's First Case—
  United States v. Oliver North
The Run of His Life: The People v. O. J. Simpson
A Vast Conspiracy: The Real Story of the Sex Scandal
  That Nearly Brought Down a President

TOO CLOSE TO CALL

TOO
CLOSE
TO CALL

*The Thirty-Six-Day Battle to
Decide the 2000 Election*

JEFFREY
TOOBIN

RANDOM HOUSE · NEW YORK

Grateful acknowledgment is made to Universal Music Publishing for permission to reprint excerpts from "Tight Rope," words and music by Leon Russell. Copyright © 1972 by Irving Music, Inc. (BMI). Reprinted by permission of Universal Music Publishing.

Library of Congress Cataloguing-in-Publication data is available.

ISBN 0-375-50708-6

Random House website address: www.atrandom.com

Printed in the United States of America on acid-free paper

98765432

FIRST EDITION

Book design by Carole Lowenstein

To Ellen,
future voter

"Our consideration is limited to the present circumstances, for the problem of equal protection in election processes generally presents many complexities."

—Unsigned majority opinion,
United States Supreme Court,
Bush v. Gore,
December 12, 2000

CONTENTS

CAST OF CHARACTERS   xiii

CHRONOLOGY: RECOUNT 2000   xvii

PROLOGUE   **FLORIDA SUNRISE**   3

ONE   **A BIG PROBLEM**   9

TWO   **THE FLIGHT OF *RECOUNT ONE***   26

THREE   **"PEOPLE GET SCREWED EVERY DAY"**   40

FOUR   **IN FOR A LANDING**   58

FIVE   **THE PALM BEACH STORY**   77

SIX   **SHALL VERSUS MAY**   94

SEVEN   **"THIS IS GUATEMALA"**   108

EIGHT   **COLD WINDS IN TALLAHASSEE**   123

NINE   **MAYOR LOCO, CRAZY JOE, AND THE BATTLE OF MIAMI**   139

TEN   **THANKSGIVING STUFFING**   160

ELEVEN   **RSTONE@GOAMERICA.NET**   177

TWELVE   **LOSE SLOW, LOSE FAST**   192

THIRTEEN   **GREAT AMERICANS**   206

FOURTEEN "FOURTH DOWN AND LONG"   224

FIFTEEN IRREPARABLE HARM   238

SIXTEEN "AL SHARPTON TACTICS"   254

EPILOGUE MOVING ON   271

SOURCE NOTES AND ACKNOWLEDGMENTS   283

INDEX   287

CAST OF CHARACTERS*

THE CANDIDATES

Republicans
Governor George W. Bush
Richard B. Cheney

Democrats
Vice President Albert Gore, Jr.
Senator Joseph I. Lieberman

THE CAMPAIGNS

For Bush
Donald L. Evans, campaign chairman
Joseph Allbaugh, campaign manager
Karl Rove, senior strategist
Karen P. Hughes, communications director

For Gore
William M. Daley, campaign chairman
Carter Eskew, Robert Shrum, media consultants
Tad Devine, strategist
Mark Fabiani, Chris Lehane, spokesmen

*Descriptions reflect actual duties rather than official titles.

Michael Whouley, chief field operative
Nicholas Baldick, Florida field operative
Donna Brazile, campaign manager
David Ginsberg, research director

THE STATE OF FLORIDA

Jeb Bush, governor
Frank Jimenez, acting chief counsel
Al Cardenas, chairman, Florida Republican Party

Robert A. Butterworth, attorney general

Katherine Harris, secretary of state
J. M. "Mac" Stipanovich, senior adviser
Joseph Klock, lead counsel
L. Clayton Roberts, director, Division of Elections
Benjamin McKay, chief of staff

THE BATTLE IN FLORIDA

For Bush

James A. Baker III, chief strategist
Robert Zoellick, Margaret Tutwiler, deputies to Baker
Benjamin Ginsberg, chief counsel
George Terwilliger, deputy chief counsel
Theodore B. Olson, federal appellate attorney
Barry Richard, lead local counsel
Michael Carvin, appellate attorney
Philip Beck, Irv Terrell, Fred Bartlit, counsel for contest case

For Gore

Warren Christopher, initial representative
Ronald Klain, chief strategist
David Boies, lead attorney
Laurence H. Tribe, federal appellate attorney
Jack Young, Chris Sautter, recount attorneys
Mitchell Berger, Dexter Douglass, John Newton, Joseph
    Sandler, Mark Steinberg, Robert Bauer, Stephen Zack,
    Jeremy Bash, attorneys

PALM BEACH COUNTY

Canvassing Board
  Charles E. Burton, county judge
  Carol Roberts, county commissioner
  Theresa LePore, supervisor of elections

Bob Montgomery, Bruce Rogow, counsel to LePore
Jack Corrigan, Benedict P. Kuehne, David Sullivan,
  Dennis Newman, attorneys for Gore
Mark Wallace, attorney for Bush

MIAMI-DADE COUNTY

Canvassing Board
  Lawrence D. King, county judge
  Myriam Lehr, county judge
  David Leahy, supervisor of elections

Kendall Coffey, Joseph Geller, attorneys for Gore
Miguel DeGrandy, Tom Spencer, attorneys for Bush

BROWARD COUNTY

Canvassing Board
  Robert W. Lee, county judge
  Suzanne Gunzburger, county commissioner
  Jane Carroll, supervisor of elections (stepped down)
  Robert Rosenberg, county judge (replaced Carroll)

JUDGES

Supreme Court of the United States
  William H. Rehnquist, chief justice
  John Paul Stevens
  Sandra Day O'Connor
  Antonin Scalia
  Anthony M. Kennedy
  David H. Souter
  Clarence Thomas
  Ruth Bader Ginsburg
  Stephen G. Breyer

United States District Court, Southern District of Florida
  Donald M. Middlebrooks, judge

Florida Supreme Court
  Charles T. Wells, chief justice
  Leander J. Shaw, Jr.
  Major B. Harding
  Harry Lee Anstead
  Barbara J. Pariente
  R. Fred Lewis
  Peggy A. Quince

Leon County Circuit Court
  Nikki Ann Clark
  Terry P. Lewis
  N. Sanders Sauls
  L. Ralph Smith, Jr.

Palm Beach County Circuit Court
  Jorge LaBarga

CHRONOLOGY: RECOUNT 2000

	STATEWIDE DEVELOPMENTS	PALM BEACH COUNTY	MIAMI-DADE COUNTY	BROWARD COUNTY
TUES. 11/7	Election Day			
WED. 11/8	First complete election figures show Bush leads Gore in Florida by 1,784 votes; Secretary of State Katherine Harris orders automatic recount of all votes in state			
THURS. 11/9	Automatic recount cuts Bush lead to 327 votes	Democrats ask for manual recount	Democrats ask for manual recount	Democrats ask for manual recount
FRI. 11/10				
SAT. 11/11	Bush files suit in federal district court in Miami to stop the manual recounts			
SUN. 11/12		Canvassing board votes in favor of manual recount		
MON. 11/13	Federal court rejects Bush's request to stop the recount; Harris's office issues legal opinions stating 1) deadline for election certification is November 14, and 2) manual recounts should not be permitted			Canvassing board votes against a full manual recount

	STATEWIDE DEVELOPMENTS	PALM BEACH COUNTY	MIAMI-DADE COUNTY	BROWARD COUNTY
TUES. 11/14	Volusia County completes manual recount; Bush lead reduced to 300 votes; Judge Lewis ("Lewis I") rules Harris must exercise discretion in deciding whether to accept late ballots; Attorney General Butterworth issues opinion stating manual recounts should be allowed	Canvassing board suspends manual recount in light of Harris's legal opinion	Canvassing board votes against manual recount	Canvassing board votes to reconsider decision not to conduct a manual recount
WED. 11/15	Harris denies requests by Broward, Miami-Dade, and Palm Beach counties for manual recounts to be included in the statewide certification			Canvassing board votes in favor of manual recount and begins counting
THURS. 11/16	Florida Supreme Court rules that the manual recounts in all three counties may proceed	Manual recount begins		
FRI. 11/17	Judge Lewis ("Lewis II") allows Harris to certify election results without the inclusion of the hand recounts; the Florida Supreme Court enjoins certification and sets hearing date for 11/20; overseas absentee ballots increase Bush lead from 300 to 930			
SAT. 11/18			Canvassing board reverses position, votes in favor of manual recount	
SUN. 11/19				Canvassing board changes to more liberal standard for recognizing votes

	STATEWIDE DEVELOPMENTS	PALM BEACH COUNTY	MIAMI-DADE COUNTY	BROWARD COUNTY
MON. 11/20	Lawyers for Bush and Gore argue before the Florida Supreme Court on the issue of whether hand counts should be included in the final tally of election results		Manual recount begins	
TUES. 11/21	Florida Supreme Court rules unanimously that the hand recounts must be included; court sets November 26 as new deadline for certification			
WED. 11/22	Bush appeals Florida Supreme Court decision to U.S. Supreme Court	Canvassing board suspends recount for Thanksgiving holiday	Amid protests, canvassing board votes to cancel recount	
THUR. 11/23	Florida Supreme Court denies Gore's request to require the manual recount to continue in Miami-Dade			
FRI. 11/24	U.S. Supreme Court agrees to hear Bush appeal of Florida Supreme Court decision	Recount resumes		
SAT. 11/25				Recount shows that Gore gained 567 votes in Broward County
SUN. 11/26	Harris denies Palm Beach County's request for more time; she certifies Bush the winner in Florida by 537 votes	Board fails to complete recount by deadline; Gore would have gained 215 (or 176) votes		
MON. 11/27	Gore files suit in Tallahassee to contest the election in Florida; Judge Sanders Sauls assigned			

	STATEWIDE DEVELOPMENTS	PALM BEACH COUNTY	MIAMI-DADE COUNTY	BROWARD COUNTY
TUES. 11/28	Judge Sauls rejects Gore's request to begin hand recount of ballots in Miami-Dade and Palm Beach			
WED. 11/29				
THURS. 11/30				
FRI. 12/1	U.S. Supreme Court hears arguments on Florida Supreme Court decision to extend deadline certification			
SAT. 12/2	Contest trial before Judge Sauls begins			
SUN. 12/3	Contest trial concludes			
MON. 12/4	U.S. Supreme Court remands case to Florida Supreme Court for clarification; Judge Sauls rejects Gore's contest			
TUES. 12/5				
WED. 12/6				
THURS. 12/7	Arguments before Florida Supreme Court on Gore's contest of the election			

	STATEWIDE DEVELOPMENTS	PALM BEACH COUNTY	MIAMI-DADE COUNTY	BROWARD COUNTY
FRI. 12/8	Florida Supreme Court rules 4–3 in favor of Gore's appeal; court orders immediate manual recount of all ballots in the state for which no vote for president was recorded			
SAT. 12/9	Statewide manual recount begins; at 2:45 P.M., responding to Bush's appeal, U.S. Supreme Court, by 5–4 vote, orders a stop to the manual recount			
SUN. 12/10	Lawyers for Bush and Gore file briefs with U.S. Supreme Court			
MON. 12/11	U.S. Supreme Court hears arguments in *Bush v. Gore*			
TUES. 12/12	U.S. Supreme Court overturns Florida Supreme Court decision 5–4, rejecting further manual recounts			
WED. 12/13	Gore concedes			

TOO CLOSE TO CALL

FLORIDA SUNRISE

THE SUN RISING over the Atlantic casts a peach glow on the Lake Ida Shopping Plaza. Its architectural motif is typical of the lesser strip malls in Florida's Palm Beach County—ersatz stucco, with a roof of battered tiles. The first rays of dawn land on Good Stuff Furniture, where factory-closeout sofas and love seats are sold on layaway. One storefront over, engineers and hard hats arrive early at the construction office for the job of widening I-95, the truck-choked superhighway whose low rumble and smoggy haze never entirely leave this commercial square. The medical office of Dr. Jean-Claude Tabuteau is open only at night, to serve his working-class Haitian clientele, men and women who spend their days changing sheets and watering lawns at the resorts on the other side of the highway.

On the morning of November 7, 2000—Election Day—the mall had none of its usual subtropical torpor. One of the storefronts was home to the Democratic Party of Palm Beach County, and its offices served as the base for the biggest get-out-the-vote operation that anyone could remember. The plan called for one group of volunteers to work the phones in the party offices and another to disperse to the precincts. The poll workers were to be given their assignments, as well as their leaflets and signs, at a long folding table just outside the front door. A woman named Liz Hyman was in charge of the table.

Hyman had spent a few years as a junior lawyer in the Clinton administration and was now a young associate at a prominent law firm in Washington. She had taken a few days off to help the Democrats try to retain the White House. The plan in Palm Beach County called for the volunteers to vote in their own precincts as soon as the polls opened at seven and then to report to party headquarters for instruction and deployment. It was only a few minutes after the hour when the first of them pulled into the parking lot.

Several—many—were distraught. There was something confusing about the ballot, they said. They weren't sure if they had actually voted for Al Gore and Joe Lieberman. In keeping with the demographics of Delray Beach, the town where the mall was located, virtually all of the volunteers were elderly and many were Jewish. They had been especially motivated to support Lieberman, who was the first Jew to be nominated by a major party for vice president. What made the problem especially upsetting was that some of the volunteers thought they had voted for Pat Buchanan, a man they regarded as an anti-Semite. What, they wondered, could they do?

Liz Hyman had no idea. Indeed, she didn't really understand what these people were talking about, and neither did anyone else at campaign headquarters. The local staff of the party had all voted by absentee ballot, so they had not seen the same voting machines as the volunteers who were arriving this morning. Like most politically attuned people, Hyman had a vague sense that voters were sometimes confused at the polls, but this seemed . . . different. These were experienced voters, indeed political veterans. Shouldn't they have understood what they were doing? It was puzzling.

So Liz Hyman called her dad.

Lester Hyman had been a successful, if not famous, Washington lawyer for several decades. He had a bustling commercial practice, but he also offered discreet volunteer assistance to Democrats in the White House. He helped vet potential nominees for high-profile positions, reviewing their disclosure statements and personal histories for possible areas of embarrassment. Hyman had helped screen candidates for Bill Clinton's first appointment to the Supreme Court of the United States—the seat that ultimately went to Ruth Bader Ginsburg. During that assignment, Hyman had met a young lawyer on the White House staff who was shepherding the nominee through the process. Now, when Hyman heard the peculiar report from his daughter in Palm Beach County, he remembered that the White House lawyer had gone on to work for Al Gore. "I'll give him a call," Lester Hyman said.

Ron Klain's cell phone rang just as he was pulling into the parking lot of Gore headquarters in Nashville. It was 8 A.M.

Eleven hours later (twelve in parts of the Panhandle), the polls closed in Florida and the presidential election came to its scheduled conclusion in that state. As it turned out, however, the race for president was so exquisitely close in Florida that no winner could be determined with assurance on election night. Because the electoral-vote margin between the candidates was so narrow across the nation, it quickly became apparent that the victor in the Sunshine State would win the presidency. The battle raged in and over Florida for thirty-six more days, until Vice President Gore conceded the race to his Republican opponent, Governor George W. Bush, of Texas.

It is impossible to discuss the presidential election of 2000 without superlatives. The race between Bush and Gore was the closest presidential election in the modern history of the Electoral College. It prompted the greatest and fastest mobilization of legal and political talent that the nation had ever seen. It featured the most dramatic and numerous swings of fortune—not only during the post–Election Day period, but often over the course of single days. It included the most unlikely cast of characters for a major national drama—from once-obscure judges who held the fates of the candidates in their hands to the governor of Florida, who happened to be the younger brother of the Republican candidate for president. Even considering the infamous 1876 contest between Rutherford B. Hayes and Samuel J. Tilden, the race of 2000 was the most extended period of true uncertainty about the winner of a presidential election. And, of course, the battle between Bush and Gore was fought for the highest political stakes.

The election of 2000 also produced the most sprawling and complex political and legal drama. In Florida, the cynosure was the state capital of Tallahassee, where the chief strategists for both sides plotted their appeals to the governor and secretary of state as well as to trial judges and the state supreme court. At the same time that the candidates were making their cases in the capital, there were equally tortuous and significant skirmishes being fought at the county level. Three of them were so dramatic that the counties themselves seemed almost to take on human qualities— the bumbling and childish Palm Beach, the efficient and mature Broward, the mysterious and sinister Miami-Dade. And yet this contest stretched far beyond the borders of Florida, consuming the entire country and concluding behind the closed doors of the United States Supreme Court.

The election of 2000 also produced the greatest controversy about the "true" result and the "real" winner—in Florida and thus in the election as a whole. This dispute gave rise to still another superlative. The ballots in Florida received more extensive scrutiny from outside—non-governmental—organizations than in any other American election. Alas, even those elaborate inquiries did not produce definite answers; indeed, the recounts conducted by the news media only deepened the confusion about who "really won." Moreover, the news-media recounts, while understandable and worthwhile enterprises, at some level misconceived and misportrayed the way this election was really decided. Those recounts were based on the notion that the goal of the thirty-six-day battle was to identify an objective truth locked within the state's ballot boxes. Under this approach, the election was over on November 7, and the candidates' subsequent efforts were devoted to counting the votes that had already been cast.

A more useful way of thinking about this election, and understanding the final result, is to recognize that the campaign simply continued for more than a month after Election Day. The thirty-six-day battle was fought using many familiar tools, including speech making, image management, crowd building, and lobbying. The Bush campaign not only recognized this reality; its leaders did a great deal to create it. The Democrats treated the recount in a different way—as a discrete event, separate from the race for the White House. It was this fundamental difference in orientation that contributed most to George W. Bush's victory. The Republicans were more organized and motivated, and also more ruthless, in their determination to win. From the very beginning, the Democratic effort was characterized by a hesitancy, almost a diffidence, that marked a clear contrast to the approach of their adversaries. In a situation like this, where the result was long in doubt, the distinctive attitudes made an important difference.

The reasons for these contrasts start with the candidates themselves. Al Gore had lived in Washington for most of his life, and he had absorbed, as if by osmosis, many of the attitudes of the establishment. He agonized about the views of the columnists, newspaper editorialists, and other elite opinion makers among whom he had lived for so long. Gore cared as much about their approval as he did about winning, and he ran his recount effort accordingly. Ironically, and poignantly, Gore's solicitude toward the Washington establishment was never reciprocated. To a great extent, the vice president lacked passionate supporters among journalists and politicians, and even ordinary citizens. In the intense conditions of the Florida recount, this absence was notable. The recount required sacrifice, devotion, even a measure of fanaticism from those on the ground. At best, Gore inspired only a distant admiration from his supporters, and he paid the price in Florida.

In almost every respect, Bush was Gore's opposite. The Texas governor was blithely disengaged from the details of the recount and, instead, trusted his subordinates, chief among them James A.

Baker III, to deliver the correct result. Elite opinion mattered little to him; Bush was steeled by a sense of entitlement that protected him from criticism. He was shielded, too, by the devotion of those around him. His campaign and legal staff included a great number of people who were willing to do almost anything to see George W. Bush elected president of the United States. His supporters were willing to take risks, bet their careers, and bear almost any burden for a Republican victory. One candidate had supporters in the streets of Florida, and it wasn't Al Gore.

This passion gap was the product of forces broader than the different personalities of the candidates. It had been eight years since Republicans controlled the White House, and their hunger for restoration was stronger than the Democrats' desire to hang on. The presidency of Bill Clinton also gave Bush supporters an extra measure of intensity in this fight. The Republican Party had not just disagreed with Clinton's policies during his administration; it had regarded him with an almost feral loathing. From the day Clinton was elected, Republicans described him as morally unfit and politically illegitimate, though they met a singular lack of success in persuading the greater American public that they were right. Republicans vented much of their anger against Clinton in legal settings—in lawsuits, investigations, and, ultimately, an impeachment. For Republicans, the Florida struggle against Gore, much of which also took place in courtrooms, served as a useful proxy for the failed onslaughts against Clinton.

Still, inasmuch as the post-election battle reflected the character of the candidates, the nature of their parties, and the state of contemporary politics, there was something else, too: random chance. The vote in Florida was bizarrely, freakishly close, and all the other states fell into place in such a way that the presidency turned on the result in that state alone. Florida itself is an anomalous, singular state, and the place where the electoral crisis of 2000 began—Palm Beach County—is a strange locale even by the standards of the Sunshine State. Error piled upon error, oddity upon oddity, surprise upon surprise. The trigger—the first trigger, anyway—was pulled in a strip mall.

CHAPTER ONE

A BIG PROBLEM

"I'LL SEE WHAT I CAN DO," RON KLAIN TOLD LESTER HYMAN. Klain was not a Washington native, which tended to surprise people. He was certainly born to the capital, even if he didn't happen to be born in it. At thirty-nine, he had spent most of his adult life there. Like most law firms, O'Melveney & Myers embraced a casual dress code, but Klain wore a regulation blue suit every day of the week. If one had asked Klain, on his first day at Georgetown, what he wanted to do when he graduated, his answer might have been: law school at Harvard, clerkship on the Supreme Court, and a series of increasingly important jobs with Democratic politicians. Through two decades, that was exactly what happened.

Klain was born and raised in Indianapolis, where his father ran a plumbing supply business. One day in 1968, shortly before the Indiana primary, advisers to Robert F. Kennedy's presidential campaign were looking for a place to film a commercial about small business and they happened upon the Klain emporium. Klain's father had never cared much for politics, and he could be seen sitting quietly in the back row of the black-and-white commercial, but the visit fueled six-year-old Ron's budding interest in politics. Just after graduating from college, he was already running cam-

paigns for the likes of Massachusetts congressman Ed Markey, and
the stakes in Klain's work just kept rising.

There once was a time when young attorneys like Klain had to
choose between law and politics. But Klain's relatively brief career
demonstrated that the line between the two fields had blurred almost to indistinction. Following his clerkship with Justice Byron
White of the Supreme Court, he had gone to work as the chief
counsel for the Senate Judiciary Committee—just in time for the
tumultuous hearings on the nomination of Clarence Thomas.
After that ordeal, he became a principal deputy to Warren Christopher on the presidential transition following Clinton's election and
then won a post as an associate White House counsel, in charge of
selecting the new president's first group of federal judges. Klain
spent the early Clinton years as a kind of troubleshooter, doing a
spell as chief of staff to Attorney General Janet Reno and another
with the Democratic leader in the Senate, Tom Daschle.

Finally, in 1995, Klain was named chief of staff to Vice President Al Gore, a choice that revealed something about both men.
The central responsibility of the job was to tend to the launch of
Gore's campaign for president—and for this critical assignment,
the vice president chose someone he barely knew. Through more
than two decades of public life, Gore had never engendered the
kind of personal loyalty that prompted talented staffers to sign
on with him for the long term. His campaign, unlike that of
George W. Bush, would be run by relative strangers. For Klain, the
job with Gore represented a chance to be more than just someone's protégé—it was an opportunity, in Washington terms, to be
judged on his own.

And for the first time in his life, in the very public setting of a
front-runner's campaign for president, Klain failed. Under his
leadership, the Gore campaign stumbled from its first steps. As is
usually the case in politics, the fault belonged mostly to the candidate, because Gore never found a way both to embrace Clinton's
political legacy and to reject the president's personal misdeeds. Because of these early troubles, in May 1999 the vice president

turned to former congressman Tony Coelho (another relative stranger) to resuscitate the campaign. Gore never officially fired Klain—indeed, the vice president asked him to remain on staff in some capacity—but Klain's position became untenable. In the end, Klain's leave-taking from the White House, in September 1999, resembled a job departure once described by Casey Stengel: "We call it discharged because there was no question I had to leave." A partnership at O'Melveney (Warren Christopher's law firm) awaited him.

But a political junkie can stay away from a presidential race for only so long, and Klain returned to the battle for the last several months. He was asked back by Coelho's successor as campaign chairman, William M. Daley. (True to form, Gore knew Daley only a little better than he knew Coelho, who left because of ill health as well as his abrasive personality.) Klain went to Nashville to help run the campaign's communications center, which was responsible for delivering messages to the press each day. It was an interesting enough job, but a far cry from his former position at the center of power in Gore's inner circle. The frantic home stretch in Nashville had let Klain enjoy a measure of redemption, but on Election Day he was more than happy that the campaign was over and he could go home for good.

For all his years in campaigns and elections, there was one thing Klain knew little about: the actual casting and counting of votes. Indeed, this arcane part of the political world was a mystery to even the most experienced operatives. So as soon as Klain walked through the door of the campaign headquarters on what he thought was his final morning in Nashville, he looked for someone else who might help Liz and Lester Hyman with their problem.

Klain told Michael Whouley, who growled that he would look into it.

Whouley (pronounced HOO-ley) had a long, narrow face that seemed frozen in an expression of perpetual skepticism, if not disgust. To hear him talk for a minute or two was to be certain he was a Boston longshoreman, because his speech often consisted of little more than interconnected profane tirades, with most of the consonants missing. At forty-two, Whouley was probably the most accomplished political field operative of his generation. His Election Day phone-bank plan for Gore—which was designed to roll out, with the time zones, reminder phone calls across the country—was the most sophisticated ever designed for a campaign. His political-consulting firm, the Dewey Square Group, though little known to the broader public, had no peer in the get-out-the-vote business. (The firm also appeared to have an unofficial policy requiring employees to use some form of the word "fuck" in every sentence they uttered.)

The tension in Gore headquarters on Election Day was even greater than usual because of the closeness of the race. The campaign's final round of private polls showed thirteen states to be within the margin of error. The night before, Whouley had convened a conference call for more than a hundred of his workers across the country, and he promised them the tightest election in history. "We are going to win it on the fucking ground," he vowed. He closed with the famous words of the St. Crispin's Day speech from *Henry V*: "We few, we happy few, we band of brothers; / For he to-day that sheds his blood with me / Shall be my brother . . . " (In keeping with the gender sensitivities of the Gore campaign, and proving that he was no longshoreman, Whouley improved on Shakespeare by adding, ". . . and sister . . .") No state was closer, or more important, than Florida, so Whouley took Ron Klain's warning to heart. He called Natalie Zellner, who was in charge of the Democratic Party's coordinated campaign in Tallahassee.

Rumblings were just then reaching Zellner. She, too, was a veteran of many campaigns, but she had never heard anything like the outpouring that was coming north from Palm Beach. Early complaints on Election Day usually concerned late poll openings or malfunctioning voting machines, not ballot configuration. Zellner tried to call the supervisor of elections in Palm Beach County,

Theresa LePore, but she couldn't get through. There were sixty-five phone lines to the Palm Beach office, but they were all busy—all the time.

A Democratic county commissioner from Palm Beach, Burt Aaronson, had also been pestering his staff to get to LePore. When Aaronson himself had voted that morning, he had called over the curtain to his wife, "It's a tricky ballot. Be careful." His office was getting calls, and Aaronson wanted them referred to LePore, but his staff got nothing but busy signals.

Finally, close to noon, Zellner located a pager number for Le-Pore, who responded after about a half-dozen pages. As Zellner began to talk, all LePore could say, in a quiet, wounded voice, was, "I know, I know, I know."

Theresa LePore had never worked anywhere except the Palm Beach County elections office. In 1971, when she was sixteen and a junior at Cardinal Newman High School in West Palm Beach, she took a part-time job as a file clerk. She went on to a local college, but never graduated. She marked her professional life by the rhythms of primaries, runoffs, and general elections in Palm Beach County. LePore had a delicate constitution—she was plagued by sinus infections and her eyes reacted badly to sunlight, a serious problem in South Florida. But she had a friendly demeanor, and though she was a registered Democrat, she enjoyed cordial relations with members of all parties. In 1996, when the supervisor of elections announced she was stepping down, LePore's long tenure made her a natural candidate for the job. (In all of Florida's sixty-seven counties except Miami-Dade, the position is an elected office.) LePore won the job, unopposed.

In the years leading up to the election of 2000, LePore had served on a federal task force on blind and handicapped voters. There she gained a special sensitivity to the problems of the visually impaired, which was a particular concern in a county, like Palm Beach, that had so many senior citizens. LePore had the lessons of the task force in mind when she approached the problem of designing the ballot for president in 2000. (Like twenty-four other Florida counties, Palm Beach used a punch-card system of voting: Voters pushed a stylus through perforated cutouts to poke holes in a computer card. Palm Beach actually used a brand of machines called Data-Punch, which was a cheaper, more mistake-prone version of the original Votomatic machines.) There were ten presidential candidates, who all had running mates, and each ticket had to be identified by party.

In late September, when the primaries were over, LePore asked the voting-system manager, Tony Enos, to design a ballot. As was customary, Enos lined up the names of the candidates along the left side of the ballot, with their corresponding punch-holes to the right; but because there were so many candidates, he had to use ten-point type, the smallest allowed under Florida law. Concerned that her many elderly voters wouldn't be able to read such small type, LePore decided to use bigger letters, which meant that the names were spread out over two pages: six candidates on the left and four on the right, with the punch-holes in the middle. In electoral circles, this design configuration is known as a facing-page ballot, but it had another name as well: butterfly ballot.

On this particular butterfly ballot, the punch-hole for the first name on the ballot—that of George W. Bush—appeared to the right of his name. The next hole belonged to Patrick J. Buchanan, whose name was on the facing-page side of the ballot. The third hole belonged to Gore, whose name was under Bush's, on the left side. Gore's name was right below Bush's, but the punch-hole for Buchanan was between them. This was a source of confusion, even for experienced voters. The Florida ballot always listed the governor's party first—in this case, Jeb Bush's Republican Party; the other major party always came second. (New York State, where many of the older Palm Beach citizens had voted before retiring, listed candidates in the same way.) This time, because of the butterfly ballot, Buchanan rather than Gore had the second hole. Theresa LePore had used butterfly ballots in the late 1980s for complicated constitutional initiatives, but neither she nor any other election supervisor in Florida had ever used one in a presidential race.

The ballot included little arrows to direct voters to the appropriate hole for their candidate, but many were still confused. Unlike many states, Florida does not allow voters to cast "provisional" ballots; instead, disgruntled voters can only call the elections office and argue. Thus, the unending busy signals. By lunchtime, delegations of angry voters were converging on LePore's office in downtown West Palm Beach. A local television-news crew caught one of these confrontations on tape; the broadcast of the story prompted even more complaints. By mid-afternoon, Randi Rhodes, a Brooklyn-born talk-show host on WJNO-AM radio, had taken up the call. A raucous, outspoken Democrat with a large following in the mostly Jewish condominiums, Rhodes confessed to her listeners, "I got scared I voted for Pat Buchanan, I almost said, 'I think I voted for a Nazi.' "

At around that time, Congressman Robert Wexler and state senator Ron Klein stopped in to protest to LePore. It was the kind of problem that a supervisor unaccustomed to controversy might have dismissed with an acronym familiar to elections officials. These malcontents were probably TSTV, or too stupid to vote. But the growing number of complaints soon made LePore realize she was facing a crisis.

But what could be done about it? Democrats were demanding that LePore provide special instructions to workers at all of the county's 531 precincts. But LePore had no viable way of reaching her employees; most polling places were not equipped with fax machines or cellular phones. By early afternoon, Democratic volunteers had hastily printed up leaflets explaining the butterfly ballot, hoping to distribute them to all polling places, but it seemed impossible to do in a county larger than the state of Delaware. Moreover, the week before the election, LePore had forgotten to mail poll-worker credentials to Democratic headquarters; she had delivered them in person on the Sunday before the vote, but that didn't leave enough time for the credentials to be distributed to their intended recipients. Thus, the Democrats had fewer people on the ground than they had anticipated. For a while, the Gore campaign also directed one of its phone banks—one that happened to be located in Texas—to call voters in Palm Beach and warn them about the ballot. By mid-afternoon, LePore agreed that her people should try to distribute the leaflet explaining the butterfly ballot to all polling places—or at least to those close enough to reach.

In truth, none of these remedial measures could have mattered very much. The turnout in the Gore-Lieberman ticket's best precincts was overwhelming—and very early. The campaign had dispatched Nick Baldick, another Dewey Square partner, to Florida to supervise the final push there, and he reported the numbers back to Whouley in Nashville: 80 percent turnout by ten o'clock in the morning. "Fucking unbelievable," they agreed. If the ballot had confused those voters, there was nothing anyone could do about it now.

When Whouley finally got back to Ron Klain, all he could say was, "It's a problem. It's a big fucking problem."

As Whouley (and everyone else) had predicted, the election was very close. On the final day of the campaign, the vice president had hopscotched through Florida, making stops all night long, and then landed in Tennessee at around seven in the morning. The original plan called for Al and Tipper Gore to take a helicopter to Carthage, his boyhood home, to vote, then return to the Loews hotel in downtown Nashville to relax and await the returns. In light of the tightness of the race, however, Gore's media team decided to schedule the vice president to give about twenty live satellite interviews from the hotel to local television stations across the country. Gore was so exhausted that he dropped off, in his chair, into a kind of half-sleep between interviews, but he never asked to stop. Interspersed with the television interviews, Mark Fabiani, who directed Gore's press operation, had also scheduled a series of radio chats, mostly with African-American stations, to build turnout. (Whouley determined the regions where Gore should appear, based on where votes were needed most.) As the polls began to close in the Eastern time zone, the senior campaign staff joined Gore at the Loews; Whouley and a small group from his team stayed at headquarters, to push turnout on the West Coast and to monitor the vote count.

The separation—between Whouley and the campaign leadership—was more than just geographic. Like Gore himself, the top management of his campaign were Washington insiders. His media consultants—people like Robert Shrum and Carter Eskew—were permanent fixtures in the city; so, by then, was William Daley, notwithstanding his roots in Chicago. Although Whouley had moved to Washington, he named his firm, Dewey Square, after a place in Boston. He brandished the spirit of an outsider, and he fought to win, with whatever tools were available. "All I know," he liked to say, "is that the one who stops fighting first always loses." Before Election Day, there was plenty of tension between the two factions in the Gore campaign—between the insiders and the outsiders, the technocrats and the ideologues, the establishment players and the street fighters. This conflict would define the Gore effort in the battle to come.

The television networks' exit polls ranked among the nation's worst-kept secrets. All day long, operatives from both campaigns pestered their contacts in the news media for the results as soon as they were released. (George Bush's cousin John Ellis was in charge of the political coverage for Fox News, and he kept the Texas governor posted on exit-poll results throughout the day.) The first numbers came in at 1 P.M. Eastern time, noon in Nashville. In the week before the election, Whouley had had buttons made for his staff—THE TRIFECTA: MICHIGAN, PENNSYLVANIA AND FLORIDA—for that was where he felt the election would be decided. In the first exit-poll numbers, Michigan looked close, but Bush had a clear lead in Pennsylvania. (As a result, Whouley summoned Jesse Jackson, who had been scheduled to make Election Day stops in Wisconsin, and redirected his campaign plane to Philadelphia.) As for Florida, which even then loomed as the biggest electoral prize, Gore had a narrow but clear lead. That margin held steady in the next two releases of exit-poll information, at two and four o'clock. (The afternoon news was so good that Shrum and Eskew went out and bought suits to wear to the victory celebration.)

It was thus no great surprise when NBC called Florida for Gore at 7:49:40 P.M. Eastern time. CBS agreed thirty-one seconds later, and ABC joined the consensus at 7:52. (These announcements took place a few minutes before all the polls closed in the Florida Panhandle, but there has never been any proof that the predictions discouraged anyone from voting during those remaining few minutes.) The Gore and Lieberman families were in tenth-floor suites in the Loews, with the staff scattered in rooms nearby. On the seventh floor, a suite was set aside for senior campaign officials to gather, watch television, and compare notes. Many campaign workers had brought in their families for the big night, and the atmosphere was festive—more so after the first results came in. All the networks called Michigan for Gore just after the polls closed at 8 P.M., and nine o'clock brought more good news—Minnesota. It now became clear to virtually everyone that Gore needed only one more of the close states to be elected president. At 9:44 P.M., ABC and NBC called one of those states—New Mexico—for Gore. There was pandemonium in the seventh-floor staff room. As Chris Lehane, Gore's campaign spokesman, later recalled, it was "our seven-minute presidency."

Shortly before ten o'clock—during the halcyon moments of the Gore presidency—Whouley called his partner Nick Baldick in Tallahassee to congratulate him on winning the state.

"I don't know, Michael," Baldick answered. "We got a problem here. This is going to be really close."

Like Whouley a veteran of many campaigns, Baldick had run Florida for Clinton in 1996, winning it for the Democrats for the first time in twenty years. He had built a model of the state's voting patterns and now tested it against the results that were coming in. Baldick told Whouley, "My model has us at negative 54 votes"—a statistically insignificant margin, but a significant cause for discomfort. "Keep this line open," Whouley ordered. And so it remained for the next five hours.

The voting results that worried Baldick had come to the networks' attention, too. One after another, they pulled the state of Florida out of the Gore column and put it into undecided. As the hour approached midnight and the other states began to fall into place, it gradually became clear that Florida's twenty-five electoral votes would determine the presidency.

As midnight passed, the high command of the Gore campaign was spread out over four locations, with imperfect communication links established between them. Whouley, who was at campaign headquarters, was talking to Baldick in Tallahassee; the staffers on the seventh floor of the Loews hotel were in touch with Gore and Lieberman on the tenth floor. But contact between field operatives and their bosses in the hotel was sporadic. Everyone was watching television and trying to log on to the website of the Florida secretary of state, which kept crashing.

No one had the same numbers. Notwithstanding the networks' early call of the state for Gore, it was Bush who had the lead in the raw vote totals all night long. But as the attention of the campaigns, and the world, focused on Florida, the Bush lead appeared to be shrinking—from nearly 100,000 votes to 50,000, then even lower. At one o'clock in the morning, the Florida website showed a Bush lead of 29,000 votes. But the Associated Press, which collected votes independently in each county, showed an even smaller margin. Five percent of the vote was still outstanding, mostly in Miami-Dade and Broward (Fort Lauderdale) counties, both Democratic strongholds. Then, abruptly, the trend turned around. At 2 A.M., the secretary of state posted complete returns from Volusia County (Daytona Beach), which pushed Bush's lead back up to 51,433 votes. Ninety-seven percent of the vote was in.

Al Gore happened to be in the staff room on the seventh floor when the votes in Florida spiked up in Bush's favor. Dressed casually, the vice president was watching the television while lying on the floor, with his chin propped up in his hands. As a result of the Volusia votes, Fox News called Florida—and the presidency—for Bush at 2:16 A.M. CBS and NBC followed suit a minute later, and ABC came in at 2:20 A.M. There was silence in the room as Gore and the others absorbed the news. After a moment, Gore said, "I'm really grateful to you all." Then, as he lumbered to his feet, he said, "I want to concede. I want to be gracious about this." He returned to his suite, where his family was waiting.

In a desultory way, a few Gore staffers called their contacts at the television networks, just to assure themselves that the call on Florida was for real. Yes, they were told; Bush has won. After hearing the network calls confirmed, several staffers turned off their cell phones.

Bill Daley and Eli Attie, Gore's speechwriter, went up to the vice president's suite. That afternoon, Attie and Gore had spent a brief time rehearsing Gore's victory speech, but the speechwriter had prepared something for the other eventuality as well. (Out of superstition, this speech was never discussed or circulated.) When Daley and Attie reached the room, the vice president opened the door. He had a piece of paper with a telephone number in his hand. "Is this the number?" he asked Daley. Yes, Daley said; that was the number where Gore could reach Bush to concede. A moment later, Gore made the call. It took less than two minutes.

All night, a crowd had waited in a cold drizzle at Nashville's War Memorial Plaza, where Gore was going to make a statement when the results were known. After the call to Bush, Gore took a minute to read through Attie's concession and then spent a little time comforting his children. "Let's go," the vice president said, and the staff followed him to the lobby to take their places in the motorcade for the ten-minute trip. Ron Klain, too depressed to move and put off by the rain, decided instead to go to his room.

In a way, the most important thing about this concession tableau was something that didn't happen—the dog, as it were, that didn't bark. Gore and his campaign lived by the authority of the Washington establishment. If the television networks, the broadcast wing of that establishment, said the election was over, then the election was over. If they said it was time to concede, it was time to concede. Gore cared more about even those abstract vote counters than about the man he had hired to watch the actual votes.

In other words, no one had thought to check with Michael Whouley.

In its half-year of existence, the Gore campaign headquarters in Nashville had developed its own nomenclature. The boiler room— the main open space—was known as "the hockey rink." The people who ran the field operation were known collectively as "the couch," after a ratty sofa where Whouley and others frequently held court. (As in "I don't know. Check with the couch.") The communications room, where Klain worked, was known as "the kitchen," even though it wasn't one. The term came into use because no one wanted to use "war room," which was associated with Clinton. Finally, there was "the closet," which was indeed a closet, where Whouley had set up his television, computer, and telephone to hunker down for the last hours of election night. There, he heard the networks' calls.

In the closet, there was the same stunned silence that greeted the news over at the hotel. Whouley started stacking his papers, ready to pack up and go home. Then, out of loyalty, disbelief, or sheer stubbornness, he said, "Get me Baldick on the phone."

The line to Tallahassee was still open.

"They're wrong, Michael," Baldick said to him. "It's not 50,000. The networks have the wrong numbers from Volusia." Baldick had dispatched one of his people to county headquarters in Daytona Beach, and she was reporting back that Gore was ahead by 13,000 votes in Volusia, and they were still counting. "If you fix Volusia," Baldick went on, "we're only down 6,000 votes."

Just then, Baldick's cell phone rang in Tallahassee. Nick Baldick was thirty-two years old, but he had a time-honored tradition of inviting his mother to help him out on every Election Day. Jackie Baldick answered the phone and blanched.

"It's Bill Clinton," she whispered to her son. He was calling from New York.

"Tell him to hold," Baldick, still on the phone with Whouley, whispered back.

Her eyes widened. "I am not telling the fucking president to hold!" Mrs. Baldick said, adapting nicely to the Dewey Square idiom. In a small way, the president's call demonstrated his superior political instincts. Gore trusted the so-called experts; Clinton, who also spoke to Whouley twice during the course of Election Day, knew to go to the source.

"Then tell him I'll call him back," Baldick said to his mother. She did.

Baldick had already checked Florida law on recounts. Any margin of less than a half-percent set off a mandatory recount. With about 6 million votes cast in the state, that amounted to 30,000 votes—far more than the 6,000-vote difference Baldick claimed. Whouley gathered his team in the closet and said, "It's time to push back with the networks on this thing. It's not over." He looked for Monica Dixon, a senior communications aide, but she had already left for the hotel. Whouley asked his assistant, Jeff Yarbo, to get him Michael Feldman, who was Gore's traveling chief of staff and the person responsible for the vice president's whereabouts at all times.

Yarbo got no answer because Feldman, disconsolate, was one of those staffers who had turned off their cell phones. Remembering that Feldman was officially a government employee, the resourceful Yarbo called the White House signal office and demanded that he be paged. Feldman's van was about two blocks from the War Memorial when his pager flashed a message: PLEASE CALL SWITCH-BOARD FOR MICHAEL WHOULEY ASAP. He called.

"Where the fuck are you?" Whouley demanded.

"We're in the motorcade," Feldman answered. "He's going to give his speech."

"A speech about what?" Whouley demanded. After Feldman said that Gore had conceded to Bush—which was the first Whouley had heard of it—Whouley explained that the margin in Florida had shrunk, practically to invisibility. A recount was certain.

Feldman recognized that Whouley had to get this news to campaign chairman Bill Daley. In the confusion at the hotel, staffers had just piled into whatever vans were available, so no one knew precisely where anyone else was. Feldman tried Daley's cell phone, but it went to voice mail. So he tried Daley's aide, Graham Streett, who put Daley on the phone. Feldman conferenced Whouley into their conversation.

Daley immediately understood the implications of the call. "We've got to keep him from going onstage," he said. But he, too, was behind Gore's limousine, which was just then pulling up to the War Memorial.

If they didn't find Gore in the next minute or two, he would probably take the stage and begin his concession. How could they stop him?

Feldman thought of David Morehouse, Gore's lead advance man, who generally opened the door to the vice president's car and informed him where to go. Morehouse, a former ironworker from Pittsburgh, was burly enough to break through the crowd and stop Gore.

But Feldman had no idea how to reach Morehouse, who was, it turned out, in the campaign's spare limousine, right behind Gore's. At the time, Morehouse had the car phone in one ear and a walkie-talkie in the other, both connected to advance people on site at the War Memorial.

By the sheerest coincidence, Feldman was in the same van as Morehouse's girlfriend, Vanessa Opperman, who was also along to see the concession speech. His panic rising, Feldman asked Opperman if she knew how to reach Morehouse, and she used her own cell phone to call Morehouse on his personal line. He was talking on two phones, but not on that one. "You can't let him go onstage!" Feldman shouted into Opperman's phone.

Morehouse sprinted though a tangle of family members and Secret Service agents and caught up to Gore at the base of the stairs, just as he was about to walk up to the stage.

"Sir," the breathless Morehouse said. "We need to go to hold."

"What for?" Gore said, irritated. "I just talked to Bush. I told him I would give this speech. He's waiting for me. I don't want to keep him waiting."

Morehouse planted himself in front of the vice president. "Daley needs to talk to you for five minutes, just five minutes," Morehouse said.

Gore shook his head in disgust and walked back toward the hold—a dingy office in the basement of the War Memorial.

The room was chaos itself. About thirty family members, staffers, and Secret Service agents wandered around, simultaneously bewildered, exhausted, grief-stricken, and, strangely, hopeful. Daley explained the gist of the issue to Gore, and they found a speakerphone, from which they called Michael Whouley.

The race in Florida had grown even closer in the meantime. The margin was now down to less than 2,000 votes. This was no time to concede, Whouley insisted. A recount was certain, and Gore might even pull ahead. From the same phone, Daley called Bush's campaign chairman, Don Evans, and said, "We've got a situation here. You've got to give us a few more minutes." Daley preferred to handle the whole thing with Evans, but Gore wanted to talk directly to Bush.

Evans put the Texas governor on the telephone. It was 2:30 A.M. local time, almost exactly an hour since Gore's first call to Bush. Everyone in the basement could hear the vice president's side of this extraordinary conversation.

"Circumstances have changed dramatically since I first called you," Gore said. "The state of Florida is too close to call."

"Are you saying what I think you're saying?" Bush asked. "Let me make sure that I understand. You're calling back to retract that concession?"

Picking up on Bush's tone, Gore said, "You don't have to be snippy about it."

Bush explained that his "little brother," the governor of Florida, had assured him he had won the state.

"Let me explain something," Gore said, his tone stiffening. "Your little brother is not the ultimate authority on this."

"You do what you have to do," Bush said icily. The conversation ended a moment later.

Gore had turned his back to everyone in the room as he spoke to Bush. Except for the vice president's voice, the basement office was silent during the brief call. The group was still quiet as Gore turned around and placed the receiver back in its cradle.

Then Al Gore looked up and smiled, and the room exploded in a raucous cheer.

CHAPTER TWO

THE FLIGHT OF RECOUNT ONE

NOW WHAT?

It took a little while to get around to that question. Daley had to go out and tell the rain-soaked crowd that the election wasn't over. With aides and staffers scrambling to get seats, the motorcade was turned around and sent back to the hotel. Mark Fabiani, one of the campaign's chief spokesmen, had missed the trip from the Loews to the War Memorial and had commandeered an entire bus to chase after the candidate. As the bus was chugging toward the plaza, Fabiani saw all the cars coming back in his direction. He jumped out of his bus and staggered back to the hotel in the rain.

Gore reached Fabiani on his cell phone and inquired what the press was saying about the turn of events—a question the vice president often asked Fabiani and others. "They're stunned, like everyone else," Fabiani said. Then, with a chuckle, the vice president quoted Winston Churchill: "Nothing in life is so exhilarating as to be shot at without result."

Campaign chairman Daley asked the senior staff to convene at headquarters at around four o'clock in the morning. Giddy exhaustion prevailed as the high command gathered, a group that in-

cluded media consultants Eskew and Shrum, and strategist Tad
Devine, Whouley, Klain, spokesmen Fabiani and Lehane, and campaign manager Donna Brazile—among the top political operatives
in the Democratic Party. It was therefore all the more peculiar that
the conversation was dominated by someone who was unfamiliar
to them all. A few minutes into his monologue, Daley leaned over
and whispered to Klain, "Who the hell is this guy?" The Washington luminaries may have been plagued by confusion and doubt
about this unprecedented tangle of an election, but this red-haired
stranger was not.

His business card said simply JOHN HARDIN YOUNG, ATTORNEY &
COUNSELLOR. Then fifty-two years old, he had been in the coast
guard in the sixties and still occasionally lapsed into naval jargon,
referring to the campaign leadership, for example, as the "flags" of
the operation. A trial lawyer for most of his career, Jack Young had
worked as counsel to several large minority-owned firms. Through
the years, he had also done volunteer legal work for the Democratic Party, and during one of these assignments, in 1989, he discovered the avocation that would become his life's work: recounts.
He had come down to Nashville just in case—this case.

There were only a handful of lawyers—Democrats and Republicans—who handled recounts, and their list of battles established a sort of catechism: the Nevada senatorial race of 1998; the
Maryland governor's contest of 1994; the Connecticut congressional race, that same year, won by Democrat Sam Gejdenson by
21 votes; Douglas Wilder's victory in the Virginia governor's race of
1989 (Young's introduction to the field); and, the greatest struggle
of them all, the epochal 1984 race for Indiana's Eighth Congressional District. It took a special breed of eccentric to specialize
in the law of recounts. There was, to be sure, no money to be
made in the field, and no guarantee that a lifetime's work would
amount to more than a handful of cases. The rules of recounts
were arcane, with their own distinctive vocabulary. (Several people

later remembered Young's speech as the first time they heard the word "chad.") But when you needed a recount lawyer, Young was it. He was on fire.

Young held in his hand a small book entitled *The Recount Primer* that he and co-authors Timothy Downs and Chris Sautter had self-published in 1994. Unlike most writers, the trio had intentionally limited distribution of the forty-three-page book. They slipped copies only to Democrats confronting recounts—and kept them away from Republicans in the same straits—and now Young tried to distill its lessons for the most important group that he had ever tutored.

Jack Young's manic energy and unnerving fluency with the most obscure concepts had an invigorating effect on the sleepy and disoriented campaign workers. His confidence was contagious, even if no one knew exactly what he was talking about. Young said there would probably be a "recanvass," followed by a "recount" of the Florida votes—with the meaning of both terms unclear. "If you're ahead on election night," Young said, "you want the rules of the recount to be as narrow as possible, and the rules and procedures should be the same as those used on election night. But if you're behind"—which was where Gore seemed to be—"you want the scope of the recount to be as broad as possible. You want the recount to be a kind of audit of the election. You want the recount to monitor the election for fairness."

Several Gore staffers wanted to know about the butterfly ballot. Some outside lawyers had already come forward to say that they wanted to sue Palm Beach County because of the poorly designed ballot. Ron Klain asked Young whether the Gore campaign should be doing the same thing. Indeed, shouldn't they be in court on Wednesday morning? Young counseled caution, for he had seen the political price that losing candidates paid in running to court after elections. In 1994, Young had helped Parris Glendening defeat Republican Ellen Sauerbrey in the Maryland governor's race; after resorting to litigation, Sauerbrey was mocked as Ellen "Sore Loser" and her political career had never recovered. Young advised against a headlong rush into court; they all had to learn a great deal more about what had actually happened in Florida. The automatic recount would take a day or two. After that process was completed, Florida law also gave them a chance to file a "protest" (another mysterious term) within seventy-two hours of Election Day.

According to Young, there were no firm rules in recounts except one: "You have to gather the information. You have to get on the ground, look at the machines, look at the tally sheets, talk to the people who were there on Election Day. Recounts only succeed if you find out what happened." He had one concrete recommendation in the meantime: Get people to Florida—now.

Daley liked the idea. It conveyed the sense that Gore remained in the race, but at the same time it did not commit the campaign to doing anything specific, such as filing a lawsuit. The logistical obstacles, however, were daunting. Who would go to Florida? By what means would they get there? Where, precisely, would they go, and what would they do once they got there?

Daley turned these questions over to Jill Alper, who had been responsible for executing Whouley's Election Day operation. (Alper had also worked with Young on the 1989 Wilder-for-governor campaign in Virginia. On a bet, Young had celebrated their victory in that race by drinking champagne out of Alper's shoe.) She now came up with the idea of using Joe Lieberman's campaign plane, which was awaiting orders at the Nashville airport. She also put the word out to junior campaign staffers that volunteers were needed to fill the plane's seventy-two seats. At four-thirty in the morning, more than a hundred of these recent college graduates showed up. (Several of those who didn't make the cut left in tears.)

While Alper assembled the troops, Daley took Klain aside for a private word. "This is a big fucking piece of business," he said, "and we need someone to run it"—someone other than Jack Young. "Go get your clothes," Daley instructed. "It'll probably be a couple of days."

As dawn broke, the Florida secretary of state's website showed Bush leading by 1,784 votes.

. . .

While Klain led the crusade to the airport, Daley, Eskew, and Shrum repaired to the Loews bar, just in time for breakfast. The conversation there set the tone for the battle that would follow. The campaign was over, they agreed. It was important to be statesmanlike, not confrontational. In Daley's words, Gore had to preserve his "credibility" with the journalists and politicians of Washington. If the campaign was to continue after Election Day, Gore had to be cast in a completely different light and represented by different people.

Eskew suggested that they bring in former secretary of state Warren Christopher, now a lawyer in private practice, who had an unassailable aura of rectitude. Daley was so sure Gore would like the idea that he didn't even bother to wake up the vice president to ask his permission. Instead, Daley went up to his room and woke Warren Christopher at 4 A.M. in Los Angeles. As it turned out, Christopher had been watching the returns and had only fallen asleep about a half hour before Daley's call. He agreed to take the next flight to Nashville.

The morning news shows had been clamoring for Gore campaign representatives to appear on their Wednesday broadcasts. Now, with those programs shortly before airtime, the Gore press operation started delineating the party line. Campaign operatives Chris Lehane and Monica Dixon sat at a word processor at campaign headquarters and banged out a first draft of talking points:

- *Gore won the national popular vote.* This was not widely known on Wednesday morning, and the Gore staff felt it was important to drive home this point at every opportunity. The popular vote had no legal significance, but it provided a sort of political imprimatur to keep the fight going.
- *We are a nation of laws.* The election could be resolved in a reasonable, fair manner, according to well-established procedures.

- *Let's take our time and get it right.* There was no crisis. The nation had a president, and there was no need for an immediate determination of the next one.

To a great extent, these hastily composed themes became the thrust of Gore's appeal for the next thirty-six days. More than anything, the campaign wanted to make sure that its candidate did not appear ungracious or presumptuous. It is worth noting what Gore and his surrogates did *not* say: They did not claim victory; they did not claim unfair treatment at the hands of Florida officials; they did not even predict with certainty what the final result would be. A more aggressive campaign, working from the same set of facts, might have made all of those assertions. But the campaign had decided to focus on the election process rather than its result.

The Lieberman plane, dubbed *Spirit of America,* took off from Nashville on Wednesday morning without anyone knowing exactly where in Florida it was going to land. As the young volunteers tried to catch a few minutes of sleep in the back, Klain and Young, along with Jill Alper and Joe Sandler, the chief lawyer for the Democratic National Committee, tried to figure out what to tell them to do. Taking Young's suggestion to collect information, Klain decided to try to spread his troops to all sixty-seven counties in the state. The plane's first stop was Tallahassee, followed by Orlando, then Fort Lauderdale. Young's book had forms for monitoring recounts, but his was the only copy on the plane, so they had to go through the agonizingly slow process of making copies on the plane's fax machine.

Klain knew that Daley wanted to keep the trip below the radar and, if possible, invisible to the press. Using the public address system, he reminded the plane's young passengers that they were entering a new chapter in the election—and in American history. "This isn't a campaign anymore," Klain said. "Take off your buttons. We are good Democrats who want a proper process to be conducted. We are going to do this the right way."

As the plane made its first stop in Tallahassee, Young whispered some instructions to the flight attendant. When the first group stepped out into the light of a new Florida morning, she saw everyone off in the same way: "Thank you for flying *Recount One.*"

In front of the general aviation terminal, Klain's leadership team, along with a handful of the volunteers, stepped down to the tarmac and found that there was no one there to receive them: no taxis, no rental cars, no means of leaving the airport, much less completing their mission. As Alper worked her cell phone to organize ground transportation, another private plane pulled in the terminal. Out stepped Governor Jeb Bush and his family, returning from his brother's abbreviated victory celebration in Austin. They waved at the brightly painted campaign plane before they were whisked away by a group of cars that had been waiting for them. So much for a secret mission, thought Klain.

In time, Klain and the others made their way to the ramshackle house in Tallahassee that was the headquarters for the Democrats' coordinated campaign in the state—the place where, less than twelve hours earlier, Nick Baldick and his mother had been reporting results to Michael Whouley in Nashville. With more than a dozen people fighting over only a few phone lines in the two usable rooms, the accommodations were inadequate. So Klain and Sandler made it their first priority to find lawyers—and a law office. They organized a meeting with Martha Barnett and Chesterfield Smith, two top partners at Holland & Knight, the biggest firm in Florida. During a quick series of phone calls, Barnett seemed to agree to take the assignment and promised to come by Democratic headquarters later that day for the first legal strategy session.

.   .   .

On that first day after the election, almost everyone on Gore's campaign—both those in Florida and those remaining in Nashville—was obsessed with the butterfly ballot in Palm Beach. Buchanan had received 3,704 votes in Palm Beach—nearly 2,700 more than he'd won in any other county in Florida. (By comparison, Buchanan received just 561 votes in Miami-Dade County and 789 in Broward, both of which have larger populations than Palm Beach.) Buchanan himself promptly acknowledged that many of his Palm Beach votes were probably not intended for him.

In the chaotic scene on Wednesday, Klain learned another startling fact. More than 29,000 presidential ballots in Palm Beach had been thrown out because of "undervotes"—that is, because no preference was recorded—or "overvotes"—because more than one preference was indicated. (Klain later noted that this was probably the first time he had ever heard those terms.) In all, Klain saw this as a massive disenfranchisement of Gore voters, and he felt even more strongly that the campaign should go to court to prove it. As the day wore on, he passed these statistics to Mark Fabiani, in Nashville, who lobbied for reporters and editors at *The New York Times* to get the butterfly-ballot story on the next day's front page, and thus at the top of the national political agenda.

Klain had scheduled a conference with the lawyers from Holland & Knight at five o'clock that afternoon, but Barnett and Smith never appeared. At 6:30 P.M., the lawyers called to say they couldn't take the case after all because of a "conflict of interest" involving the firm's representation of a county canvassing board. It seemed to Klain like the kind of conflict that could have been overlooked if the firm had really wanted to represent Gore. The brushoff from Holland & Knight was a sign that Tallahassee would not be friendly territory for Gore's team. Implicitly, or explicitly, the big firms did not want to offend Governor Jeb Bush by siding against his brother in perhaps the greatest legal-political battle of all time. Two of the state's most powerful firms—Greenberg Traurig, and Steel Hector & Davis—signed up, respectively, to represent the George W. Bush campaign and Secretary of State Katherine Harris.

Klain, by contrast, was left to improvise and build, person by person, what he came to call his virtual law firm. He called Kendall Coffey in Miami, a former United States attorney in the Clinton administration, who had succeeded in overturning the results of a Miami mayoral election by proving fraud. They were joined by Mitchell Berger, a longtime Gore fund-raiser, who ran his own medium-size firm, based in Fort Lauderdale. Klain also got on the phone to Nashville and told Daley that he and Christopher had to get to Tallahassee as soon as possible. Secretary Harris was not ordering a separate "recanvass" and "machine recount" of the votes. It turned out there would only be a single automatic "machine recount" of the vote. It was already under way, and it would probably be over in a day or two. "Things are moving a lot faster than we expected," Klain explained to Daley.

As the United States secretary of state, Warren Christopher had enjoyed perhaps the most elegant suite of offices in Washington. In his memoirs, he described the aerie on the seventh floor of the State Department building, with its "large, graceful rooms . . . furnished with museum-quality American antiques." When Christopher and Daley arrived in Tallahassee on Wednesday night, there was still enough light for the former diplomat to see how far his circumstances had fallen. Local supporters had rented a vacant retail space, nestled between the Bloomingtails Pet Salon and the Nu Dimensions Salon (for humans) in an aging strip mall on a busy commercial thoroughfare that led to downtown. Inside, a makeshift room had been carved out of crumbling drywall. Someone located a few folding chairs and Daley, Christopher, Klain, Mitchell Berger, and Jack Young were joined by Chris Sautter, Young's co-author of the recount book, whose work in the field had earned him the nickname King of the Chads.

With the exception of Young and Sautter, the group was made up entirely of lawyers with no experience in election-law procedures such as recounts. The Gore lawyers were, however, familiar with lawsuits, and the manifest injustice of the Palm Beach situation seemed to cry out for a legal remedy. Several voters had already filed cases earlier that day. But in this, the first calm reflection on the emerging situation in Florida, the difficulties of litigation started to become clearer. There was the danger that Gore, in running to a judge, would be branded a sore loser. There was also the question of what to ask a court to do about the butterfly ballot. Three possibilities emerged. First, they could request a judge to reapportion some of the miscast votes. The court could parcel out some of the Buchanan votes to Gore and the other candidates based on their respective statistical showings in the county at large. Second, the court could hear testimony from individuals who may have cast mistaken votes and then reapportion their votes accordingly. Third, the court could simply order a new presidential vote in the county, with a clearer ballot.

In outlining these options, the group recognized their dubious prospects. Statistical reallocation of votes was without precedent in Florida or in a presidential election, as was the individual-testimony route. Besides, what judge would have the moxie, or the authority, to use statistics to award the presidency of the United States to one candidate or another? And how could voters prove that their secret ballots were cast for someone other than the candidate they had preferred? There had been revotes in minor races, but never in a presidential contest. Moreover, a revote might conflict with the declaration in the Constitution that Election Day "shall be the same throughout the United States." In short, even if the vice president's team could establish that the butterfly ballot was improper, it was by no means clear that a lawsuit in Palm Beach could propel Gore to the presidency.

Young listened to the lawsuit scenarios in uncharacteristic silence until his frustration got the better of him. "What about the recounts?" he asked.

According to Florida law, Gore had seventy-two hours from the closing of the polls to ask for manual recounts—recounts of the vote by hand—in each of the sixty-seven counties. These requests for recounts were called protests. Since Florida government offices would be closed on Friday for Veterans Day, the campaign faced a deadline of Thursday to ask for recounts—and it was now Wednesday night. Recounts, not lawsuits, were the way to win this election, Young said.

All right, Daley and Christopher agreed; give us a list tomorrow morning of which counties you want to recount.

It wasn't exactly a ringing endorsement, but it was all Young and Sautter had. The meeting broke up shortly before midnight, and the two recount lawyers found a Bennigan's open late, where they strategized over steak and beer.

Klain took Christopher to the Governor's Inn, Tallahassee's only semi-luxury hotel. The former diplomat made it almost all the way to his room without commenting on the dismal setting for their last meeting. Finally, he couldn't resist. "Ron, don't you think we should be in a law office from now on?"

Barely eight hours passed before the same group, plus Kendall Coffey, reconvened in the more congenial Tallahassee Room, set up for conferences, at the Governor's Inn. By now, circumstances had changed in one important way. The machine recount of the vote had narrowed Bush's advantage considerably. Instead of a margin of 1,784, the machine recount had left Gore trailing by just 327 votes—a margin that offered a much more realistic chance of being eliminated in a recount.

Despite the improved prospects, Christopher and Daley presided with their trademark caution. Daley in particular was concerned about Gore's prospects even as the gap narrowed. One party controlling the electoral machinery, the other struggling even to find out what was going on, vote totals fluctuating mysteriously—it all had a familiar ring. "Shit, I've been here before," Daley said. "This is not good." He was talking about Chicago.

Perhaps no figure in modern American history was more associated with the theft of a presidential election than Mayor Richard J.

Daley, of Chicago. In 1960, John F. Kennedy won the state of Illinois by only 8,000 votes, thanks to his overwhelming 450,000-vote margin in Daley's Cook County. Did Mayor Daley manipulate the outcome? The Illinois vote was extensively investigated at the time, and no proof of misconduct, or even substantial mistakes, was ever uncovered. But as years passed, myths flourished. American politics has yielded few richer ironies than another Daley from Chicago—Richard's son—recounting the votes for president.

The first son of Richard and Eleanor "Sis" Daley's seven children, Richie Daley was the child destined to be his father's political heir. When Richie secured his birthright in 1989, Bill Daley, the fourth son, served as his brother's campaign manager, but he always had more refined ambitions than the gritty electoral dreams of his older brother. Bill spent much of his career as a partner in the white-shoe Chicago law firm of Mayer, Brown & Platt. When Clinton won the presidency in 1992, Bill Daley hoped for a position in the cabinet, but he had to settle for an interim assignment instead—chief architect of the administration's effort to pass the NAFTA trade bill. The unions that had backed the first Mayor Daley's rise to power generally opposed NAFTA, but lawyers, bankers, and newspaper editorial boards—in short, the Washington establishment—supported the measure enthusiastically. NAFTA passed and Daley soon received his reward—the job of secretary of commerce. He had found success in Washington.

When Al Gore's campaign was floundering under the mercurial leadership of Tony Coelho, the vice president turned to Bill Daley to help him. At fifty-two, Daley was a reluctant political operative, who tried to balance his inbred desire to win with his long-cultivated hope for respectability. The recount forced the opposing sides of his character into even greater tension. Washington—Daley's city, the capital of the NAFTA coalition—cared little for Al Gore and even less for the kind of uncertainty that Florida represented. Moreover, Daley's Chicago experience told him that recounts rarely succeeded, especially when the opposing party controlled the government. So Daley was skeptical when Jack

Young and Chris Sautter began outlining their plan for the recount that would take Al Gore to victory.

Their plan was straightforward: They wanted Gore to request manual recounts in all sixty-seven counties. This idea reflected the thesis of their book—that trailing candidates should ask for recounts everywhere, not just where they were ahead. The larger the number of votes we examine, Young said, the greater the number of previously uncounted votes we will find. The more uncounted votes we find, the more we can pick up.

Daley and Christopher were unenthusiastic. By law, Gore could not make a single request for a statewide recount; rather, he had to ask each county individually, which meant sixty-seven separate proceedings in which the local canvassing boards would decide whether or not to recount the votes. It was a recipe for chaos. R. W. Apple, Jr., a veteran correspondent for the *The New York Times* and a faithful chronicler of the Washington conventional wisdom, began his coverage of the Florida situation with a challenge: "Now we learn . . . who the grown-ups are around here." Christopher was the definition of a grown-up, and Daley longed to be one, and they both believed that grown-ups didn't pick sixty-seven fights at once.

Besides, Ron Klain pointed out, there was no guarantee that all, or even most, of the canvassing boards would agree to conduct recounts. Florida law said only that the boards "may" order the recounts "if there is an error in vote tabulation which could affect the outcome of the election."

No one knew precisely what the standard meant, but some counties were sure to refuse to recount. The press would treat a substantial number of refusals as a fatal loss of momentum for Gore, Klain said. Better, he suggested, to focus requests on the places where they were likely to have them accepted—and, of course, where they were likely to pick up votes.

So Young and Sautter went to their fallbacks. Volusia's vote totals had fluctuated all night long; at one point, the county's computer said that the Socialist Worker candidate had 10,000 votes. It was Volusia's errors that had prompted the networks to recant their calls of the state for Bush. By then, the problems in Palm Beach were also well known. Certainly, Gore had to ask for recounts in those two counties. Klain agreed immediately, and in time Daley and Christopher joined the consensus.

Young pointed out that several of the biggest counties also had big undervotes—large numbers of ballots that hadn't been counted for president. Based on the vote breakdown, Young did some rough projections of how many votes Gore could expect to pick up in each county: 302 to 400 in Palm Beach, 80 to 100 in Miami-Dade, and 272 to 500 in Broward. (The predictions proved highly prescient.) There were reports that Duval County, which included Jacksonville, had an especially high number of undervotes in African-American neighborhoods. Could Gore really walk away from this many potential votes?

Ultimately—reluctantly—Daley and Christopher agreed to add Miami-Dade and Broward to the request.

At this point, just forty-eight hours after the polls had closed, Klain allowed himself a moment of satisfaction, if not optimism. Bush's margin in Florida, which was tiny to start with, had shrunk by 80 percent. Though the Gore campaign had not yet decided to file a lawsuit based on the Palm Beach butterfly ballot, the story had made the front page of *The New York Times* and a legion of journalists were now looking into the problems in that county. Also, the recount process was under way, and Klain had every reason to believe that at least some counties would immediately begin recounting their ballots.

The meeting at the Governor's Inn broke up quickly. Mitchell Berger, joined by the recount specialists, left to draft their requests to the four counties. Kendall Coffey had to rush back to Miami to attend an important ceremony that evening. As for the "flags," Christopher and Daley stayed where they were. Another visitor was due in the Tallahassee Room: James A. Baker III.

CHAPTER THREE

"PEOPLE GET SCREWED EVERY DAY"

JAMES BAKER SPENT ELECTION DAY in the same way he spent most of his days—in a shimmer of discreet privilege, a half-step removed from the spotlight that had been his for so long. He began the day in Washington, with a meeting of the board of directors of the Howard Hughes Medical Institute. Baker also served on the board of Rice University, where a public-policy institute bore his name, but even at age seventy, he did not devote himself exclusively to philanthropy and good works. He was a senior (and active) partner at Baker Botts, the Houston law firm that was founded by his great-grandfather, and he also worked as senior counselor to the Carlyle Group, a merchant-banking firm in Washington that had quietly assembled controlling interests in leading defense contractors. Baker didn't need the money, but he couldn't live without the action.

The Hughes meeting broke up about an hour earlier than usual, because one trustee, Hanna Gray, had to return home to Chicago to vote. With a nod toward that city's colorful political history, Baker bade her good-bye with the instruction "Vote early and often."

After the meeting, Baker flew to Austin to await the election results. It was a familiar ritual for Baker, who had run five consecutive Republican presidential campaigns between 1976 and 1992.
No other American had come close to that record, nor had anyone
equaled Baker's trajectory in high-level government service. He
was the White House chief of staff, then treasury secretary, under
President Reagan, and secretary of state for most of President
Bush's four years in office. Toward the end of Bush's single term,
Baker served a rather unhappy tour as White House chief of staff,
in an unsuccessful effort to salvage the 1992 election. Baker had
had no great enthusiasm for leaving the realm of diplomacy for the
contest to defeat Bill Clinton (and Ross Perot), and the resounding
failure in the election created a widely perceived chill in the Bush-
Baker relationship.

But the passage of eight years healed a lot of wounds, and Baker
and the former president had put their differences aside. Indeed,
just a few days after the 2000 election, former President Bush
planned to join Baker and H. Norman Schwarzkopf for several
days of pheasant hunting in Europe. When the trip was planned
some months earlier, Dick Cheney had been a fourth invitee, but
in light of his vice-presidential nomination, he hoped to be otherwise engaged. When Baker arrived in Austin on Election Day, he
went to Dick and Lynne Cheney's hotel suite to wait out the results.

At last, at the end of the long evening, Cheney and George W.
Bush went to claim their victory. Baker had a cold and didn't want
to wait in the rain to hear the speeches. Instead, he found some
hotel stationery and wrote letters of congratulation to the new
president and vice president. Baker handed them to a staffer just
moments before it was announced on television that Gore had
withdrawn his concession. Still, this wasn't Jim Baker's fight, so all
he could do was go to bed. (He retrieved the letters before they
were delivered.)

In any event, Baker had to be up early. He was due back in
Houston on Wednesday morning to meet with the new foreign

minister of Mexico, just the kind of connection that served Baker's parallel roles as elder statesman and still-hustling businessman. The two men never got together, because as Baker and his wife, Susan, were driving into town from the Houston airport, his cell phone rang. It was Don Evans, Bush's campaign chairman, calling to say that the Bush team had learned from the *Today* show that the Gore campaign had hired Warren Christopher to represent the Democrats in Florida. Would Baker represent Bush in Florida? Evans didn't have to ask twice.

Joe Allbaugh, the Bush campaign manager, secured a private plane and flew to Houston later on that Wednesday to pick Baker up for the trip to Florida. Shortly after the plane took off, Allbaugh asked Baker how he thought the controversy would end. "It's going to be decided by the Supreme Court," Baker said.

Ben Ginsberg was watching the *Today* show, too. He had also spent election night in Austin, following the ebb and flow of the projections from campaign headquarters. At the age of forty-nine, he was the top lawyer on the Bush campaign, and he had been on duty since the morning, monitoring reports from around the country for signs of irregularities. Most of the day, his attention had been focused on Missouri, where complaints from Democrats prompted a judge to keep the polls open later than planned in St. Louis. He had heard about butterfly ballots at some point during the day, but never in a way that seemed to require his attention.

Ginsberg had made the nine-block trek in the rain to listen to Bush claim victory on election night, and then the long walk back when he heard that Gore had decided to continue the fight. At around four-thirty—just about the same time that Jack Young was lecturing the Gore troops in Nashville—Ginsberg was performing much the same function for the Republicans in Austin. As Evans, Allbaugh, chief strategist Karl Rove, and a handful of others listened in stunned silence, Ginsberg explained the rudiments of recounts to them.

Ginsberg was waiting at the Austin airport for his flight to Florida when he heard Bill Daley and the other Democrats on the *Today* show. Surrounded by a group of recount neophytes, Ginsberg knew there was no one who would really understand what he was thinking, so he kept it to himself. *They are doing it again,* he thought. *They are doing it again.*

People would ask Ginsberg, with varying degrees of subtlety, What's a nice Jewish boy like you doing . . . in the Republican Party?

It wasn't in his genes. His father was a microbiologist and his mother was one of the first female graduates of Columbia Law School. Both were Democrats, and so was their son when he entered the University of Pennsylvania in the class of 1974. As editor of the school newspaper, though, Ginsberg found himself attending, and enjoying, the press conferences of the mayor of Philadelphia, Frank Rizzo. He appreciated Rizzo's gruff honesty, especially in contrast to the dilettante student protesters who dominated the Penn campus. The mayor also took a liking to the bushy-haired student journalist and gave him a summer job helping gang members scrape old political signs off lampposts. (Later, Ginsberg realized that Rizzo simply wanted to make room for his own signs in the coming fall campaign.)

Ginsberg decided to make a career in journalism, but the reporting life soon lost its charms, and he drifted into law school at Georgetown. He joined a Washington law firm in 1982 and decided to give a little pro bono legal assistance to the beleaguered Republican minority in the House of Representatives. In preparation for the election, Ginsberg was asked to review the precedents on recounts in congressional elections, just in case there were any really close races that year. There weren't. Two years later, in 1984, there was one.

. . .

The Eighth Congressional District in Indiana stretches along the southwestern corner of the state, from the university town of Bloomington to the industrial city of Evansville. The district had been so evenly balanced between Democrats and Republicans that it elected four different congressmen in four consecutive elections in the 1970s. In 1984, the incumbent Democrat, Frank McCloskey, was seeking his first re-election against an aggressive challenge from a Republican named Richard McIntyre. The election-night totals put McCloskey ahead by 72 votes, but it quickly became apparent that the votes in one precinct had been counted twice. When the votes were retallied, McIntyre was ahead by 34. A recount—and a political war—followed.

An army of Washington lawyers trooped out to the district for the battle, and young Ben Ginsberg wound up leading the Republican crusade. (The Democrats included Chris Sautter, who would later co-author *The Recount Primer* with Jack Young.) The recount showed McIntyre ahead by 418 votes, and the Indiana secretary of state certified the Republican victory, but the Democratic House, led by a rising star named Tony Coelho (later Gore's campaign chairman), refused to seat McIntyre. In January, when the new Congress began work, "Indiana 8" was left vacant while the Democrats scrambled for a new way to count the votes. The House majority set up a task force to "study" the election results, a process that dragged on until April. Ultimately, the House voted along straight party lines to certify the Democrat, McCloskey, as the winner by 4 votes. As even many Democrats would acknowledge later, it was as close to an outright theft as had occurred in modern American political history.

Newt Gingrich said that the fight over Indiana 8 marked a turning point in the radicalization of the Republican minority in the House. (At the time, Representative Dick Cheney, of Wyoming, said of the recount battle, "I think we ought to go to war. There's unanimity. We need bold and dramatic action.") In a broad sense, Indiana 8 helped convince an entire generation of Republicans in Washington that the Democratic Party was not just politically misguided but fundamentally cynical and deeply corrupt. Fights like this one set the rhetorical tone of the Gingrich years in the House, and the Republican air of moral certainty had only grown stronger through the Clinton years and into the election of 2000. In a way, there was a bracing absence of cynicism in the Republican style of this era. Whether the subject was Monica Lewinsky or the vote in Florida, Ginsberg and his colleagues operated at a sustained pitch of perpetual outrage.

"Recounts change lives," Ginsberg would often say. Indiana 8 changed his. Ginsberg's anger over the Democrats' tactics in that race turned him from a part-time volunteer to a full-time Republican Party activist, and he spent the next decade as the general counsel to various campaign committees, leading up to the Republican National Committee. In 1993, he joined the large lobbying firm of Patton Boggs, but he kept a close hand in party activities. He signed on early with George W. Bush's campaign. Over the years, Ginsberg's once-full head of hair retreated to a few wisps around a bald dome, but his passion never faded. As he listened to the honeyed phrases come forth from the Democrats on the *Today* show ("Count all the votes"), Ginsberg knew it was time once again, in Dick Cheney's words, to go to war.

When James Baker first caught his breath after accepting the Florida assignment, he decided to place a call to Warren Christopher. At one level, it was just a courtesy to another former secretary of state, but it was also a way to size up his rival and perhaps get an edge. The two men had little in common aside from their service in the State Department. Christopher had spent most of his career as a corporate litigator, with occasional detours into government service and almost no time on campaigns. Baker, by contrast, was the leading political operative of his generation as well as a lawyer. Their temperaments differed, too—Christopher was cautious and judicious; Baker, relentless and partisan. Over the years, they had had little contact, just enough to recognize that they did not care for each other.

Drawing on his store of political knowledge, Baker remembered that Christopher's secretary at O'Melveney & Myers was a woman named Kathy Osborne. Baker knew her because she had been Ronald Reagan's secretary at the White House. However, Osborne was loyal to Christopher, and she wouldn't tell Baker where he was—even though his trip to Nashville was all over the news. So Baker left a message, and when his call wasn't returned promptly, he told reporters that Christopher had failed to call him back. It was a little jab, intended to irritate Christopher (which it did), but it was also an early signal that Baker was playing hardball.

It was about five o'clock when Baker finally assembled his team around a conference table at the George [H.W.] Bush Republican Center, the recently renovated three-story brick building that served as state party headquarters in Tallahassee. Ben Ginsberg was there, and perhaps half a dozen others. Surveying the group, Baker had a simple question: Is this everyone? He knew that the Democrats had sent a planeload of campaign operatives into Florida hours earlier. (He didn't realize that the plane held mostly college kids.) Baker was appalled that the Republicans had assembled such a meager team after a full day of activity. He wanted more lawyers, more political people, and a communications staff. "We need a PR strategy," Baker said. "We're getting killed on 'Count all the votes.' Who the hell could be against that?"

After the meeting drifted to an unsatisfactory conclusion, Baker took off for his next appointment—at the governor's mansion. Baker wanted to get the thoughts of the man he called Jebbie, since he'd known him as a boy. Governor Jeb Bush painted a dark picture of his brother's prospects in Florida. The canvassing boards in most of the counties—the people who would be supervising the recounts—were mostly Democratic, especially in the most populous, southern part of the state. The Florida Supreme Court, which would probably have the last word on the election, was a disaster area for Republicans.

In the 1980s, Baker had become friendly with then-senator Lawton Chiles, and the two men had gone turkey hunting together. Through Chiles, Baker had met a Tallahassee lawyer named Dexter Douglass, who went on to become Chiles's general counsel when the senator won Florida's governorship. They were nice guys, Baker said, but they were partisan Democrats who had selected the entire state supreme court in their image. As Baker made his way to his room at the Doubletree Hotel, a couple of blocks away from the Democratic stronghold at the Governor's Inn, he regarded the situation as dire.

Christopher and Baker, in their first nights in Tallahassee, each saw the odds as stacked against his own side. Christopher regarded the governor, the secretary of state, and the entire machinery of state government as an advancing army of Republicans; Baker counted the canvassing boards and the courts as warriors for the Democrats. There was merit in both views, though geography alone suggested that Baker was playing down his advantages on that first evening. After all, Baker went from a gleaming party headquarters to the governor's mansion, while Christopher was dodging paint chips in a strip mall. All in all, it was clear that the situation was unstable and unpredictable—and that both former diplomats had a wide range of options to turn the situation to their candidates' advantage. The very different manner in which each man chose to confront adversity would become the crux of the battle.

The mark of a superior strategist is the ability to plan for both immediate and long-range challenges. It would have been easy for Baker, for example, to get caught up in the manifold small issues that quickly enveloped the Bush campaign in Florida—staffing, public relations, and working space, to name just a few. But within Baker's first twenty-four hours in Florida, he seized on the idea that would, almost six weeks later, turn the battle decisively in his favor. On the plane to Tallahassee, Baker had predicted to Joe Allbaugh that the election would wind up in the United States Supreme Court. Now, on the ground, Baker wanted to start the process—by filing a lawsuit in federal court.

Federal courts have limited jurisdiction—that is, they are not compelled to hear every case that is brought before them. Elections are generally considered to be state matters, so it was far from clear that Baker could even persuade any federal court to become involved in the Florida dispute. In addition, the Republican Party in general had an ideological aversion to judicial activism in any setting, but especially when it involved federal courts telling states what to do: State sovereignty, sometimes called federalism, was Republican gospel. Also, there was a special stigma against political candidates going to court to win elections. Finally, the United States Supreme Court could decline to hear any case, even one that was properly before a lower federal court, and the justices generally steered away from immediate political controversies. It was, in all, a daunting array of obstacles.

The following day, Thursday, November 9, Baker gathered his team to face the same question that Christopher's group was weighing in the Governor's Inn, a few blocks away. In which counties, if any, would the campaign ask for recounts? Many in the Democratic camp predicted that Baker would simply try the reverse of the Gore strategy—that is, seek recounts in the counties where Bush had done best. That, after all, would be classic recount strategy, and it would almost certainly produce some new votes for the Republican ticket. But Baker was thinking several steps past the handful of votes that a few recounted counties might produce. Once the machine recounts were completed—and they were almost finished on Thursday—Baker wanted to send the message that the election was over and that any further recounts were attempts to undermine the system. Indeed, Baker thought the Bush campaign should go to federal court to stop hand recounts in any county and bring the entire election to a swift conclusion.

Baker's plan took stunning bravado—or, seen in a different light, hypocrisy—as he himself was soon to learn in dramatic, if private, fashion. The Republicans, like the Democrats, were inundated with offers of legal assistance in the immediate aftermath of the election. In the Republicans' first legal-strategy conference call, Ginsberg picked up the receiver in the first minute and found that he was the seventy-fifth person on the line. In the rough allocation of responsibility that grew out of the first call, the federal case went to Theodore Olson, a prominent conservative lawyer based in Washington. Baker knew Olson and liked him, but he was worried that Olson didn't have enough stature for such a case. So Baker suggested that Don Evans, the campaign chairman, put in a call to former Missouri senator John Danforth, a part-time clergyman widely regarded as a national figure of rectitude.

Evans found Danforth in Cancún, Mexico, where he and his wife had just arrived at their hotel for a vacation. The maître d' tracked him down at the restaurant. Evans said he wanted Danforth to represent Bush in federal court.

Though Danforth expressed himself in the low-key manner for which he was known, it was clear that he was appalled. Off the cuff, he predicted that Bush's chance of winning in federal court was "close to zero." Federal courts just don't tell states how to run their elections, especially before a candidate has proved that the process harmed him in a particular way. Still, Danforth was a loyal Republican and he didn't decline outright. He had a follow-up conversation with Baker, in which the former senator unburdened himself about the risks of filing the case. "Candidates don't sue," he told Baker. "You could ruin Governor Bush's career. He's only fifty-four years old, and the decision to file a court case like this one would be a black mark that followed him forever. And it would destroy the reputation of everyone involved on the Bush side."

His voice growing tight, Baker insisted that the Bush team wanted Danforth for the public advocacy he could bring to the case. They had lawyers who would prepare the arguments, but none of them had Danforth's reputation. This was a political war, and Baker needed Danforth as a spokesman for the cause. Finally, Danforth proposed a deal. He wanted to speak to Bush himself, explain the risks of the case, and if the candidate still wanted to go forward, Danforth would serve as his lawyer. Fine, said Baker. Two minutes later, the phone in Danforth's hotel room rang. It was Don Evans. "It sounds like your heart really isn't in this," Evans said. Then he paused before adding a postscript dangling with icicles: "Why don't you enjoy your vacation." There was no room in the Bush campaign for ambivalence. Ted Olson would do just fine as Bush's representative in court.

Still, the question remained: What would the lawsuit say? In asking for manual recounts, the Gore campaign was simply following long-established Florida law. How was that a violation of federal law, much less of the United States Constitution? The issue was farmed out to the ever-expanding group of lawyers chiming in from all over the country. George Terwilliger, the deputy attorney general in the first Bush administration, had joined Ginsberg as a kind of chief operating officer of the legal effort in Tallahassee. Olson was leading a task force in Washington. John Manning, a professor of law at Columbia University, was contributing from New York.

Then, late Thursday, the Republicans got a break. Word reached them that the Gore campaign had filed for recounts in four counties—and not just any counties.

The Democrats were asking for recounts in the places where Gore had done best. Suddenly, Olson's team had a theory—of sorts. These "selective" recounts violated the equal-protection clause of the Fourteenth Amendment, because they emphasized the votes of some counties over others'. The votes of Bush supporters were thus diminished in importance, because they were only counted by machine; no one was out looking for Bush votes by hand.

That was the theory. And as the most clear-eyed Bush lawyers recognized, it was a pretty weak one. The law allowed the Republicans to select their own counties to recount, so they were on an equal footing with the Democrats. Courts had long allowed different counties within the same state to use entirely different voting systems, so there was likely no problem with different standards within a state. Indeed, the Florida recount laws resembled those of most other states, and the Supreme Court had never before suggested any problem with those laws.

But Baker, thinking ahead, liked the equal-protection theory, and on Friday, November 10, he told the lawyers to prepare a complaint for federal court. Baker's reasoning was only partly based on the law. He saw that Democrats were getting political traction out of the demand to count every vote; he wanted to turn that around and put the counting of the votes on trial. The great advantage of the Democrats' count-every-vote argument was that it had the ring of neutrality. Because they chose only Democratic counties for hand recounts, though, Baker recognized that the Democrats didn't want "every" vote counted; they wanted every Gore vote counted. Baker saw that even if Bush lost his legal claim in federal court, his argument was at least sufficiently compelling to change the tenor of the political debate in the country.

Back in Austin, Karl Rove was doing his part to send a complementary message—that the election was over and Bush had won. On Wednesday, Rove and Karen Hughes, Bush's communications director, invited television cameras to watch his economic and national-security advisers brief the Texas governor. The message was that Bush was moving out of campaign mode and into his transition to the White House. Rove also wanted to make sure that Bush supporters knew the Republican Party was going to keep fighting to win this election. So Rove asked local organizers to make sure that pro-Bush protesters were in the streets—in Austin, Florida, and Washington, especially outside Gore's home at the Naval Observatory. The strategy was summed up by a little card that Rove's wife, Darby, gave him just after Election Day, which he carried with him for the duration: DON'T GET OFF YOUR GAME. NONE OF YOUR BUSINESS WHAT *THEY* SAY. DON'T TAKE THE BAIT.

When the first hints of this Republican attack on "selective" recounts began leaking out, Christopher and Daley—still hunkered down at the Governor's Inn—were flabbergasted. They had thought they were being statesmanlike by asking for recounts in only four counties. They had expected to get credit for not subjecting the state, and the country, to a recount of votes in all sixty-seven

Florida counties. Instead, they were castigated for cherry-picking only the areas that would help their candidate the most. It was indicative of their limited political acumen that they did not anticipate the Republican line of attack. But this failure by the leaders of the Democrats also hinted at a larger problem in their entire post-election effort. Gore and his lieutenants were so worried about appearing too aggressive that they were always hedging, compromising, and, in effect, undercutting their own work. To some extent, this weakness could be seen as a strength. After all, the vice president worried about the consistency and integrity of the arguments his team was putting forward. At the same time, Gore wanted to win. The result was a legal and political campaign gnarled by self-doubt and self-censorship.

James Baker suffered no such agonies. He believed that his candidate had won the vote on Election Day, and his job was to preserve that victory—by any means necessary. If he had to repudiate decades of Republican thought about judicial activism and state sovereignty, Baker would—and did—do it in a flash.

That Friday in Tallahassee the two sides met for the first and only time. Baker, joined by his longtime protégé Bob Zoellick and Bush campaign manager Joe Allbaugh, were greeted by Christopher, Daley, and Klain in the Tallahassee Room of the Governor's Inn. "We're going to have disagreements, but I hope we can keep it civil," Baker said. "Let's keep the tone civil." Christopher concurred, and there was nothing more to say. As both sides recognized, this was not a contest that lent itself to compromise. There could only be one winner.

Saturday, November 11, marked the first major turning point in the post-election period. Both sides took major steps that day— Bush in public, Gore in private. Their actions set the tone for the remainder of the battle. At this moment, the race had never been closer. The machine recount had shrunk Bush's margin to just 327 votes out of almost 6 million cast. But if the vote totals were mov-

ing the candidates closer together, the events of the day showed
that the two candidates were otherwise heading in opposite directions.

James Baker began the day as he would start almost every morning until the battle was over a month later. From his room at the
Doubletree Hotel (the campaign later found him an apartment in
Tallahassee), Baker conducted a before-breakfast conference call
with George W. Bush and Dick Cheney. Often, Baker would speak
to the candidate several more times during a given day; sometimes,
they wouldn't talk until the following morning. To an extraordinary
degree, Bush left the operation to Baker. On this day, as on so
many others, Bush was at his ranch in Crawford, Texas, near
Waco. Bush spent the post-election period mostly as a morale
booster, placing many telephone calls to people who were working
hard for the campaign. This was not a trivial thing, and the recipients of the calls treasured them. But as far as the actual operations
of the post-campaign campaign went, Baker was in charge.

On this Saturday, Bush gave final approval for the federal lawsuit the campaign was going to file in Miami. Baker held a news
conference in which he tried to spin the filing as a defensive measure. "This morning, we have asked that the United States District
Court for the Southern District of Florida preserve the integrity
and the consistency and the equality and the finality of the most
important civic action that Americans take, their votes in an election for president of the United States. We feel we have no other
choice." Notwithstanding this rhetoric of reluctance, there was no
mistaking the audacity of the Republicans' decision to take a presidential election to court—for the first time in American history.

While Baker was giving his press conference in Florida, back in
Washington Vice President Gore had set up a command post in
the library of the Naval Observatory. All he really needed were his
telephone and his television (which was usually muted), for Gore
had a somewhat undeserved reputation as a computer whiz. He
surfed the Web occasionally, sent e-mail on a wireless BlackBerry
device (which largely replaced his Palm Pilot), and used a laptop

computer now and then. His habits were not totally unlike those of George W. Bush, who was an inveterate e-mailer. The differences between the two men reflected temperament more than technology. Bush made decisions; Gore studied problems. Bush cared about results; Gore relished process. Each man created a recount effort in his own image.

Among Gore's early calls was one to Erin Brockovich. In the case that made her famous, Brockovich had rallied a large number of citizens to join together in a lawsuit. The Democrats were now considering doing something like that in Palm Beach County. Why not, Gore wondered, put Brockovich's expertise to work in Florida? (Gore actually spoke to Brockovich twice before Klain and Whouley stepped in to bury the idea. The Florida recount offered enough material to late-night comedians without the recruitment of a woman who was best known as Julia Roberts's real-life counterpart. Klain told Gore that Brockovich would create an unhelpful sideshow, and the vice president reluctantly agreed.)

Still, even as early as this Saturday afternoon, Al Gore was in his element. Throughout his political career, he had relished the opportunity to study complex problems that had multiple, changing variables. His own election proved to be the most compelling puzzle of them all. To the surprise of many around him, the vice president never seemed agonized by the possibility that the presidency might slip away by the smallest of margins. Rather, he was invigorated by the challenge of assimilating so much new data. Gore dutifully performed the public aspect of political life—glad-handing, speech making, and the like—but he lived for intellectual challenges such as this. He couldn't understand why everyone didn't revel in it as he did.

On this day, Gore convened his top advisers to take stock. Christopher and Daley had flown up from Florida, and they settled in around the dining room table. They were joined by media consultants Carter Eskew and Bob Shrum and by Tipper Gore and Frank Hunger, the widower of Gore's late sister and probably the vice president's closest friend. Gore sat at the head of the table, flanked by two pads of butcher paper set up on easels.

For his part, Bill Daley was not thriving. At his first press conference in Tallahassee, he had read a statement (written by Klain) that sought to project a resolute tone without committing Gore to any specific action. In addition to asking for manual recounts in the four counties, Daley had said, regarding the butterfly ballot, "We will be working with voters from Florida in support of legal actions." The statement was intentionally vague, but it prompted a vigorous denunciation from the *New York Times* editorial page. Daley's remarks had "escalated the atmosphere of combat," by suggesting a "worrying . . . rush to litigation." Daley had no stomach for criticism from that cherished forum, and he grumbled for days that he never should have made the statement in Florida.

Daley was piqued about something else, too. At a press conference in Austin, Karl Rove had said, "I really thought it was ironic that Chairman Daley went to great lengths to decry the butterfly ballot . . . because I have here a copy of the Cook County, Illinois, judicial ballot, which is a butterfly ballot." The comparison was specious; Cook County only used a butterfly ballot in unopposed elections. Still, Rove had tweaked Bill Daley with the legacy of his father, and that was something Daley couldn't stand.

Still, Daley opened the meeting in Gore's dining room by reviewing the political situation and the vote totals. Gore dutifully transcribed the numbers on the butcher paper for everyone to see. The heart of the session was Christopher's review of the campaign's legal options. He began with the butterfly ballot, offering a pessimistic assessment of the prospects for winning any relief on the issue. All of the most favorable legal remedies—such as a new election or a reallocation of the votes—were unlikely; they had maybe a 10 percent chance. Gore wasn't a lawyer, but he had studied the issues carefully and consulted other attorneys on his own, and he challenged some of Christopher's conclusions.

"Ten percent," Gore said. "That's too low."

"Well, maybe twenty," Christopher allowed.

"See," Gore said brightly. "I got you up 10 percent."

But Christopher had made his point: Litigation would likely fail. Even though the automatic recount had cut Bush's lead dramatically during the previous three days, Daley and Christopher offered little hope that the margin could be eliminated completely. "Look, you got screwed," Daley said. "But people get screwed every day. They don't have a remedy. Black people get screwed all the time. They don't have a remedy. But sometimes there's no remedy. There's nothing you can do about it."

Early in the morning, Gore had made clear that he wanted his running mate to join the conversation. However, Lieberman didn't drive on the Sabbath, so he was a little late, having walked up the hill from Georgetown to the vice president's residence.

Lieberman did not share the advisers' reluctance to push forward on all fronts. This became a recurring theme of the post-election period: The Connecticut senator always sounded like a warrior—in private settings. (Much to the frustration of the hawks on Gore's team, Lieberman sounded very different before the cameras.)

Gore, too, rallied against the prophesies of hopelessness he was hearing from Daley. He drew a series of concentric circles on the butcher paper to illustrate what he thought was the scope of his responsibilities. Inside the smallest circle were Gore and Lieberman; their closest supporters were in the next circle, then Democrats generally, and finally the country as a whole. Gore said his actions had to serve all of these groups, not just those closest to him. An immediate surrender would be a violation of his obligations to the people who had supported him, he said—all the people in all the circles.

The conversation drifted for hours without resolution. Christopher, with his eye for compromise, proposed that Gore ask Bush for a manual recount of the whole state, with both candidates agreeing to forgo any legal challenge of the result. Lieberman pressed for more forceful action. "There are Holocaust survivors down there who didn't get their votes counted," he said. "We can't just walk away from them."

Finally, Christopher put his view straight to Gore. "I'm seventy-five years old. You're only fifty-two," he said. "You can run again.

But you don't want to be known as a sore loser. You don't want to fight for too long. You've got to have your eye on history and the future."

In the end, Gore said he thought they shouldn't make any "momentous decisions." But it was clear that Daley and Christopher felt that a victory for Gore was nearly impossible, even though more people in Florida had gone to the polls there intending to vote for the vice president than for Bush. Gore and Lieberman couldn't wage a battle alone, of course, and their two principal deputies were telling them, in effect, that they ought to give it up.

This Saturday had begun with Bush and Gore locked in a closer contest than earlier in the week. Indeed, the vice president had made gains over the past three days. But the day ended with James Baker leading the attack—and Bill Daley and Warren Christopher making the case for surrender. And this was even before Gore realized there was another formidable adversary before him—a formerly obscure elected official named Katherine Harris.

CHAPTER FOUR

IN FOR A LANDING

KATHERINE HARRIS went to bed on election night believing that her work was done and George W. Bush would be the next president.

Harris had a whirlwind of an Election Day—bouncing from her office to the round of parties that filled the restaurants of Tallahassee's South Adams Street—but frenzied activity was routine for Florida's secretary of state. At the age of forty-three, Harris had more energy than anyone in state government. She'd give six or seven speeches a day, in as many as three different cities, and leave voice mails for her staff well after midnight. No one could offer up accomplishments to match all the activity, but that wasn't really the point. Her position came with so little power that there was scarcely anything Harris could do. Indeed, in 1998, the year Harris won the job of secretary of state, the electorate voted to abolish the office at the end of her term. No; Harris herself—her life, her career—was the accomplishment, and she was determined to make it a success.

She was born into the Florida aristocracy, the granddaughter of Ben Hill Griffin, Jr., who was one of the state's turn-of-the-century

robber barons, a citrus farmer, cattle rancher, and, rather inciden-
tally, member of the state senate. The football stadium at the University of Florida, as important a structure as any on the Gator
campus, is named for Griffin. Her father, George W. Harris, Jr.,
still runs the family bank in Polk County, in central Florida, where
Katherine was raised. The bank is called the Citrus and Chemical,
named after the county's famous orange groves and the even more
lucrative mines that were carved out of the Bone Valley, North
America's richest deposit of phosphate. Katherine was both an ath-
lete and a beauty queen in high school, and she attended her
mother's alma mater, Agnes Scott, a small women's college outside
Atlanta that has long been popular with well-born daughters of the
South.

Harris had an unsettled, if not atypical, life in the 1980s. She
studied art in Spain, moved to Tampa, worked as a marketing rep
for IBM in various cities, and married a businessman who lived in
Sarasota. In the early 1990s, she took, then quit, a job in commercial real estate and divorced her husband. For all her energy, Harris was basically looking for something to do—and found it,
courtesy of Florida's most important Democrat at the time. In
1991, Governor Lawton Chiles, for whom Harris had been a summer intern when he was a senator, named her to the board of Sarasota's Ringling Museum of Art. Despite its famous collection of
paintings by Peter Paul Rubens, the museum was in financial trouble, especially with the region mired in a recession. But Harris net-
worked and raised funds with gusto. Later, she was set up on a
blind date with the man who would become her second husband,
Anders Ebbeson, a Swedish businessman. Ebbeson made his living
in the same rarefied world in which Harris had spent her life; he
ran companies that made miniature appliances—stoves, washing
machines, and the like—for yachts.

As part of her duties on behalf of the museum—Harris told
this story often—she visited her state senator to lobby for more
funds. But the senator, a Democrat named Jim Boczar, allegedly
told her that as far as he was concerned, a Rubens was a sandwich.

According to Harris, she was so offended by Boczar's attitude that she decided to run against him in 1994. She raised more than half a million dollars—a record for a state-senate race—and swept into office in a landslide, boosted by a national tide for the Republican Party that year. Harris's election tipped the balance in the state senate from the Democrats to the Republicans. In the course of the campaign, Harris was the leading beneficiary of illegal campaign contributions (more than $20,000) from an insurance company called Riscorp, which spread more than $400,000 among Florida candidates that year. In the eventual trial of Riscorp executives, Harris's campaign manager was named an unindicted co-conspirator in the scheme, but Harris herself denied knowledge of any improprieties.

Like many North Floridians, Harris simply evolved from Democrat to Republican without being especially ideological. She supported funding for the arts, but sponsored a bill to require parental consent before a minor could have an abortion (vetoed by Chiles). She also spearheaded an effort to cripple Riscorp's out-of-state competitors in Florida. Her one-term legislative career was marked principally by her effort to find a higher office to seek in 1998. As it turned out, Jeb Bush—planning a second run for governor—chose the incumbent secretary of state, Sandra Mortham, as his running mate. Harris promptly declared for her job. But Mortham became embroiled in a controversy over whether she used the office to promote herself, withdrew from the lieutenant-governor's race, and decided to run for re-election. Many expected Harris to bow out in favor of the incumbent (as another candidate did), but displaying the resilience and energy that were her trademarks, she chose to fight on against Mortham.

The Republican primary between the two women was bitter, notwithstanding (or perhaps because of) their virtually identical stance on issues. In an act of great political bravado, Harris attacked Mortham for accepting illegal campaign contributions—from Riscorp. (Mortham had accepted $5,000 from the company, about a quarter of what Harris received.) Harris won her primary and general election easily, as did Jeb Bush at the top of the ticket.

While a state senator, Harris had studied part-time at Harvard's John F. Kennedy School of Government and received a master's in public administration. As secretary of state, Harris made trade the focus of her energies, traveling to South America, the Sydney Olympics, and the Caribbean in efforts to drum up business for Florida companies. It was difficult to point to any concrete benefits from these undertakings, but the costs amounted to over $100,000—more than any other public official in Florida spent on travel in the same period. In light of the built-in term limit to her job as secretary of state, Harris spent a great deal of energy focusing on the possible next step in her career, just as she had in her brief tenure in the state senate. Because of her international interests, some sort of federal service—an ambassadorship, perhaps—seemed the best possibility, so her attention turned to the 2000 presidential race. Though they had run on the same ticket, Harris and Jeb Bush were never particularly close, but it was clear that a George W. Bush administration represented her route out of Tallahassee.

So Harris waded into the presidential campaign for the same reason that a lot of people joined—in equal parts, it seems, because of what George W. Bush would do for the country and because of what he could do for her. Harris's work for Bush was sporadic, but enough to mark her as an active supporter. She joined Jeb Bush and a big group of locals to travel to New Hampshire on a one-day "Freezin' for a Reason" tour for George W. Bush. (A fourth-generation Floridian, Harris neglected to wear socks and nearly got frostbite.) She served as a Bush delegate to the Republican National Convention and as one of eight co-chairs of the Texas governor's campaign in Florida. "I am thrilled and honored to announce my support of George W. Bush for the presidency," she said in a press release posted on the Bush campaign's website.

When the election controversy began, Gore supporters pointed to Harris's ties to the Bush presidential campaign as evidence of her bias, a legitimate point. On closer inspection, Harris's activities offered insight into her operating style. Her title as "co-chair" was purely honorary and involved no responsibilities on the campaign; the delegate assignment involved nothing more than attending the convention in Philadelphia. Even Harris's quote in the press release was written by someone else. Katherine Harris didn't do substance; it was done for her.

All in all, then, it wasn't surprising that Harris's final stop on election night was at the Doubletree Hotel, where the state Republican Party was holding its victory celebration, hosted by state chairman Al Cardenas. It was there that she watched the networks call the state, and the election, for Bush. After the cheering subsided, she went home to bed, falling asleep at about 3 A.M.

Harris's home phone rang about a half hour later. It was Don Evans.

Bush's campaign chairman, who was with the candidate in Austin, wanted a briefing. What is going on in Florida? When are we going to get some final results? After Harris mumbled an answer, Evans handed the phone to Jeb Bush, who was also standing vigil in Texas.

"Who is Ed Kast," the governor asked, "and why is he giving an interview on national television?"

Harris knew that Kast was the deputy to Clay Roberts, the director of the Division of Elections in her office. (She didn't know that Kast had just been cut off from explaining Florida election law on CNN because Frank Jimenez, general counsel to Jeb Bush, had called Roberts and told him to get Kast off the air.) But why the panicked phone calls? Last she had heard, George W. Bush had won the election.

Harris raced back to her office on the ground floor of the Capitol, in the corner of the building that also housed the governor and the attorney general. The Division of Elections was way up on the eighteenth floor, and the separation was more than just geographic. In the hodgepodge of her responsibilities, which included such things as the registration of corporations and historic preservation, Harris paid little attention to her elections portfolio. As a rule, neither the press nor the state legislature had much interest in the mechanics of elections, so she more or less let the division run itself. Like her predecessors, Harris did not see the need to acquaint herself with the minutiae of election law and vote-counting procedures. She rarely traveled up to eighteen.

When Harris took the elevator up to Clay Roberts's office before dawn on November 8, she found chaos. Reporters were clustered by the receptionist's desk, and a bevy of Republican politicians were huddled with Roberts in his office. Like the candidates' entourages in Austin and Nashville, like the reporters outside, like the millions of people still watching the baffled network anchormen, everyone in that office was asking some version of the same question: Who won?

It was Clay Roberts's first election, and he was feeling his way. He spent several of the early-morning hours trying to get a legitimate result from Volusia County, whose misreported early numbers had caused the networks' premature call for Bush just after 2 A.M. By 6 A.M., Roberts was able to report the results for the state—2,909,135 votes for Bush, and 2,907,351 for Gore, a difference of 1,784 votes, or three one-hundredths (.03) of 1 percent. Because the margin was less than one half (.5) of 1 percent of all votes cast, Florida law required the canvassing boards in each of the sixty-seven counties to "order a recount of the votes cast." This would become known as the "automatic," or "machine," recount of the ballots.

In all the tumult of the next thirty-five days, this automatic recount supervised by the secretary of state's office represented one apparent point of consensus. The ballots were counted once on election night and again pursuant to this statutorily mandated repeat procedure. As James Baker said any number of times during the post-election battle, "The vote in Florida was counted . . . the vote in Florida has been recounted . . ." No one from the Gore campaign ever challenged this view. There was only one problem. It simply wasn't true.

. . . .

When Harris took office at the beginning of 1999, she cleaned house by installing her own people. For the most part, Harris gave a more partisan tilt to traditionally apolitical appointments. This included the new man at the Division of Elections, Clay Roberts.

Roberts was typical of the new guard—youngish (thirty-five), Republican, and a former staffer for some conservative members of the Florida legislature. He had graduated from West Point, but went to law school after an injury forced him out of the army. He was not a political operative, per se—he had never worked on campaigns—but he wasn't a career civil servant, either. He owed his job to Harris—and to the Republican Party.

Unlike his boss, Roberts really knew Florida election law, both the codes on the books and the unofficial rules of how things actually operated. Most important, for present purposes, Roberts knew that there had been some controversy about the very procedure the state was about to begin, the machine (or automatic) recount. Nothing less than the presidency might turn on this once-obscure matter.

Back in 1999, several supervisors had requested guidance on conducting automatic recounts. Specifically, in counties that used optical scanners for voting—where voters marked their ballots by penciling in ovals, as in standardized tests—should the local officials recount the ballots themselves or simply check that the totals on the machines were added correctly? In Key West, the supervisor of Manatee County said he thought machine recounts should involve only a checking of the summaries, not an actual recount of the votes.

Ethel Baxter, who was in 1999 near the end of her days as Roberts's predecessor as director of the Division of Elections, gave a formal reply. "You have asked for an official opinion or rule, with specific procedures for conducting a recount on an optical scan voting system," Baxter's letter, dated April 28, 1999, stated. The opinion offered in response was unequivocal. "It is our opinion that each ballot must be reprocessed," Baxter wrote, explaining that Florida law "requires that there be a *recount* of the votes cast with respect to the office where a candidate was defeated or eliminated by one-half of one percent or less of the votes cast for the office. It is our opinion that 'recount' means to count again."

The subject came up again at the annual summer conference of all the election supervisors on June 22, 2000, in Key West. How should optical-scan counties conduct automatic recounts? At a workshop, in front of all the supervisors, Clay Roberts and his colleagues in the Division of Elections were emphatic in response: *Checking the totals is not enough. In order to do a recount, you should run every ballot though the machines again. The secretary of state's office believes that this is the only correct way to conduct an automatic recount.*

The question illustrated the delicate balance of power between the supervisors in the counties and the secretary of state's office in Tallahassee. The supervisors were elected officials in their own right, so Harris's people could not simply issue orders to them. But the state officials, in turn, exercised ultimate authority over certifying elections, so the local officials could not ignore the Division of Elections, either. As was often the case, the county supervisors didn't have the time, resources, or inclination for recounts. The supervisors viewed recounts as little more than expensive second guesses of their work.

All of this was fresh in Roberts's mind as he sat down, early Wednesday morning, November 8, to instruct the counties on how to conduct their recounts. At 9:30 A.M., he issued a "Memorandum to All Supervisors of Elections," explaining that because of the margin of 1,784 votes between the candidates, "Florida law requires an automatic recount of all votes cast." He said the deadline was the close of business on the following day, Thursday, November 9. The memo included a paean to Harris, "the constitutionally independent officer elected by the people of Florida as the chief election officer of the state." As such, the document went on, "it is her responsibility to obtain and maintain uniformity in the application, operation, and interpretation of the election laws. Florida law has rules and procedures to ensure the integrity and accuracy of the recount process . . ."

But what were those rules and procedures? As for the answer to that question—how the recount should proceed, and what the counties should actually do—Roberts said nothing at all. Most notably, Roberts did not say that optical-scan counties had to re-process the votes. There was no reference to his office's established policy that " 'recount' means to count again." Amateurs in Florida election law—virtually everyone at that point—did not notice the omission.

In fact, many counties—a total of eighteen—did not recount their votes on the day after the election. Those counties accounted for 1.58 million votes, more than a quarter of all the votes cast in the election. The significance of this omission can scarcely be overstated. First, as recount expert Jack Young never tired of pointing out, increasing the size of the pool of votes in a recount invariably increases the chances for the lead to change. In other words, if Roberts had insisted that the counties follow the procedures that Harris's own office had established, Al Gore may have been leading in the vote totals by Thursday afternoon. Moreover, the process may have prompted some counties to re-examine their ballots more closely. In Lake County, which did not run its ballots through the machines, the *Orlando Sentinel* found 376 uncounted ballots clearly intended as votes for Al Gore—and 246 uncounted ballots showing clear votes for George W. Bush. The swing in just this one county—where Gore would have netted 130 votes—illustrates how important a true recount might have been.

Baker, and Bush himself, invariably cited the automatic recount as proof that the votes had been "counted and recounted." But, of course, those votes had not been recounted, and to this day, the votes in the eighteen counties still have not been officially recounted. A central theme of the Republican public-relations effort was that Gore was demanding third and fourth examinations of ballots that had already been rigorously scrutinized. And it was false.

This subterranean story of the automatic recount marked just the first time that Harris's office performed heroic, if necessarily unsung, service to the Bush campaign. In the days that followed, Clay Roberts and Debbie Kearney, Harris's general counsel, would exchange nervous glances whenever the subject of the automatic recount came up. They knew that it had not been a full recount. But neither they nor their superior, Katherine Harris, ever corrected the public record.

The chaos, and the crowds, in Harris's office only grew as Wednesday turned into Thursday and the margin between Bush and Gore continued to shrink—down to 327 votes—as a result of the limited automatic recount. Voters were filing lawsuits in Palm Beach County, and some cases named Harris as a defendant. As lawyers for both sides tried to understand Florida law better, there was talk of manual recounts, certification of the election, and a host of other concepts that most people, including Harris and many of the people who worked for her, barely understood themselves.

Of course, reporters by the dozen were now camped by Harris's door in the Capitol. Adam Goodman, a political consultant who had worked on Harris's race for secretary of state, wanted to lend a hand, so he called Ben McKay, her chief of staff. "Let me speak to your press and communications people," Goodman requested.

"You are," said McKay.

On Thursday, Harris herself demonstrated how much she needed guidance. She gave a press conference of sorts at the Capitol, but she knew so little about the law that she answered few questions. To those who knew Harris, the stiff, awkward presentation was especially odd, because it contrasted so much with her usual gregarious demeanor. In her nervousness that day, Harris also overapplied her makeup, which cemented her public image in another unfortunate way.

Also on Thursday, lawyers from the Bush campaign were catching up to the Gore team's head start and starting to spread out to all the counties in the state. A Tallahassee lawyer named Kenneth Sukhia was deputized by the Bush team to go to Gadsden County, just outside the capital. He wasn't impressed by the state of the Bush effort. He wanted the advice of a real professional, so he called his law partner, J. M. "Mac" Stipanovich.

"This is a disaster," Sukhia said. "You gotta get involved."

In the public sector, Mac Stipanovich hadn't done much more than serve as chief of staff and campaign manager for Bob Martinez, Florida's Republican governor from 1987 to 1991. (He also helped run Jeb Bush's first—unsuccessful—campaign for governor, in 1994.) But for corporate interests in the Sunshine State, Stipanovich was the man to see for the project that absolutely had to be approved, the bill that simply had to pass. Stipanovich generally worked behind the scenes as the most effective and ruthless lobbyist in Tallahassee, but he had a theatrical demeanor. Walking outside the Capitol with Governor Jeb Bush after the 1999 legislative session, Stipanovich boasted to Lucy Morgan of the *St. Petersburg Times,* "I got everything. I don't know what the poor people got, but the rich people are happy, and I'm ready to go home."

With his trimmed goatee and muscular physique, Stipanovich at the age of fifty-one seemed to be going out of his way to look like Mephistopheles. It helped that he was smarter than just about anyone in town. He decided, in midlife, that he wanted to learn about the Crusades, so he took time away from his clients every week to study Latin and medieval history at Florida State. He had a special interest in the Council of Toulouse, of 1229, when the elders of the Church decided that the laity would be forbidden from reading the Bible—the people in charge would tell them everything they needed to know.

Stipanovich, who took the call from his colleague on his way to Latin class, couldn't very well sit out the biggest political battle ever, much less one that happened to be raging on his home turf. So while he still had his cell phone out, just outside of class, Stipanovich called a friend on the Bush campaign—where he knew just about everyone who mattered—and asked what he could do to help. He received his assignment.

He was to be Katherine Harris's minder.

The three main rooms in Harris's suite on the ground floor of the Capitol looked out on a broad plaza, and reporters quickly discovered that her windows offered views into the world of the woman who would be certifying the next president. (Looking out, Harris herself could see the Florida Supreme Court, just across Duval Street, where she would soon be doing battle.) Harris and McKay, her chief of staff, had curtains in their offices, which they used to keep out prying eyes, but the conference room had no such protection. So McKay found some big pieces of cardboard and taped them over the glass. He also rounded up all the delivery-food menus he could find. It was going to be a long haul.

Mac Stipanovich arrived in that conference room late on Thursday and would scarcely leave it for the next several weeks. His first stop, though, was Harris's office, for a heart-to-heart with the secretary of state. He had a single piece of advice for her, a phrase that should guide all of her actions in the drama to come. He would say it so often in the secretary's suite that others began to use it, too. Months later, Harris and McKay would explain their actions with this phrase, but without attribution to its author.

"You have to bring this election in for a landing," Stipanovich said.

The instruction may have sounded banal, but there was a substantive core to the message, which Stipanovich spent the next several days spelling out. In a general sense, Stipanovich knew that Harris shared his overall goals for a Republican victory, but he still feared that she would act as most politicians do in a crisis—vacillate, test public opinion, watch what other people did first, "see how it all plays out," a cliché much beloved by officeholders. Harris knew so little about the legal and procedural issues that the chances of this kind of hesitancy from her were even greater. Such behavior would have been unacceptable to both Stipanovich and the Bush campaign. Rather, they wanted Harris to take strong action, narrow the issues, make decisions, cut off debate, set and enforce deadlines, and pick a winner. That was what "bring the election in for a landing" meant.

Stipanovich had served as an informal adviser to Harris for several years; he was one of the few heavyweights in the state who had stuck with her after Sandra Mortham re-entered the race for secretary of state in 1998. Stipanovich knew to play to Harris's dramatic sense of herself, insisting that she was the only person in America who could bring order to the growing chaos of this election. She would be the one to vindicate the rule of law. Harris suffered from one of the perils of a privileged life: self-confidence unburdened by self-knowledge. So she was primed to hear what Stipanovich had to say. Yes, she agreed with her adviser; it was her duty to bring this election in for a landing.

Thursday, November 9, was an extraordinarily busy day for Harris, even by her usual standards. In addition to welcoming Stipanovich to the team, she held her news conference and conducted brief meetings with the protagonists on both sides—Baker and his team for the Republicans and Christopher and his for the Democrats. Harris assured the visiting dignitaries that she would follow the law, but she didn't go into any greater detail. Neither meeting lasted longer than ten minutes, though Jim Baker, flaunting his Southern bona fides, made time to sip a Dr Pepper. As he would throughout the crisis, Stipanovich remained out of sight during these meetings, tucked away in Harris's conference room.

Given the tensions of the day, Harris wanted to unwind with a good dinner, so she and her husband invited Stipanovich to the best restaurant in town, Cypress, where her cousin was the co-owner. As it happened, Christopher, Daley, and Klain, having just agreed on the four counties where they would seek manual recounts, chose the same place to eat. (Tallahassee, after all, did not enjoy an overabundance of fine restaurants.) Christopher had noticed Harris's nervousness earlier in the day in her office and the way she looked to Clay Roberts whenever any matter of substance was raised. He was therefore all the more surprised when a very different Katherine Harris came to his table that night and pulled up a chair.

This was the effervescent Harris that Tallahassee knew so well. In a fifteen-minute monologue, Harris explained how she had been all over the world and how she was going to make Miami the headquarters of the Western Hemisphere, the Brussels of the Americas. She went on and on in such a breathless way that Christopher could only study her in wonderment. She was completely unself-conscious in rattling on about these matters, and reached the climax of her oration when she said that the Congress of the United States had passed a *resolution* supporting her effort to make Miami the headquarters of a free-trade region. It didn't take an extreme cynic to note that congressional resolutions were usually devoted to such urgent matters as designating National Bird-Watching Week. Daley, who was sitting across from Christopher, was rolling his eyes at Harris's performance, but she wasn't finished.

"Isn't it funny," she mused, turning to Daley, "that here I do all this foreign trade and you were secretary of commerce." And then, shifting back to Christopher, Harris added, "And I'm a secretary of state, and you were a secretary of state!"

By Friday morning, there was work to do back at the secretary of state's office. Gore had filed four protests, requesting manual recounts in Broward, Miami-Dade, Palm Beach, and Volusia counties. Recounts, of course, represented a risk to the Bush campaign, which was now clinging to a preposterously small margin. Stipanovich's reaction to the Democrats' requests was simple. They should be denied. There shouldn't be any more recounts. Harris should just certify Bush's victory on the following Tuesday, November 14, seven days after Election Day, as mandated by Florida law. No to recounts; yes to certification. *Bring it in for a landing.*

But it wasn't up to Stipanovich, or even Harris, to decide

whether there would be manual recounts in the four counties. It was up to the counties' three-member canvassing boards—each of which was comprised of the local elections supervisor, a county judge, and an elected county commissioner. So Stipanovich asked Clay Roberts to explain the grounds for granting or rejecting a manual recount of the vote.

As ever, Florida law was cryptic. If the county canvassing boards found "an error in vote tabulation which could affect the outcome of the election," they were supposed to conduct a manual recount. But the statute didn't define "error in vote tabulation." There were, basically, two interpretations. First, these errors could be mistakes in counting, for example, leaving out ballots that really should have been included in the final tally. This standard would meet the broad objective in all of Florida's election laws to make sure that every vote was counted. Gore's lawyers assumed that this was the meaning of the rule. Second, the errors could be breakdowns in vote-tabulation *systems,* such as computer software. If this were the case, then recounts would be much less common, and there would be none in 2000. Republicans, of course, would prefer this connotation. Broad recount standard versus restrictive recount rule. Count all the votes versus bring it in for a landing. Gore versus Bush.

Stipanovich and Roberts discussed what constituted "an error in vote tabulation," and they quickly agreed, not surprisingly, that the restrictive (i.e., Bush) standard was the correct meaning. Counties should not order manual recounts unless there had been flaws in their entire mechanical or software systems. But now they faced the problem of imposing this view on the counties, in particular Palm Beach, which was going to be the first to decide whether to proceed with a manual recount. They decided to send one of the secretary of state's lawyers, Kerey Carpenter, down to Palm Beach to be their eyes and ears on the ground.

Harris could try to prohibit the manual recounts by issuing opinion letters. As the chief elections officer for the state, she could offer binding interpretations of Florida election law—but only if she was asked for them. Carpenter, the Republican emissary to Palm Beach, made it her business to guarantee that the county would seek the secretary of state's guidance. All day on Saturday, as the Palm Beach County canvassing board met in a raucous session in West Palm Beach, the personable Carpenter made her views available to Judge Charles Burton, the chair of the board—all the while taking instructions by cell phone from Clay Roberts, back in Tallahassee. By midday, in a series of private conversations, Burton asked Carpenter whether she thought a recount was justified in Palm Beach. Like her patrons in the Capitol, Carpenter said no. The information pipeline was up and running—from Roberts to Carpenter to Burton, with Mac Stipanovich at the source.

More important, as Carpenter and Judge Burton caucused privately during the afternoon, the lawyer introduced the judge to the subject of opinion letters. By nightfall, Carpenter had persuaded Burton to make a formal request for an opinion letter on the appropriateness of a manual recount in Palm Beach. "Assuming we asked for an opinion, when could we receive it?" Burton asked Carpenter as the board was preparing to recess for the day. "Tomorrow," she said—that is, Sunday. But in the chaotic conclusion to the board's meeting, there was never a formal vote of the three members to ask for an opinion from Harris's office. Still, Judge Burton said that as chair, he intended to ask for the opinion from the secretary of state on Sunday. It looked like Stipanovich might get his chance to shut down the manual recount before it even started.

In his town house in Tallahassee, Jeb Bush's acting general counsel, Frank Jimenez, flipped on CNN and watched the proceedings of the Palm Beach canvassing board in an exhausted stupor. But he perked up when he heard Kerey Carpenter say that the Division of Elections could have an advisory opinion to Palm Beach on Sunday. Jimenez knew how useful an advisory opinion from Harris would be on the question of manual recounts. It could shut down the recount in Palm Beach and help the Republicans' federal lawsuit, which was going to be heard the next day in Miami. When he dragged himself into the state Republican headquarters on Sunday morning, he looked forward to reading the opinion that Kerey Carpenter had promised the previous night.

A generation ago, people like Frank Jimenez scarcely existed. If you were a young lawyer interested in using the courts to effect social change, you were a Democrat. But Republicans eventually realized that they too could reach their goals through legal action, and the notion of the conservative public-interest lawyer was born. Jimenez was born in Miami to a family of Cubans who had fled the revolution. He received his undergraduate degree from the University of Miami, then attended Yale Law School, once the great citadel of the legal left. But thanks to vigorous organizations such as the Federalist Society, conservatives like Jimenez had their own networks. After law school, Jimenez worked on both of Jeb Bush's campaigns, and in 2000, he found himself the thirty-six-year-old acting general counsel to the governor.

Jimenez decided to take an unpaid leave of absence almost as soon as the recount saga began. He moved to Republican headquarters to serve as a key adviser on Florida law, government, and politics to Ben Ginsberg and others on the Bush legal team. Jimenez's formal leave of absence notwithstanding, the presence of Jeb's top lawyer at the elbow of his brother's legal strategists illustrated the tight weave of the Republican power structure in Tallahassee.

But as the morning stretched into the afternoon, no opinion appeared from the Division of Elections, and Jimenez was getting antsy. So the young lawyer called Clay Roberts and asked why it had not been issued. Roberts explained that Judge Burton had said he was going to write to ask for the advisory opinion on Sunday, but no letter had arrived. The draft of the opinion was ready, but the Division of Elections could not issue it until someone made a request in writing. How could Jimenez pry the opinion out of the Division of Elections?

He began to wonder whether someone besides Burton could formally request the opinion. Working together, Roberts and Jimenez discovered that virtually anyone with a connection to an election could ask for a formal opinion such as this. Jimenez came up with the idea that Al Cardenas, the state chairman of the Republican Party, could ask Katherine Harris for her opinion about when manual recounts were justified. That sounded fine to Roberts, and within minutes Jimenez himself had drafted a request for an opinion for Cardenas's signature. (The opinion was not produced until Monday morning, however, because Mac Stipanovich thought it would appear unseemly for Harris's office to open on a Sunday to issue an opinion favorable to George W. Bush, in a letter to the chairman of the state Republican Party. Evidently, doing that on a Monday was fine.)

The advisory opinion, when it was released on Monday, November 13, read as if it had been written by the Bush campaign. "An 'error in vote tabulation' means a counting error in which the vote tabulation system fails to count properly marked" ballots, Clay Roberts wrote to Cardenas. In other words, the mere existence of undervotes and overvotes would not justify a board's voting to go forward with a manual recount. So, since joining Harris's team on Thursday afternoon, Stipanovich had achieved a critical goal by Monday morning—an apparent prohibition on the manual recounts that were Gore's only hope of victory.

Less than a week after the election, the office of Katherine Harris began acting as a wholly owned subsidiary of the George W. Bush campaign. In retrospect, it is clear how this happened. First, the Bush campaign installed the state's premier Republican power broker (Stipanovich) as the chief adviser to the Republican secretary of state. Her office then schemed to elicit a request for its own binding opinion that would virtually guarantee the victory of the Republican candidate for president. When that request was not made promptly, the responsibility shifted briefly to the Republican governor of the state, who happened to be the brother of the Republican presidential candidate. The chief lawyer for that Republican governor (who was on a brief and meaningless "leave of absence" from his official duties) figured out how to ask for the same opinion on behalf of the state chairman of the Republican Party. In an almost comically meager act of deference to notions of decency and fair play, the Republican power broker ordered that the opinion materialize on Monday morning rather than Sunday night. The events all took place without the knowledge, much less the participation, of the Gore campaign. In the battle for Florida, this was how Bush won—through superior knowledge of the Florida electoral system; through tight (and secret) coordination between Republican officeholders and Bush lawyers; and, in short, through ruthless determination to exploit any advantage. There was also the crucial participation of the nodding figurehead, Katherine Harris.

On Sunday night, November 12, Judge Burton's letter asking for an advisory opinion eventually turned up on Clay Roberts's desk. The judge and Al Cardenas received the same opinion on Monday morning: no manual recounts. But that wasn't the end of the matter. Things in Palm Beach were a little more complicated than they had first appeared.

CHAPTER FIVE

THE
PALM BEACH
STORY

"Vote for Gore."

Theresa LePore slid a punch-card voting machine across the table. It was four o'clock in the afternoon on Election Day, and Judge Charles Burton had arrived to oversee the testing of the vote-counting equipment. By that point in the day, LePore had already been deluged with complaints about her butterfly ballot, and she wanted an objective opinion from her new colleague on the three-member county canvassing board.

"Vote for Gore," LePore instructed Judge Burton.

Burton pulled the stylus from the holder and punched through hole number five on the sample ballot.

"I don't think it's that *haad*," Burton said with a smile and a thick Massachusetts inflection. At the age of forty-two, Burton had already spent two decades in South Florida, but his accent remained. He had followed his brother south from the Boston suburb of Newton and stayed in Florida to attend law school. He practiced in cheerful obscurity, mostly as a prosecutor in the state's attorney's office, and as 2000 began, he threw in an application to become a county-court judge—the lowest level in the state judiciary. (The court handles misdemeanors and civil cases where less than $15,000 is at issue.) Burton was a Democrat who had interned for Senator Edward Kennedy as a college student, but he passed Governor Jeb Bush's screening panel, and on May 3, the governor called Burton to say that he would be appointed. It was their only conversation.

Burton looked like a big, friendly lug, which is exactly what he was. He had never courted controversy, never pretended to be a scholar, never drawn attention for either especially hard work or undue ambition, but had drifted contentedly through the sunshine—another snowbird who had found his corner of paradise. When, a couple of months into his judgeship, the chief judge asked Burton to serve as the judicial member of the Palm Beach canvassing board, he agreed without hesitation. He only had one question. "What's a canvassing board?"

Under Florida law, each county had a three-member canvassing board responsible for certifying the fairness and accuracy of all elections. By law, the boards were made up of a local judge, a county elected official, and the county supervisor of elections. Like most Floridians, Burton had never heard of the boards, because they worked in near-total obscurity. Most elections passed without controversy, and the supervisors generally handled most issues themselves. In Palm Beach County, the chief responsibilities of the canvassing board were to verify the signatures on absentee ballots and to preside over the "L-and-A test"—the logic and accuracy test of the vote-counting machines, which was done before and after the ballots were tallied. The sum total of Burton's preparation for his new assignment was to plan to take Wednesday off—because he knew he'd be up late on election night.

But the closeness of the election ruined Burton's hopes for a one-day vacation. On Wednesday morning, LePore called him to say that the margin in the presidential election was less than half a percentage point, which triggered the automatic-recount provision of the law. County workers were going to run the ballots through the machines a second time, and Burton had to observe the L-and-A test before and after the counting. (In the test, a pre-counted set of ballots is used to see if the machines are properly calibrated.) So Burton trooped across the street from the courts building to LePore's office in the government center and watched the cards blur through the counters once more. In keeping with LePore's hapless performance in the entire election, the machine recount did identify a serious error—865 ballots that hadn't been counted on election night. Gore netted a 643-vote gain from the new Palm Beach totals, an important factor in Bush's statewide margin slipping from 1,784 to 327.

This machine recount on Wednesday took place while the county—and the country—was still in a kind of shock about the uncertain outcome of the election. By Thursday, however, the nation's anger and confusion had a focus: Palm Beach County.

In a lot across the street from the government center, the Reverend Jesse Jackson stood on a makeshift platform and announced, "There was a misalignment in the process. If you drive your car down the road in a little car and your wheels are not aligned, you have a wreck. That was a wreck in West Palm." The analogy may have been imperfect, but cheers rang out nonetheless. Not everyone was sure why they were protesting, but the frustrations of the unresolved election crested on Thursday, November 9, in West Palm Beach. By late afternoon, the crowd had swollen to nearly a thousand, mostly pro-Gore demonstrators, shouting, "Gore got more!" and "Revote!" and "This is not a game!"

The election controversy had settled in what may be, if such a thing is possible, the least typical county in the United States. The oddities begin with the town of Palm Beach itself, the fourteen-mile spit of sand that was first developed by the legendary early-twentieth-century magnate Henry Flagler. To a remarkable extent, Flagler's vision for the tiny island endures. Lockjawed socialites still sip cocktails on Worth Avenue, where, as it happens, the Bloody Mary was invented at the restaurant Taboo, to cure Barbara Hutton's hangover. The *Palm Beach Daily News,* known as the Shiny Sheet, remains the only daily newspaper in America printed on glossy paper, so that the ink will not rub off on its readers' designer clothes.

But the town of Palm Beach houses only about ten thousand of the county's 1-million-plus residents. Ninety minutes inland, by the coast of Lake Okeechobee but in the same county, is perhaps the poorest community in America. In 1960, Edward R. Murrow set his famous documentary *Harvest of Shame* in the sugar groves of Belle Glade, and the mostly black inhabitants of the area have not fared much better in subsequent decades. In their own ways, the towns of Palm Beach and Belle Glade have evolved little over the years, but the rest of the county has been transformed. Retirees from the North, many of them Jewish, have been the chief engines of change as they filled vast condominium complexes in Boca Raton and elsewhere, bringing their mostly Democratic politics with them. Twelve thousand people live in one development alone, Century Village. Thanks largely to these senior citizens, and the businesses that sprang up to serve them, the population of the county has doubled since 1980.

Some condo commandos, as the politically active among the retirees are known, made their way to the Jackson protest in downtown West Palm Beach, but the real focus of their energy was Democratic Party headquarters, in Delray Beach. When Liz Hyman received her first hints of trouble there on Tuesday morning, there was just one folding table on the sidewalk to receive volunteers. By Thursday, however, the Democrats had to shut down an entire corner of the parking lot to accommodate all the aggrieved voters who were streaming in to tell their stories. The one table grew to three, and soon a volunteer army of lawyers and notaries had arrived to take affidavits from voters who said they were confused by the ballot. Gore sent spokesman Chris Lehane to Palm Beach during this first post-election crush, and he found himself surrounded by a swarm of friendly admirers. Lehane had little to tell them or the press, but the crowds were such that he found that he couldn't even leave the headquarters building. Half-jokingly, he called Mark Fabiani in Nashville and said, "It's like the embassy in Vietnam! You're going to have to get a helicopter and pluck me off the roof!"

To be sure, there was an element of hysteria in the reaction to the butterfly ballot. Democratic lawyers ultimately compiled more than twelve thousand dossiers from disgruntled voters in Palm Beach County, even though Buchanan received only 3,407 votes there. That means that not all of the voters made the mistake they thought they had, although some of them surely contributed to the high totals of undervotes and overvotes. Still, there was a special poignancy in the notion that so many elderly Jews, who had lived through the Holocaust in the United States, if not in Europe, had to face the possibility that they had voted for Buchanan, who had spoken sympathetically about Hitler's Germany. Their pain and anger were real.

Few people understood these feelings better than Carol Roberts, who, alongside LePore and Burton, was the third member of the Palm Beach County canvassing board. Born Carol Klein sixty-four years earlier, she was in one respect a true oddity in this county of immigrants—she was a native of South Florida. She had married a doctor, and after they raised six children—all of whom, she liked to point out, had become professionals of one kind or another—she began a career in politics. She worked her way from minor posts in the West Palm Beach city government to the mayoralty of that bustling city and finally, in 1986, to the county commission, which is the ruling body in Palm Beach. Trained in the bubbling cauldron of condo politics, Roberts had a thick head of orange hair, a nicotine-ravaged voice, and a rugged confidence in her own opinions. In county meetings, she had a favorite phrase: "I'm not a lawyer, but . . ." In the days ahead, she would have the chance to use it often.

The Gore campaign requested recounts in Palm Beach and the other three counties late on Thursday, November 9. Friday was Veterans Day, so it wasn't until Saturday morning, November 11, that the Palm Beach canvassing board convened to decide how, and whether, to recount the votes that might determine the next president of the United States. For the Democrats, time mattered almost as much as votes. Katherine Harris had vowed to certify the results of the election on Tuesday, November 14. Any votes counted later might never figure into the final tally. But even if Harris's deadline was extended by a day or two, the Gore team in Washington was especially worried about hanging on to its national political support for more than a week. As the Palm Beach board prepared to meet, R. W. Apple, Jr., writing in *The New York Times*, again informed the vice president that the Washington establishment was losing patience. "Another week and no more," Apple's front-page story intoned. "By next weekend, a group of scholars and senior politicians interviewed this weekend agreed, the presidential race of 2000 must be resolved, without recourse to the courts." As on election night, the Gore campaign was hobbled by its blind faith in elite opinion, which had reached a consensus that the election had to be resolved in the next few days.

"If we could have quiet in here, we could get through this meeting as quickly as possible and get to the matter at hand," Burton said over the din in the lobby of the government center. "Today is November 11, 2000. It is approximately 9:05 A.M. My name is Judge Charles Burton." Roberts and LePore flanked him on an improvised platform.

The hysteria and uncertainty had only grown since Jesse Jackson's visit on Thursday, though following a request from Donna Brazile, Gore's campaign manager, Jackson himself had left Palm Beach and never returned. (Gore regarded Jackson's efforts, and all street protests, as incompatible with the solemnity of the recount process. The Bush campaign had an entirely different view of this subject.) In Tallahassee, on Friday, November 10, Harris had announced that she was going to certify the election on the following Tuesday, regardless of any vote counting still under way. The secretary of state, per Mac Stipanovich, was bringing the election in for a landing. Still, the four counties were struggling with the Gore requests for manual recounts. Volusia was committed to a manual recount. (Jack Young was running the Gore effort there.) Broward was deciding how to proceed, while Miami-Dade had put off any decision on what to do until Tuesday. Unbeknownst to Burton on Saturday morning, the Bush campaign was just then filing a lawsuit in Miami federal court to stop all the recounts. Yet for all this activity around the state, the conviction remained among many that Palm Beach would determine the outcome of the election. With its controversial ballot and thousands of uncounted votes, Palm Beach was the place that had the numbers to make the difference.

The crowd in front of the canvassing board spilled through the lobby and outside into a small courtyard, where a long picture window provided a clear view of the vote-counting machines. There were more journalists than earlier in the week, but the real reason for the crush of people around the three board members was the lawyers. Each side, including the board itself, now had a squadron of attorneys to monitor the process. Benedict Kuehne, from Miami, came up to lead the team for the Democrats, and Mark Wallace, also from Miami, was the top Republican. LePore had two of the best-known lawyers in South Florida representing her— Bob Montgomery, a flamboyant personal-injury attorney (and prominent Democratic fund-raiser) from Palm Beach, and Bruce Rogow, a high-profile appellate specialist who was also a professor at Nova Southeastern University law school. All of them stood huddled awkwardly at the shoulders of the board members as they began their deliberations, in full view of a live nationwide television audience.

One key figure in West Palm Beach that day hung back in the shadows, as was his custom. Jack Corrigan had called Michael Whouley on the day after the election and muttered a single question: Where do you want me? Corrigan and Whouley had dueled the Jesuits together at Boston College High School and then pursued careers in politics. Corrigan had taken off so many semesters to work on campaigns that it took him about a decade to make his

way through Harvard College and Harvard Law School, but he ultimately became deputy campaign manager of Michael Dukakis's
1988 campaign for president. (Whouley sent the campaign manager of the Dukakis effort, John Sasso, to work the recount in
Broward.) If anything, Corrigan had an even darker, more conspiratorial view of the world than his old friend from Boston. He
spent most of the next month closeted in a borrowed union office
that suited his sinister sensibility—the Plumbers'.

Corrigan had pored over the election-night returns to find
Gore's best precincts in Palm Beach. Under Florida election law,
the Democrats had a right to request manual recounts in three
precincts, totaling 1 percent of the county's 461,000 ballots. Then,
based on the results of that tally, the board would decide whether
to recount the whole county. It took most of the morning for the
board to organize the 1-percent count, which was to be done at a
series of tables in LePore's office—all closely monitored by more
than a dozen television cameras pressed against the long picture
window. It was, as Burton called it, "our world-famous view from
the outside."

While the count began, Montgomery, one of LePore's lawyers,
invited a handful of the other attorneys to join him for lunch at the
Palm Beach Country Club. Amid the bowing and scraping of the
club's liveried staff, Montgomery and his colleague Rogow did a
discreet interrogation of a lawyer they had just met, Kerey Carpenter, from the state's Division of Elections. She had been dispatched to the Palm Beach session by her boss, secretary of state
Katherine Harris, whom LePore's lawyers knew to be a co-chair of
Bush's campaign in the state. Though the luncheon conversation
was friendly, it bore out Montgomery and Rogow's suspicions
about Carpenter. They believed (correctly) that Harris had sent
her down to sabotage the Democrats' attempt to get a full manual
recount in Palm Beach.

Back at the government center, there were about a dozen tables
where LePore's subordinates examined ballots under the stern
gazes of Democratic and Republican observers. Disputed ballots

went to the three board members to be decided. From the start, the Republican strategy was clear—to object both to recounts generally and to the reconsideration of each individual ballot. Mark Wallace and his team fought virtually every new vote that was found for Gore. Through the first several hours of counting, the trend was clear. After the examiners finished just half a precinct, Gore netted 50 new votes—a dramatic change at a time when the margin in the entire state was only 327 votes. Burton presided grumpily, complaining how long the process was taking. "I'm losing it, I tell you," he said to no one in particular in mid-afternoon.

At 5:25 P.M., Burton disappeared from the counting room altogether—and no one, it seemed, knew where he went. As it turned out, he went to speak privately with Kerey Carpenter. At the time, Burton didn't know Carpenter personally, and he wasn't even familiar with the state Division of Elections, where Carpenter worked. The judge later said that when he first started talking with Carpenter on that Saturday, he had no idea that Carpenter worked for Secretary Harris or that Harris chaired Bush's campaign. Later, many Gore supporters in Palm Beach, who grew to loathe Burton, found his ignorance of these matters impossible to believe. Rather, the Democrats thought, Burton was placing himself in the pocket of the Tallahassee Republicans who had appointed him to the bench. Yet Burton was just oblivious enough not to have known that Carpenter—and especially her boss—had a clear agenda in this election. And he was ignorant enough about election law to seek out anyone who represented something called the Division of Elections.

There was, however, nothing naïve about Carpenter. She had the ear of the chair of the canvassing board, and she was going to use it to serve the needs of her boss. In their private meeting, Carpenter lobbied Burton on the standard the counters were using to determine whether votes had been cast. Since Burton regarded Carpenter as an impartial election expert, the judge came back to the table convinced that the count had to begin again. The counters had been using what was known as the "sunshine standard":

If sunlight could be seen through the bulge in the chad—the little piece of paper that is supposed to be punched out by the voter's stylus—then the vote was counted. In 1990, following a disputed election in Palm Beach, the canvassing board in place at the time had adopted a stricter standard for interpreting whether votes had been cast. According to that policy, a hanging chad could be counted as a vote, "but a chad that is fully attached, bearing only an indentation, should not be counted as a vote." Hanging chads, yes; bulging or pregnant chads, no. On one level, this was an extremely obscure issue. The national audience was still learning the meaning of the somehow amusing word "chad." (Its origin was never determined with certainty, although *The New York Times*'s William Safire suggested that it came from a Scottish or Provincial English dialect, and that "chad," "chit," and "chaff" share a common origin and all mean "small residue.")

The matter of the Palm Beach standard had enormous significance on that Saturday afternoon, and during the rest of the post-election period. If Burton had merely let the counting proceed as it had been going for the previous few hours, Gore might have pulled ahead by the end of the 1-percent review. If Gore had led in the total vote count less than a week after the election, that might have transformed all the events that followed. But after Burton's moment of revelation, courtesy of Kerey Carpenter, he directed that the previous votes be re-examined under a stricter standard. As a result, Gore's net gain until then plunged from more than 50 to just 6 or 7.

The significance of this decision on the standard went well beyond the 1-percent review. After the election, *The Palm Beach Post* recounted the ballots in the county and determined that if a lenient standard had been used on all the undervotes, Gore would have gained 784 net votes. Since Gore lost the state by 537 net votes, it is no exaggeration to say that Kerey Carpenter and Charles Burton won the presidency for George W. Bush with their decision on Saturday afternoon.

The questions, then, were why Burton changed his mind about

the standard and whether he was right to do so. Contrary to the suspicions of many Democrats, there is no evidence that Burton simply wanted to help the party of the governor who had appointed him to his job. Rather, Burton's actions reveal a subtler disadvantage that the Gore team faced throughout the recount fight. Insecure, ignorant of the law, paralyzed by the magnitude of the task before him, Burton was floundering for advice and turned to what he thought was an objective source—the official voice of Florida state government. But as Burton seemed not to have known, the whole machinery of that government, including Kerey Carpenter, was under the tight control of the Republican Party. In countless big and small ways, like this one, the power of state government worked to the advantage of the brother of the Florida governor.

As for the standard itself, it would turn out to be one of the central controversies of the post-election battle. Should vote counters have recognized bulging or pregnant chads on the punch-card ballots? It is tempting to say that voters should have been required to follow the rules that were right in front of them. In the Palm Beach voting booths, for example, voters faced a bold-faced sign: AFTER VOTING, CHECK YOUR BALLOT CARD TO BE SURE YOUR VOTING SELECTIONS ARE CLEARLY AND CLEANLY PUNCHED AND THERE ARE NO CHIPS LEFT HANGING ON THE BACK OF THE CARD. By one reckoning, then, voters who failed to execute this task should have paid the price with their votes. Florida law, however, required election-law officials to identify the intent of the voters, not to police their competence. This was especially true in places like Palm Beach, where the ballot was confusing and many machines were defective. Chads do not bulge on their own, and it was often possible to examine a full ballot and see a pattern of indented chads that clearly reflected the intent of the voter. Burton's rash reversal on the standard failed to capture the nuances that were integral parts of the law.

Worse, perhaps, than the merits of Burton's decision was the haphazard way it was expressed and implemented. As Saturday night fell, it was not entirely clear just what standard the board was applying, and the chaotic deliberations of the canvassing board left as vivid an impression as did the results of their work. The process did not look like a trustworthy way to determine the results of any election, much less one for the presidency. Burton was blustering and impatient; Roberts, cocksure and determined; LePore, timorous and overwhelmed. "Theresa," Bush lawyer Mark Wallace asked at one point. "Is this the way you've done it in the past?" Sighing slightly, LePore whispered in understatement, "Pretty much, but it's not been scrutinized as much."

Finally, at 11:05 P.M., Carol Roberts announced, "Shall we break out the champagne? We've got one left." The three board members studied it—it was a bulging chad and thus rejected—and after fourteen hours in session, they finally began the most important work of the evening: deciding whether to count by hand the remaining 99 percent of the ballots.

It was after midnight, Sunday morning, by the time Burton announced the results of the 1-percent manual recount. The judge said that Gore had gained 33 votes, and Bush had gained 14 votes—a net gain of 19 votes for the vice president. The board had also analyzed the overvote—that is, the ballots cast for more than one candidate. There, the results were striking. Of the 132 overvotes, 80 had been cast for Gore and Buchanan, presumably by voters confused by the butterfly ballot. The remaining overvotes indicated various other combinations. Of course, it remained unclear if anything could be done about these voter errors, but they reinforced the Democrats' sense that Gore was deprived of votes that rightfully belonged to him.

By this point, the punchy and exhausted Burton had had more than enough activity for one day, so he tried to end the session with the announcement of the results. He began, "We have been in a meeting all evening, so . . ."

But Carol Roberts cut him off. She knew how to seize a moment and she saw her chance with the net gain to Gore of 19 votes. "I would like to make a motion," Roberts announced, cutting off Burton in mid-sentence. "If we were to assume that the votes represent 1 percent of the counted ballots, and they were not picked up by the machine, then they would represent a total of 1,900 votes that is possible countywide . . . and this would affect the result of the national election, given the importance of the election and the fact that the present margin is approximately 300 votes statewide . . ." (Since, thanks to Corrigan, these precincts were among Gore's best in the county, Roberts's math may have been a bit off, but there was potential for a considerable shift in votes.)

Warming to her own oratory, Roberts went on, "I believe the people of Palm Beach County have entrusted us with the power to voice their rights to participate in their government. And given the totality of the circumstances here, I move that this board conduct a manual recount of all the ballots for the presidential election for the year 2000."

Raucous cheers from Gore supporters drowned out Roberts's last words. Burton, who couldn't even speak over the din for half a minute, was enraged that Roberts had blindsided him with this proposal. He had been hearing all day from Carpenter that the board was acting beyond its authority, and he was now worried that a vote for a full recount would make a bad situation worse. Scrambling, Burton came up with a new proposal on the spot.

"This is a situation that I think is new to everyone," he said. "I believe we have the authority to ask the secretary of state or Department of Elections [sic] for an advisory opinion, and it would be my intent as chair to do that."

An experienced parliamentarian, Roberts knew she had made her proposal first, so she said, "I'd like to call for a vote."

"Well, procedurally, I don't know if we modify a motion," Burton said. "My request is to obtain an advisory opinion prior to . . ." He trailed off. Carpenter had been lobbying Burton on more than just the standard. Based on her instructions from Tallahassee, Carpenter had been urging Burton to seek an advisory opinion— which was designed to shut down the manual recount.

"You are making a substitute motion," Roberts shot back at Burton. "You need a second."

"Is there a second?" Burton said as every eye in the room turned to Theresa LePore.

She was nearly catatonic. LePore had a sinus infection and laryngitis, she hadn't slept for three days, and she was a figure of national ridicule because of her butterfly ballot. Her contributions to the discussion had dwindled to almost nothing, so it was almost an automatic reaction when she said, "I will second the motion."

Bob Montgomery, her lawyer (and a Democratic fund-raiser), bolted to her side. "Bullshit," he whispered. "You don't need to ask for any advice. It's a nest of vipers up there in Tallahassee. You better identify who you're dealing with . . . " He was practically jabbing her in the ribs to get her to change her mind. Unlike Burton, Montgomery knew all about Carpenter's patrons back at the Capitol.

Pitifully, LePore said, "I'm withdrawing my second."

Roberts continued to play to the crowd. "I don't believe we need an opinion on what we should do, because we are here in Palm Beach County," she said. "And I believe all the people in Palm Beach County deserve to have, as well as the people in the United States, deserve to have an answer . . . I would like to call the vote since I made the motion."

In a final attempt to sway LePore, Burton recognized Kerey Carpenter to speak on whether a full recount was justified. According to Carpenter (and thus to her boss, Harris), only problems with voting *systems,* not with voters themselves, could constitute errors in "vote tabulation." The problems in Palm Beach were voter errors—"for example, a voter did not push a chad completely through. . . . That would not be a vote-tabulation error that would affect the outcome. . . . And so I believe that we could provide assistance in giving interpretation, a formal opinion."

"Assuming we asked for an opinion," Burton asked her, "when could we receive it?"

"Tomorrow."

As Burton continued to stall, Roberts asked a half-dozen more times to call the vote on her motion. It was just after two in the morning when Burton finally gave in and allowed the vote on Roberts's motion. It passed by a vote of two to one, Roberts and LePore against Burton. The motion for a manual recount of all the votes had passed. At Roberts's suggestion, the board agreed to reconvene on Monday morning to hear LePore's plans for counting all the votes.

Still seething about his defeat in the raucous board meeting, Judge Burton made a rare Sunday visit to his chambers for some legal research. There he discovered that he alone, not just the full board, could request a legal opinion from the secretary of state about the validity of the recounts. (This was the same legal research that Stipanovich and Jimenez and company were doing in Tallahassee.) There's an old saying in Florida government that you don't ask for a legal opinion unless you already know what the answer will be. Legal opinions are generally binding. Burton already knew from Kerey Carpenter that the secretary of state thought the recount should not go forward. So by asking for an opinion, Burton had, in effect, lit a fuse under the recount—and he only had to wait until Monday for it to explode.

For her part, LePore spent Sunday planning the recount process. As she announced at the board's Monday morning meeting, she would send a hundred or so paid volunteers to the county's Emergency Operations Center—a vast Mission Control–type structure that was intended for use as a command center during hurricanes. The counting, she said, would take about six days. Then, late Monday afternoon, Burton's bomb detonated. Harris's Division of Elections sent a formal opinion stating that the Palm Beach board was not authorized to order a manual recount. Would Harris's opinion succeed in stopping the recount?

On Tuesday, the board convened for the first time at the Emergency Operations Center. As if things could get any stranger, Burton decided to hold the board's meeting outdoors, in the parking lot, where a boisterous crowd surrounded the three members on all sides. To complicate matters further, the state attorney general, Bob Butterworth, Florida's senior Democrat and Gore's state campaign chairman, issued his own legal opinion that day, which said that Harris was wrong—the canvassing board *was* authorized to conduct a manual recount. A local judge, Jorge LaBarga, ratified Butterworth's view and said the counting could go forward. In light of the Butterworth and LaBarga opinions, Carol Roberts thought that Harris's view should simply be ignored. With her dramatic flair, she announced in the theater-in-the-round setting: "What happens? Do we go to jail? Because I'm willing to go to jail!"—a charge that was greeted by cries of "You go, girl!" Still, Burton and LePore would not start the count.

It was at this moment that Bruce Rogow, the law professor who was co-representing LePore, decided to effect his moment in history. Tall, lanky, with a beard and demeanor that self-consciously recalled Abraham Lincoln, Rogow had been telling people that he thought the whole election was going to wind up in front of the United States Supreme Court . . . and that he was going to argue the case. Rogow had argued eleven cases before the high court, but he had never received the attention that true legal celebrities like Laurence Tribe had received. Rogow would stop the count from going forward and file an original lawsuit, called an interpleader, before the Florida Supreme Court and let its seven justices resolve the dispute between Harris and Butterworth. Indeed, Rogow told his client Theresa LePore and others that the justices of the Florida court would be offended if the count went forward without their approval.

All of this made the Gore campaign apoplectic. The board had voted for the recount in a meeting that began on Saturday, yet days were passing without any votes being counted—all because of an entirely unnecessary lawsuit filed by an ostensible supporter of the recount. (For its part, Broward County was proceeding with its recount notwithstanding the contrary legal opinion from Harris.)

Rogow was a Democrat, and several of his friends called and asked him to drop his messianic Supreme Court scheme. Finally, on Thursday morning, Warren Christopher called Rogow from Tallahassee and implored him to let the recount proceed. For his trouble, the former secretary of state was treated to an extended monologue on Rogow's obligations to his client.

After hanging up with Rogow, Christopher said wearily to an aide, "It was easier to deal with Kim Il Sung"—the longtime dictator of North Korea.

The folly of Rogow's approach was revealed in the most direct and public way. Late on Thursday afternoon, the seven justices of the Florida Supreme Court, without even being asked to do so, issued a brief opinion saying that the decision of Palm Beach's Judge LaBarga was "binding legal authority." Thus, according to the court, "petitioners are authorized to proceed with the manual recount." Four days of possible vote counting—a process that could have put Gore in the lead for the first time—had been wasted.

Finally, at 7:16 P.M. on that Thursday, LePore's one hundred vote counters began sifting through the ballots at their tables in the Emergency Operations Center. Back in Tallahassee, Klain figured it might be too late to matter. On the following day, Friday, November 17, the overseas absentee ballots were going to be counted, a process that almost certainly was going to add to Bush's lead, because some of the votes would come from military bases. Later in the day, unless a court said otherwise, Katherine Harris was going to certify Bush as the winner of the election. "The deathwatch has begun," Klain told his colleagues—not realizing, of course, that it was only the first of several.

CHAPTER SIX

SHALL VERSUS MAY

A FEW DAYS AFTER JOE ALLBAUGH arrived in Tallahassee, he received a call on his cell phone from George W. Bush. "You know what we ought to do, Joe?" Bush asked.

"What's that, Governor?"

"We ought to count all the votes," Bush said. "Come on. You call Gore up and work it out. Let's count all the votes."

By this point, the Bush campaign had already committed itself to fighting recounts. "Uh, Governor," Allbaugh said. "That's not really how we're proceeding here."

"I know," Bush said. "But let's count all the votes."

"Governor, you know you're on a cell phone."

"I don't care. C'mon. Let's count all the votes. Count all the votes."

After a couple minutes more, Allbaugh figured out that Bush was kidding him. He was making fun of Gore's obsessive use of that phrase. Bush did this kind of thing often. As for the actual management of the Florida operation, Bush left it completely in the hands of Jim Baker.

It only took one disorderly staff meeting for Baker to decide he needed a clear management structure. As the chief executive of the Florida operation, Baker designated Bob Zoellick as his number two—a sort of chief operating officer or chief of staff. Margaret Tutwiler handled communications—preparing talking points for Baker and the Austin campaign staff, arranging for Bush surrogates to appear on television and on the ground in Florida, and translating the abundant legalese in the case into a comprehensible message. Allbaugh did politics—making sure that Bush supporters from around the country were mobilized and present in all sixty-seven Florida counties.

It took real prescience for Baker (and Ben Ginsberg) to set up their legal teams so quickly after Election Day. First, there was the federal-court team. Lacking a big name like Danforth, Baker settled for people who knew the law best and also had the greatest passion for the cause—Ted Olson, George Terwilliger, and a group of junior colleagues from Washington. The second group handled the canvassing boards, which were deciding whether to conduct manual recounts. Most of the lawyers in the second group were deployed to the counties.

Team three—for state-court litigation—became a focus of some controversy inside the Bush camp. On the morning after the election, Jeb Bush's lawyer Frank Jimenez called a Tallahassee lawyer named Barry Richard to lock him in for the Republican side. (This was part of the Florida Republicans' broader, successful strategy of trying to keep the state's major law firms out of the hands of the Gore campaign.) Richard, with his elegant swirl of gray hair, which resembled soft-serve ice cream, eventually became a familiar figure in the recount debate, but at the time, none of the national Republicans had heard of him. They knew only that he was a Democrat who had served in the Florida legislature and even run for state attorney general during the 1970s. For Republicans who had lived through the partisan acrimony of the Clinton years in Washington, a man with such a background was anathema. But Richard had done plenty of legal work for Republicans in Florida, and when Jeb Bush personally vouched for him with Baker, he was kept on the team. Richard brought the resources of Greenberg Traurig, the second-biggest firm in the state. Because Ginsberg didn't trust Richard entirely, he sent a dedicated Washington conservative named Michael Carvin to keep an eye on him.

The final group showed how much the Republicans were thinking ahead. Florida law allowed for absentee ballots sent from overseas, including military bases, to be received as late as ten days after Election Day. Even though the press and public were focusing almost exclusively on the recounts during the first week, Baker set up two teams to deal with issues relating to the overseas ballots. Warren Tompkins handled the political side of overseas absentee ballots. A protégé of fellow South Carolinian Lee Atwater, Tompkins had run George W. Bush's viciously negative primary campaign against John McCain in that state. Now, Tompkins was charged with making sure there were Bush operatives in each Florida county monitoring the ballots as they arrived from overseas.

The legal side of the overseas-ballot operation was more delicate—and secret. It was run by David Aufhauser, who came from the Washington law firm of Williams & Connolly, whose scorched-earth tactics had been put to work for clients as diverse as Oliver North and Bill Clinton. Aufhauser's work underlined the thoroughness, as well as the cynicism, of the Republican approach. His team took every legal issue relating to the overseas ballots—regarding deadlines, disqualification standards, counting procedures, and the like—and prepared arguments on both sides. In counties where Republicans won the vote on Election Day, particularly areas with a large military presence, Bush lawyers would argue for lenient standards on counting ballots. In Democratic counties, the Bush lawyers would insist on strict compliance with state rules in order for ballots to be included. For the issue, say, of overseas ballots lacking postmarks, Aufhauser even produced alternative forms for local lawyers to use—to include military ballots that lacked postmarks and to exclude civilian ballots that had the same defect.

Within a few days, the Bush team in Tallahassee was well established not only at Republican Party headquarters—with nationally known lawyers like Ginsberg, Olson, and Terwilliger—but also in the local offices of several prominent law firms. Staffers for Governor Jeb Bush, who didn't even pretend to be neutral, coordinated the recruitment of lawyers and operatives for all of the counties. There was also the staff of the nominally independent but highly cooperative secretary of state, who herself retained the services of another big firm, Steel Hector & Davis. The Bush team was an armada of legal firepower.

After a couple of days of operating out of the conference room in the Governor's Inn—and fielding rejections from the likes of Holland & Knight—the Gore team grafted itself onto a smaller operation but one whose loyalty would never be questioned. Berger Davis & Singerman had only forty-three lawyers in all of Florida, but one of them was Mitchell Berger, a longtime fund-raiser for and friend of the vice president. The Tallahassee outpost of Berger's firm had only three full-time attorneys on site, so there was scarcely any room for the new arrivals who had come to lead the charge. The setting—less than a quarter of a floor in one of the handful of office buildings in the capital—was plainly inadequate to wage a statewide legal war. Initially, there was no cable-television hookup, no high-speed Internet connection, and no room for the dozen or so lawyers who had made their way to Tallahassee after Election Day.

Christopher and Daley remained in charge—nominally. After making their pessimistic case to the vice president on the first Saturday after the election, they returned to Tallahassee the following day. But after several days of working around the clock and traveling across the country, Christopher began feeling all of his seventy-five years. The former secretary of state was simply not in a position to manage an operation as sprawling and fast-moving as this one.

Daley had a different handicap. He could scarcely contain his sense of futility about the recount operation, and he didn't like the personal cost it was imposing on him, either. Notwithstanding his background in Chicago politics, Daley was thin-skinned about criticism of himself or his family. (When a Republican congressman named Curt Weldon said to *The Washington Post,* "I will use every ounce of energy I have to deny the electors being seated if I believe the political will of the people was thwarted by the son of Mayor Daley of Chicago," Bill Daley called the congressman for eleven straight days in an attempt to confront him. Weldon never came to the phone.) After his return on Sunday, November 12, Daley remained in Tallahassee for only about a day until he decided he was needed back in Washington.

Except for a quick round trip to watch a court argument, Daley never again returned to the Florida capital. It wasn't Daley's kind of fight. He had built his post-Chicago career as a technocrat in the airy realm of international trade; he wasn't soiling his hard-won respectability for Al Gore or anyone else. Daley's curious combination of pride in his political legacy and fear of being tainted by it led to his virtual disappearance from the battlefield.

With the two former cabinet secretaries out of commission, Ron Klain became the de facto boss of the operation, with an eclectic cast around him. Dexter Douglass, former general counsel to Governor Lawton Chiles and a venerable local trial lawyer, was on board; Bob Bauer, a Washington lawyer close to the Democratic leadership in Congress, came down to help; Joe Sandler, the general counsel to the Democratic National Committee, handled the recruitment of lawyers; Mark Steinberg, a protégé of Christopher's from Los Angeles, checked that there was a Gore lawyer at every court hearing; and John Newton, a partner at Berger's firm, sat at his word processor all day and made sure that court papers were timely, complete, and coherent. A host of younger attorneys, such as Richard Lucas and Jeremy Bash, pulled one all-nighter after another to keep up with the work. Doug Hattaway, a lower-key version of Fabiani and Lehane, served as press spokesman.

The Democrats and Republicans in Tallahassee differed in one important way besides sheer numbers: The members of the Gore team had almost no personal affection for or connection to their candidate. Most of the lawyers had never even met Al Gore; others had at best awkward relationships with him. Bauer had been general counsel to Bill Bradley's campaign for president and had even played Gore in mock debates with his candidate. Klain, of course, had been all but fired by Gore in 1999. To be sure, all of the Democrats in Florida wanted Gore to win, but there was a clear disparity in the level of passion of the two sides. Many people with the Bush campaign had known their candidate for years, and adored him; several had staked their entire careers on victory in 2000. Just as important, many of the Republicans had spent the previous eight years in a futile fight against the Clinton administration; failure in that quest spurred their rage in this one. This contrast between Bush and Gore in the loyalty and ardor they inspired was just another intangible that gave the Bush forces an edge.

Mitchell Berger was the exception to the rule. He felt a strong emotional and ideological connection to Gore. He'd made a fortune as a business lawyer, but he also cared deeply about the environment, which made him feel even more of a bond. At forty-four, Berger still had the manic intensity of a kid, whether he was giving out nicknames (calling himself Hawkeye, because the office always felt like a M*A*S*H unit) or prowling its corridors looking for intruders (once evicting three bewildered Gore volunteers, because he thought they were "spies"). One day, a group of the lawyers were talking about Gore, and Berger blurted out, "You know, I would take a bullet for that guy." The silence that followed made it apparent he was the only one.

On Monday, November 13, the election battle turned into a tale of two cities—Miami and Tallahassee—and two courts—federal and state. The situation was so fluid at this point that no one really knew which one would be more important. The national media bet on Miami and the federal court. It would not be the last time the reporters were surprised.

Virtually all of the high-powered legal talent in both campaigns descended on the federal courthouse in Miami to hear the argument of the lawsuit brought by the Bush campaign. Though it had been filed less than two days earlier, the case boasted more than thirty lawyers and took place before an overflow crowd in the magnificent ceremonial courtroom, with its ruby-colored carpet, intricately carved bench, and half-dozen chandeliers. By and large, the attorneys in court that day looked alike: white guys in suits. But in the tense moments before Judge Donald M. Middlebrooks took the bench, it was simple to tell the Democrats from the Republicans. Gore's lawyers were sprawled chaotically at the tables to the judge's left, while the Bush team looked tidy and well kept on the right.

Ted Olson—his presentation as dry and cool as his Nordic appearance—made the Baker-approved argument that the very idea of manual recounts in selected counties violated the Constitution. In a frantic series of phone calls over the weekend, Klain had recruited his former mentor at Harvard Law School, Laurence Tribe, to represent the Gore campaign in the federal case. Tribe now argued that recounts had been a routine, accepted part of Florida election law for decades, and that a federal court should not go meddling in the quintessentially state-based function of running an election. It did not pass without notice that Olson, a luminary in the conservative movement, was acting like a stereotypical liberal—going to federal court when he didn't like what a state was doing—and Tribe, the great liberal, was preaching the conservative gospels of judicial restraint and states' rights.

The verdict was preordained—and prompt. Judge Middlebrooks, a moderate Clinton appointee, did not even leave his seat after oral arguments before he started reading the opinion he had already prepared. "Under the Constitution of the United States, the responsibility for selection of electors for the office of president rests primarily with the people of Florida, its election officials and, if necessary, its courts," he read near the start of a twenty-four-page opinion. "The procedures employed by Florida appear to be neutral and, while not yet complete, the process seems to be unfolding as it has on other occasions. . . . I believe that intervention by a federal district court, particularly on a preliminary basis, is inappropriate."

As many of the Bush lawyers themselves predicted, the court had completely rejected their position. But Baker recognized that there was more to this case than a judge's decision. Notwithstanding the defeat, the public-relations opportunities that arose as a result of filing the suit—and trying to discredit the recount process—would work to Bush's advantage. Indeed, in important venues like conservative talk radio, the criticism of the Florida recounts was reaching a crescendo. As for the case itself, the federal lawsuit would drift through the appeals process for the next month and never re-emerge as a significant factor in the legal resolution of the election. The real action would start in Tallahassee.

By late morning, it was clear that the Gore campaign had a bigger problem than the federal case in Miami: Katherine Harris in the Capitol.

On Monday, November 13, Harris made public her advisory opinions about the manual recounts. The Division of Elections told the Republicans' Al Cardenas, Palm Beach's Judge Burton, and a representative of Broward County that no further vote counting should take place. This, of course, was a disaster for Gore, who needed those votes to pull ahead, but Klain and the other Tallahassee lawyers believed there was an even more immediate problem on the horizon. They were running out of time.

Florida law contained an explicit contradiction about the deadline for recounts submitted to Harris's office. One section said that all votes had to be received by the Department of State by 5 P.M. on the seventh day after the election, in this case Tuesday, November 14. The law said any returns filed after that time "shall be ignored." But another section of the law said that if returns were not received by the specified time, "such returns may be ignored and the results on file at that time may be certified by the department." Such a sloppy drafting of laws is more common than one would think, but the consequences of this particular discrepancy were enormous. Which was it, *shall* or *may*? Was Harris required to certify on Tuesday, or could she wait until the manual recounts were completed?

As soon as Mac Stipanovich joined her team the previous week, he had also put his foot down on this issue, which was the paradigmatic example of his in-for-a-landing creed. Harris had to make clear that she would accept no returns after Tuesday, November 14. The deadline was absolute: *shall* trumps *may*. No extensions. Finish your recounts by Tuesday—or else. As Harris's office wrote to Judge Burton on Monday, November 13, if the canvassing board did not submit its votes by five o'clock on November 14, "the votes cast in Palm Beach County will *not* be counted in the certification of the statewide results."

On the previous Thursday, the Democrats had asked for manual recounts in four counties—the process known in Florida as a protest. Since that time, only Volusia had begun the counting process. Broward was just getting started, Palm Beach was dithering, and Miami-Dade wasn't scheduled to discuss a manual recount until Tuesday, November 14—the supposed deadline for completion. To Klain's mind, there was only one alternative: Gore had to ask a court to extend the deadline, since Harris herself would not. So the Gore team, joined by the canvassing board of Volusia County, spent much of Monday in court trying to stop Harris from certifying the election and to force her to extend the deadline.

Much later, after the Democrats had set the course of their litigation, it became clear that there had been another option for them at the beginning of that second week: do nothing. Let Harris certify on Tuesday, November 14, and then file what was known in Florida as a "contest," as opposed to a "protest." A contest, which can only be filed after a race is certified, is a lawsuit in which a trailing candidate asks a circuit-court judge in Tallahassee to review every aspect of the election. In contests, the judge has broad discretion—to order recounts in all or part of the state, throw out or include ballots, and generally take a fresh look at the votes. Instead of the county-by-county slogging involved in a protest, a contest might have offered the Gore team a relatively straightforward way to resolve all of the issues in one forum.

Of course, a contest would have been a gamble for Gore. The judge in the contest might have refused to order any recounts or otherwise ruled against the vice president. Moreover, Gore had a right to ask for manual recounts during a protest, and the canvassing boards, abetted by Harris, were denying him what he was entitled to under the law. Forgoing a protest would have rewarded this misconduct. Moreover, if the four counties just recounted their votes, the vice president might have pulled ahead in a matter of a few days. These were all legitimate reasons for Gore to protest, to fight certification and pursue the manual recounts in the four counties.

But the Gore high command also rejected the idea of a contest for a reason that revealed a deeper weakness in their effort. The vice president thought that once the result was certified, the press and public would decide that the election really was over and begin to view him as a sore loser. If they filed a contest after certification, Gore's team feared it might lead to the loss of, as Bill Daley liked to say, "credibility." Yet there was never any sign that the public cared about arcane legal concepts such as protests and contests. In the first week or so after the election, popular support for counting all the votes was very strong—much stronger, in fact, than the putative experts in the Washington establishment believed it to be. But Gore feared that a contest would alienate the editorialists and pundits whose approval he so craved and whose views, as it turned out, mattered so little.

So Klain and company went to court in Tallahassee to win an order that said Katherine Harris couldn't bring the election in for a landing for a few more days.

Judge Terry Lewis had a bushy mustache, which prevented most people from seeing whether he was smiling or frowning. He was long, lean, and conspicuously Southern, with an accent that revealed his North Florida upbringing. At forty-seven, he played basketball several times a week and still ate the same breakfast he had enjoyed in the little town of Perry, where he grew up—bacon, eggs, and grits, with American cheese. He'd been in private practice for several years, but he was one of those lawyers who seem destined early on to become a judge, and he was first elected to a county judgeship in 1988. Like all the best judges, Lewis had an instinctive sense of the limitations on his own power and, in a broader sense, of the difficulties of bringing order to the world. In 1997, he had published a novel with this theme, a legal thriller called *Conflict of Interest,* in which the flawed hero was fond of quoting a song by Leon Russell. "I'm up on a tightwire, one side's ice and one is fire," the song goes. "I'm up on a tightrope. One side's hate and one is hope."

On Monday, November 13, Lewis was trying one of those cases that remind judges of the limits of their authority. A mother was suing her daughter over a piece of property. It was a non-jury case, so Judge Lewis had to make the decision alone. But in the late morning, the door to the courtroom flew open and one of the court clerks waved frantically for his attention. The judge called a recess and found that another intractable problem had landed in his lap by random assignment—the election for president of the United States.

Gore and Volusia County wanted Judge Lewis to force Secretary Harris to extend the filing deadline past Tuesday. The judge read the few cases on the subject and called the parties to his courtroom in mid-afternoon. In what was to become a familiar ritual in Tallahassee, Judge Lewis waited to start until a phalanx of video and still cameras were set up in the jury box. Thanks to Florida's famous "Government in the Sunshine" law, every word in Lewis's courtroom would be broadcast to a waiting world. (The law doesn't apply in federal court, so there were no cameras in Miami.)

None of the lawyers had time to prepare or even file briefs, and there was a breathless quality to the presentations—by Deborah

Kearney for Secretary Harris, Dexter Douglass for Gore, and Barry Richard for Bush. Lewis immediately threw Kearney off balance with a simple question. Though the law said the votes had to be counted by Tuesday, there was also a provision that said overseas absentee ballots could be accepted as late as Friday. The Tuesday totals would necessarily be incomplete. "So you do a certification and you don't say who the winner is?" Lewis said. "What's the good of doing a certification ahead of time?" The judge was also making a larger point. Wasn't Harris just rushing to certify the election to shut Gore down?

Kearney didn't have much of an answer. No one, she said, should "allow recounts to go on and on and on. Where's the ending of it?" As far as Secretary Harris was concerned, Kearney said, the only legitimate excuse for an extension was a natural disaster like Hurricane Andrew, and that was one thing that hadn't happened in Florida during this election.

This remark gave Dexter Douglass the opening he wanted. White-haired and seventy-one years old, Douglass had charmed Southern juries for years with his down-home wit. He was, in fact, a serious legal scholar who had played a principal role in several revisions of the Florida constitution and could turn the country-boy act on and off at will.

"Let me tell you," Douglass drawled. "This is not only a hurricane, this is a bark-splitting North Florida cyclone with a hurricane tailing on the end of it." He went on, "The issue is, does Florida stand up for an honest vote that people in the other countries can look to and say that the United States has honest elections, or are there elections where some bureaucrat writes a letter and says, You lose, your vote doesn't count?"

But Judge Lewis didn't let Douglass escape, either. If Tuesday, November 14, wasn't the deadline, what was? Picking a date at random, Douglass suggested November 21. A lawyer for Volusia County said November 18. Still another lawyer said the counting should stop "when the court thinks it should end."

It seemed like Terry Lewis was smiling behind his mustache. He said he would announce his decision at ten-thirty the following morning.

Lewis's comments had been sufficiently Delphic that it wasn't possible to predict which way he was going to rule. Klain was un-characteristically pessimistic, so he decided to put in a call to Washington that Monday night.

"Walter," Klain said to Walter Dellinger. "I think we are going to lose. Who is the best appellate lawyer in America who is not Larry Tribe?"

Klain needed a contingency plan for an appeal (or defense) of Lewis's ruling before the Florida Supreme Court, and he wanted the state-court equivalent of Tribe in the federal courts. Dellinger had been a kind of legal Dutch uncle to the vice president's staff for several years. An acting solicitor general during the Clinton ad-ministration and now a law partner of Klain's (and Christopher's) at O'Melveney & Myers, Dellinger had taken himself out of con-sideration for a post in a Gore administration, but he still liked to stay in touch. He was due to argue a pair of cases in the Supreme Court, so he could not volunteer for this duty himself.

After a moment's discussion, Klain and Dellinger came up with two names. Joel Klein had just completed a tumultuous term as as-sistant attorney general in charge of the antitrust division, where he had supervised the case against Microsoft. Klein had chosen David Boies to try the government's case against the giant software company. Both men had impressive reputations. In the spirit that characterized Klain's virtual law firm, he and Dellinger decided to have a race of sorts. Klain would call Klein, and Dellinger would call Boies, and they would hire the first one who said yes. Klain struck out; Klein was off celebrating his recent marriage to Nicole Seligman, one of President Clinton's defense lawyers in his im-peachment trial. Dellinger didn't get through to Boies right away, so he made a third call—to David Strauss, a professor at the Uni-versity of Chicago Law School, but Strauss was not available, either.

But Boies called back promptly, and Dellinger didn't waste any time. "There's an important appellate argument in Florida," he said. "Can you get to Florida tonight?"

"Yep," said Boies, and he was soon on his way to Teterboro Airport, outside New York City, to catch the first available chartered plane to Tallahassee.

CHAPTER SEVEN

"THIS IS GUATEMALA"

At ten-thirty the following morning, Tuesday, November 14, the great swarm of lawyers and journalists descended on the Leon County Courthouse—an oddly cheerful modern building just across Monroe Street from the Capitol—to hear Judge Lewis's ruling on the certification deadline. But Lewis needed a little more time. Harris had made clear that she was going to certify the election at five o'clock that afternoon, so the delay was especially excruciating for the Democrats. If Lewis was going to rule for Bush (and Harris), he was going to rob Gore of crucial time to try to get an injunction against certification from a higher court. One hour passed, then two . . .

Finally, at 12:50 P.M., a court administrator named Terre Cass appeared in the lobby of the courthouse bearing several hundred copies of Lewis's nine-page opinion. Would Lewis allow Harris to certify that afternoon, or would he postpone the deadline?

The answer, it turned out, was not simple. Harris had said that she was required to reject late returns unless there was an act of God to intervene. The judge did not accept this argument. Gore had said that Harris was required to accept late returns. The judge rejected this view as well. Rather, he said, the whole question of whether to accept the late returns was within Harris's discretion. "To determine ahead of time that such returns *will* be ignored, however, unless caused by some Act of God, is not the exercise of discretion," Lewis wrote. "It is the abdication of that discretion. An Act of God has long been considered to excuse even the most mandatory of requirements. Rather, the exercise of discretion, by its nature, contemplates a decision based upon a weighing and consideration of all attendant facts and circumstances." So Judge Lewis concluded that the counties could file late returns and Harris could reject them—but only if she had a reasonable basis to do so.

Watching the announcement on their newly installed televisions in the Berger Davis & Singerman law offices, the Gore lawyers started to celebrate: We won! Harris couldn't shut the election down! It ain't over yet! Then, as the details were disseminated and the opinion itself circulated, their response was revised. Harris could still decide to reject the late returns. She was still calling the shots. Oh no! We lost!

The same reaction was happening in reverse at Republican headquarters, where Ben Ginsberg and his colleagues were tearing through their copies of the opinion. Lewis's ruling made clear that final certification could not take place that night. But Bush supporter Katherine Harris was never going to allow those late votes to be counted. (It is testament to the surreal complexity of the litigation of the election that even these lawyers had a hard time knowing if they'd won or lost.)

In Tallahassee, Terry Lewis was well known for this kind of opinion, one in which he found a solution that occurred to no one else. Lewis had cut through the partisan rhetoric and crafted a result that was true to the values embedded in the law. He had said to Katherine Harris that she had an obligation to simple fairness— that she didn't have to wait forever, but that she should give the counties some chance to count all their votes. In doing so, the judge had, perhaps naïvely, called on the better angels of Harris and all the people trying to sort out who had won this election.

. . .

Lewis's ruling guaranteed that the election was headed for the Florida Supreme Court, which made Boies's arrival in Tallahassee all the more important.

The fifty-nine-year-old New Yorker was an immediate media sensation, which prompted the Bush lawyers to start referring, rather grumpily, to the COB, the Cult of Boies. This sudden celebrity was peculiar, because Boies displayed none of the flamboyance traditionally associated with the best courtroom performers. He projected a calculated blandness. Boies had no accent (he grew up in California), no discernible ethnicity (he was distantly French), and no signature rhetorical style (arms bent in front of him, like a downhill skier, he was particularly skilled at . . . pausing before answering a judge's question, to keep attention focused on himself). Even his oft-cited eccentricities were more charming than odd. Boies dressed exclusively in cheap mail-order suits, flat-bottomed knit ties, and black sneakers. He worked solely from memory in the courtroom, in part because dyslexia prevented him from reading notes at a lectern. He lived on ice cream, sourdough pretzels, Triscuits, and Barq's Diet Root Beer, except when he was eating steak and drinking expensive red wine.

Boies had a knack for putting complex legal concepts into plain English, so Klain—as well as Gore—encouraged him to become the public face of the vice president's post–Election Day campaign. But there was another reason Boies became so prominent: Gore had no one else. Baker's team made sure that a constant stream of Bush surrogates—mostly governors and senators—filled the media pipeline. The recruiting wasn't difficult; the entire Republican Party wanted the White House so badly that its leaders panted after the opportunity to jump into the recount fray. In contrast, prominent Democrats contented themselves with vague mumblings about the rule of law. Many said nothing; few ventured to Florida.

In this way, Boies ultimately came to represent the limitations, as well as the appeal, of the legal side of the Gore campaign. On the morning of the call from Gore's representatives, Boies had been meeting with executives of Philip Morris, assisting them in their struggle to fend off tobacco lawsuits. By contrast, Gore had, in recent years, taken a public stance against cigarettes; in his acceptance speech at the 1996 Democratic Convention, he talked about his sister's death from lung cancer. Of course, Boies was a free agent who could represent anyone he pleased, but Gore might have been accused of hypocrisy if anyone had known of Boies's work for Philip Morris. In the end, though, Boies served the same role for Gore as he did for the cigarette maker. He was a technician who could present a legal case with skill, and that, ultimately, was the basis of the Gore campaign in Florida: lawyers' logic. The vice president assumed that the rest of the world saw the recount as he did—as a challenging intellectual puzzle, to be solved by the best lawyers and judges, all working in good faith.

Bush's lawyers lacked Boies's low-key panache, but Baker had designed his team so that the attorneys were not the only ones making the Republican case. Baker transformed his legal tactics into a brutally effective communications strategy, which featured politicians, protesters, and talk-show hosts marching along with the attorneys in Florida courtrooms.

In 1997, Boies left a partnership at Cravath, Swaine & Moore and started a new firm with four other lawyers. This move alone displayed startling self-confidence, since partnership at Cravath was considered the law-firm equivalent of membership in the College of Cardinals. The sinecure was so lucrative, powerful, and stable that lawyers rarely gave it up. But even though Boies had helped win some of the firm's most celebrated cases—including the government's long antitrust war with IBM and CBS's successful defense of a libel case filed by General William Westmoreland—he chafed at the firm's rigid ways. In particular, Boies in no way shared the passion for anonymity that characterized the typical Cravath lawyer. So when the firm wanted to stop Boies from representing New York Yankees owner George Steinbrenner because of a purported conflict of interest with another client, Boies walked out.

In less than three years, the original Boies quartet grew to a substantial firm of nearly a hundred lawyers. Not only did he participate in the Microsoft case, but Boies also attracted such high-profile clients as Napster, the on-line music-sharing business, and won a gargantuan fee for his firm by negotiating the civil settlement of a class-action suit against Sotheby's and Christie's, the auction houses. Before he left for Florida, Boies had asked one of the lawyers in his new firm—his son Jonathan—to make copies of everything the Florida Supreme Court ever had to say about election law.

Boies quickly immersed himself in the story of one of the more peculiar legal institutions in the United States. In the 1970s, the Florida Supreme Court's reputation was abysmal. At one point during that period, four of the seven justices were under impeachment investigation for various corrupt acts. Three of them ultimately left the bench and one was soon disbarred, just before he was indicted for his role in a narcotics investigation that involved the seizure of marijuana worth $140 million. That former justice, David McCain, died while still a fugitive from the federal charges. The fourth justice in the group, Joseph Boyd, avoided impeachment, but he had to promise to submit to a psychiatric examination before returning to the bench. (Duly reinstated, Boyd would boast that he was "the only justice on this court ever declared sane.")

This string of embarrassments led Florida voters to support a 1976 referendum that ended contested elections for the supreme court and left appointments up to the governor. Since then, a string of Democratic governors, including Reubin Askew, Bob Graham, and Lawton Chiles, had put aggressive, opinionated judges on the bench. This group of justices, known at first as the young bucks, gave the court a well-known progressive stamp—it was protective of abortion rights, hostile to the death penalty, and favorable to plaintiffs in personal-injury cases. While the state drifted to the right politically, the court did not. In 2000, as the election cases appeared on its doorstep, the court boasted seven justices who had been chosen by Democratic governors. (One justice, Peggy A. Quince, the first African-American woman to serve on the court, was appointed jointly by Governors Chiles and Bush.) In an era when most of the American judiciary had followed the conservative lead of the United States Supreme Court, David Boies found one that still looked kindly on the causes of Democrats.

On the matter of most concern to him, Boies learned that the court had taken a distinctive approach to the subject of elections. As former senator Danforth noted when he rejected Baker's overture to join Bush's legal team, most courts try to stay out of the business of supervising elections. Courts generally recognize that elections are imperfect, and if judges were to insist on anything close to perfection in the casting and counting of ballots, every close contest would likely wind up in litigation. Studying the cases, Boies found that this was also the view of the Florida Supreme Court—with one major exception.

In a famous local race in Daytona Beach in 1996, Gus Beckstrom ran for sheriff of Volusia County against an incumbent, Robert L. Vogel. A manual recount showed Beckstrom trailing 77,012 to 79,902—a margin of 2,890 votes. But Gus Beckstrom's lawyers pointed out that election officials had used black felt-tip markers to color in absentee ballots, in order to make the voters' lighter marks readable by the vote-counting machines. Beckstrom couldn't point to any fraud by the officials, but he asserted that this bizarre procedure tainted the reliability of the results. In its opinion, the Florida Supreme Court refused to throw out all the absentee ballots, because there was no proof that the shoddy procedures had changed the result of the election. Boies found his opening in the court's reasoning on this issue. "The real parties in interest here, not in the legal sense but in realistic terms, are the voters," the justices wrote. "They are possessed of the ultimate

interest and it is they [to] whom we must give primary consideration. . . . The right to vote is the right to participate; it is also the
right to speak, but more importantly the right to be heard."

Then, in words that would define the Gore legal strategy for the
next month, the court went on: "If a court . . . makes a factual determination that reasonable doubt exists as to whether a certified
election expressed the will of the voters, then the court . . . is to
void the contested election even in the absence of fraud or intentional wrongdoing." Boies saw that although the Florida court was
concerned about assuring finality in elections, it cared more about
reaching the correct results. It was pointless to try to persuade the
court that an election had not been conducted by the book. What
mattered to these justices was whether the right candidate won—
that is, the one who received the most votes.

And on this score, Boies saw, Gore had an important advantage.
The race for president in Florida was much, much closer than Gus
Beckstrom's election in Volusia or any other contest that the justices had considered. If all the votes were counted—the goal that
Gore's team was trying so hard to accomplish—there was every
reason to believe that Bush's margin of 327 votes might disappear.
The Gore mantra from Election Day forward—Count all the
votes!—may have had a dwindling shelf life as a political slogan,
but it was enduring good law in Florida. Boies made it his theme.

Katherine Harris also had to figure out how to respond to Judge
Lewis's ruling. In this she had a new helper sitting across the table
from Mac Stipanovich.

Even though Joe Klock had moved to Florida more than thirty
years earlier, his speech was still marked by the long vowels and
slurred consonants of Philadelphia. The fifty-one-year-old Klock
was the older brother of seven younger sisters. When his father
moved south as a real estate developer and motivational speaker,
Joe followed him to Miami for law school. He found himself editor-
in-chief of the law review and decided to go to work at a small but

growing firm called Steel Hector & Davis. He never left, and he became managing partner of the 170-lawyer firm in 1983. Like so many longtime Floridians, Klock was a registered Democrat, but he often supported Republicans in national races. When Jeb Bush had occasion to introduce Klock to his older brother, Jeb said, "This is a righteous Democrat."

Klock had the look and bearing of a man who had been giving orders for a long time, and he built a firm in his own image— tough, successful, and money-hungry. Early in his tenure as managing partner, Klock had sent a memo to his fellow partners that some of them took as a directive to decline pro bono work in favor of cases with paying clients. One partner was so offended that he marched into Klock's office and punched him, leaving Klock with a bloody nose. Notwithstanding the beating, Klock kept the policy, and the assailant, Sandy D'Alemberte, ultimately left the firm and went on to become the president of Florida State University.

With his graying blond hair and fireplug build, Klock resembled a cartoon version of the big-bellied plutocrats he had represented for years. The most prominent of these clients were Pepe and Alfy Fanjul, the owners of Florida Crystals, a privately held company that controls 40 percent of the state's sugar crop. It is a measure of the Fanjuls' power that, according to the Starr Report, Bill Clinton interrupted one of his trysts with Monica Lewinsky to take a call from Alfy. Joe Klock was Alfy's general counsel.

On the afternoon of Tuesday, November 14, Klock and Stipanovich had to figure out how to comply with Judge Lewis's order. How should Harris exercise her discretion on late returns from the counties conducting recounts? For all the time that Harris's advisers spent weighing this question, the work was, at its core, a phony exercise. At the end of the day, Harris, Stipanovich, and Klock were going to devise a plan to avoid counting the votes from Broward, Miami-Dade, and Palm Beach unless a court forced them to do so. The risk to Bush's candidacy was simply too great. (Volusia had actually completed its hand count by the Tuesday deadline, so its votes were included, and Gore had a net gain of 27 votes.) The question before the secretary of state and her advisers, then, was how to construct a process that looked fair enough to pass legal muster but still prevented Al Gore from getting the votes counted.

"We need a catalytic event," Stipanovich said, "something that will flush out their reasons so we can evaluate them."

"I've got a suggestion," Harris interjected. "Why don't we just ask them—ask the counties why they want a delay?"

Harris rarely contributed to her own legal strategy, but this time she came up with a clever idea. What had obviously bothered Judge Lewis about Harris's position was that she had rejected the late filings out of hand. An orderly give-and-take with the counties would contribute to the appearance, if not the reality, of fairness on Harris's part. Even better, this process would allow Harris to reject the counties' *reasons* for the recount rather than the recounted *votes*, which might have been politically perilous. On the downside, Harris would clearly be jumping the gun. Lewis's order said the counties could file explanations "after" they completed their recounts, while Harris would be asking for the counties' reasons "before" the recounts were finished. But the Harris brain trust glossed over this problem. They had their eyes on the prize—preventing Gore from getting any more votes.

So, shortly after seven-thirty on Tuesday night, Harris walked across the Capitol to the senate hearing room, stood before the familiar blue curtain, and made another painfully stilted announcement.

"Good evening," she began before thirty-six video cameras and about a hundred reporters. "I intend to read a brief statement. On advice of counsel, I will not take questions . . ."

Harris began with the vote totals. Thanks to the changes from Volusia, Bush's lead had dwindled to just 300 votes out of the nearly 6 million counted in the state of Florida. The usual practice, she said, would be to certify these results immediately, with the final resolution of the election following the filing of the overseas absentee ballots on Friday. But three counties were considering manual recounts. "In accordance with today's court ruling," she went on, "I am requiring a written statement of the facts and circumstances that would cause these counties to believe that a change should be made before final certification of the statewide vote. This written statement is due by 2 P.M. tomorrow." Having given the counties their homework assignment, Harris fled the room.

Late that night, in the exhilaration of the moment, Klock succumbed to a fit of hubris. Without telling Stipanovich—or even Harris—Klock's team of lawyers showed up on the doorstep of the Florida Supreme Court after midnight with a request on Harris's behalf to stop all hand counting of votes in the state until the cases could be transferred to Tallahassee. When Stipanovich learned about Klock's gambit the next morning, he was furious at this needless provocation of the Democrats. (Ben Ginsberg and the Bush lawyers were also angry with Klock, believing that he was stirring the pot in a potentially dangerous way.) Klock's motion suggested that Harris was contradicting herself—saying that the counties had counted too slowly and at the same time asking the court to enjoin the counties from any counting at all. Worse, Klock's late-night filing invited Gore's only potential ally in the state government—the Florida Supreme Court—into the heart of the case. The justices took advantage of this offer and rebuked Harris. In a terse order, the court unanimously refused to stop the hand counts in the three counties and refused to consolidate the cases.

Still, even this setback did not deter the Harris team from hustling the election toward a speedy conclusion. In response to Harris's announcement on Tuesday night, the counties, especially hapless Palm Beach, made her job a little easier by filing the most shoddy and cursory requests for extensions. Any lawyer with the slightest initiative could have spun out reams of rhetoric demanding the fundamental democratic right to honor the will of the voters. Yet Judge Burton in Palm Beach and his counterparts in the other counties dashed off petitions little more than one page in length.

So on Wednesday, for the second night in a row—this time at 9:15 P.M.—Harris came to the senate briefing room for a dramatic, if predictable, announcement. "After Judge Lewis's decision yesterday morning, my staff and I, along with counsel, developed criteria appropriate to the exercise of my discretion under Florida law," she said. "For the past six hours, I have applied this criteria. . . . I've decided it is my duty under Florida law to exercise my discretion in denying these requested amendments." After the counting of the overseas ballots on Friday, she concluded, the state would "finally certify the presidential election in Florida on Saturday." (Again, no questions allowed.)

With each step in the process, many on the Gore team thought that Harris would make at least a gesture of bipartisanship, perhaps throw the vice president a single bone along the way. But this assumption illustrated how differently the two sides approached the whole recount situation. In simple terms, the Democrats saw power as a responsibility, while the Republicans saw it as an opportunity. Mac Stipanovich believed that any hesitation would be seen as evidence of Harris's weakness, not as statesmanship, and he insisted that she push toward a conclusion at every opportunity. The landing was in sight.

Like Katherine Harris, Al Gore also gave a speech on Wednesday night. Since the Saturday summit meeting, he had been thinking about the idea of proposing a manual recount of all the votes in the state, with a promise that the Democrats would not file any legal challenges to the result.

The speech, delivered from his home in the Naval Observatory and timed to coincide with the start of the networks' evening news broadcasts, laid out Gore's proposal for a "resolution that is fair and final." First, Gore said that if the recounts were completed in Palm Beach, Miami-Dade, and Broward, he would agree to abide by the results without further legal challenge. Alternatively, "if Governor Bush prefers," the vice president would agree to a recount of the entire state. Finally, Gore called on Bush to meet with him, "one on one, as soon as possible . . . to improve the tone of our dialogue in America." He also took an all-but-direct jab at his spokesmen Mark Fabiani (who had accused Harris of "stealing" the election for Bush) and Chris Lehane (who had said Harris was acting like a Soviet "commissar"). "I would also like to urge all of those speaking for either of us to do their part to lift up this discourse, to refrain from using inflammatory language, and to avoid statements that could make it harder for our country to come together once the counting is over," Gore said. "That is the direction I have given to my own campaign."

At the time Gore made his speech, Bush was where he was for most of the Florida recount—in semi-seclusion at his ranch in Crawford, Texas. The high command of his campaign in Austin decided that the Gore statement necessitated a response, so they scrambled to return Bush to the Texas capital for a hastily arranged, dismissive reply. "I honor and respect the value of every single vote," Bush said. "That's why my campaign supported the automatic recount of all the votes in Florida. Everyone in Florida has had his or her vote counted once. Those votes have been recounted." Later in the five-minute speech, Bush reiterated: "The votes of Florida have been counted. They have been recounted." This was, of course, untrue.

Bush affirmed his campaign's rejection of manual recounts, which he called "neither fair nor accurate" but rather "arbitrary and chaotic." His point underlined Baker's true motivation in filing the federal lawsuit: discrediting the recount process, regardless of whether the Republicans actually won in court. Bush was sticking with the strategy that had brought him this far: no recounts, no negotiations, no extensions, no debate, and no second thoughts about harsh rhetoric. The Republicans had a campaign, and a party, in which everyone was on the same page.

It was right around this time that Klain began to feel increasingly estranged from the people in Gore's headquarters in Washington. Klain didn't object to the ideas the vice president proposed on Wednesday, but he felt they were irrelevant to what was actually happening in Florida. Once again, Gore was talking to the editorial page of *The New York Times,* which did support the idea outlined in his speech. ("Vice President Al Gore offered a sensible way out of the legal and electoral quagmire . . .") But as far as Klain was concerned, this genteel debate existed in a different country from the one in which he was now living. The Republicans not only brushed off Gore's sensible ideas about how to resolve the election, but they paid no political price for doing so. Bush's hard line never drew a hint of public dissent in the Republican ranks. It was time, Klain believed, to start trading punches.

"You don't understand," Klain would tell his colleagues in Washington. "This is Guatemala down here."

Gore's next legal step was obvious. He had to go back into Judge Lewis's courtroom on Thursday morning and argue that the secretary of state had abused her discretion in refusing to grant extensions to the three counties. The vice president's team had to persuade Lewis to force Harris to extend the deadline. But how?

At this time, Dexter Douglass was still the lead lawyer for Gore in Tallahassee. (Boies was present, but he was being held in reserve for duty before the Florida Supreme Court.) For all his old-fashioned courtliness, Douglass believed in fighting hard, so he had a simple idea: If we want to prove that Katherine Harris abused her discretion, we are going to need a witness to prove it— Katherine Harris. They ought to slap her with a subpoena and get her on the witness stand as soon as they were back before Judge Lewis, on Thursday, November 16. The other Florida lawyers on Gore's team, notably Mitchell Berger and his partner John Newton, seconded Douglass's idea. It wasn't hard to think of some potentially effective questions for Harris. Describe all your contacts, past and present, with the Bush campaign. Whom have you consulted about this decision? What was the basis for the standards you established? What do you stand to gain from a George W. Bush presidency?

These lawyers knew that dragging a statewide elected official into court would be incendiary. The reaction of the campaign leadership back in Washington was predictable: Christopher and Daley didn't care for the idea, which they found too provocative and confrontational, and it was dropped.

The hearing in Judge Lewis's courtroom was supposed to begin at noon on Thursday, November 16, but no one could find a court reporter, so the resolution of the presidential election was put off for forty-five minutes until one was dragooned into service.

The lawyers on both sides repeated the arguments they had made earlier in the week. As usual, Douglass had a folksy twist on the recent events. He reminded the judge how Harris had begun by telling the counties that they had no right to conduct a manual recount unless there was a problem with the voting machines. Then, when Palm Beach had stopped counting as a result of the first opinion, Harris issued a second opinion that said that any recount was too late because the deadline had passed. "If I can put it in a little better language, where I can understand it," Douglass drawled, "it's like the policeman says, 'Stop,' and you're driving along, and you stop. A whole bunch of cars come up behind you. And then he comes over and says, 'I'm writing you a ticket for blocking traffic.'

"That's what they've done here, basically," Douglass said.

It was an apt analogy, but it wasn't actual evidence. Since they couldn't call Harris, Douglass and the other lawyers decided to save time by not calling any witnesses at all. Lewis said little, but it was clear that he was troubled. Here the Gore campaign was asking a lowly trial judge to rule that one of the most powerful elected officials in the state had violated a court order, but as far as proof was concerned, the Democrats had said, essentially, Trust us. "I haven't received any evidence of any facts," the judge said—twice. He said he would have his ruling the following morning.

The hearing concluded at two o'clock on Thursday afternoon, and the parties retreated to their respective offices. Then, for the second straight day, the Florida Supreme Court stepped into the fray. At 4:45 P.M., the justices answered Bruce Rogow's question about whether Palm Beach had the right to keep counting the votes even though Katherine Harris said that they shouldn't. As the Democrats had insisted all along, the answer was: Of course. "There is no legal impediment to the recounts continuing," the justices said in a brief, unsigned order. "Thus, Petitioners are authorized to proceed with the manual recount." The ruling meant that Theresa LePore had, at Rogow's insistence, wasted four days of vote counting for no reason.

The brief order by the Florida Supreme Court was a victory for the Gore campaign, but the situation was still perilous—and deeply uncertain. The court had said the vote counting could continue, but to what end? Judge Lewis was in the midst of deciding whether Harris was right to refuse to receive any more votes. There had been two days of extraordinary, erratic developments in Tallahassee—mornings in the Leon County Courthouse and afternoons in the Florida Supreme Court, mornings for finality and afternoons for fairness, mornings for Bush and afternoons for Gore. On balance, though, Klain's group was on a pretty remarkable streak. On Monday, Judge Middlebrooks threw the Bush case out of federal court; on Tuesday, Judge Lewis barred certification of the election that afternoon; on Wednesday, the Florida Supreme Court rejected Klock's attempt to stop the hand counts; and on Thursday, the supreme court instructed Palm Beach to keep counting votes.

Still, on Thursday night, the only thing anyone knew for sure was that Friday, November 17, would be a turning point—perhaps the last one. Judge Lewis would rule on the deadline; the supreme court might respond; and the counties would report the tallies from the overseas absentee ballots to Katherine Harris by 5 P.M. These were the final votes cast in the election for president, and unless some court ordered her to do otherwise, she was going to end this election once and for all by Saturday morning.

CHAPTER EIGHT

COLD WINDS IN TALLAHASSEE

JUDGE TERRY LEWIS didn't keep anyone waiting on Friday morning. At 10 A.M., the court administrator, Terre Cass, again appeared in the lobby of the Leon County Courthouse in Tallahassee to distribute Judge Lewis's opinion. Unlike the first decision, which came to be known as Lewis I, there was no ambiguity in Lewis II. In a pithy ruling, just one page in length, Lewis said the Democratic plaintiffs argued that Katherine Harris "has acted arbitrarily in deciding to ignore amended returns from counties conducting manual recounts. I disagree." Klain's winning streak was over.

The ruling represented a crucial victory for Bush and Harris and a resounding defeat for Gore. "On the limited evidence presented"—which was Lewis's slap at the Gore lawyers for calling no witnesses—"it appears that the Secretary has exercised her reasoned judgment to determine what relevant factors and criteria should be considered, applied them to the facts and circumstances pertinent to the individual counties involved, and made her decision," the judge wrote. "My Order requires nothing more." Other judges might have been tougher on Harris. The secretary of state had clearly jumped the gun, demanding explanations from the counties even before they finished counting. But trial judges do not reverse the actions of elected officials lightly, and the Gore team had provided few compelling reasons—and no evidence at all—for Judge Lewis to do so.

The Gore forces in Tallahassee were devastated. As Boies, Klain, and the others retreated to the Berger law offices, they had every reason to expect that the whole contest might end that day. Watching CNN's running tally of vote totals crawl across the bottom of the screen, the lawyers saw that as expected, the overseas absentee ballots were increasing Bush's margin. (By the end of the day, Bush gained 1,380 overseas absentee votes and Gore received 750, meaning that Bush's lead increased from 300 to 930 votes.) With the absentee votes counted, and now Lewis's imprimatur, there was nothing stopping Harris from certifying the results of the election that evening, or Saturday morning at the latest.

So what, at that desperate hour, were Gore's options? In his rolling press conferences over the course of the week, Boies had been suggesting that Gore might go straight to the Florida Supreme Court and ask the justices to enjoin Harris from certifying the election. Another possibility was to wait for Harris to certify and then file a contest, which could call into question the fairness of the election. A third option was simply to appeal the ruling and see what the Florida Supreme Court would do. A few moments after Judge Lewis's ruling, Boies was weighing those options in front of a group of reporters at a Tallahassee ice cream shop while eating a large chocolate-vanilla-swirl cone.

That afternoon, the Gore lawyers gathered around a speakerphone to outline the unattractive options to Gore and Lieberman. As the rulings over the previous two days demonstrated, the Florida Supreme Court was a congenial place for Democrats, but winning an injunction against Harris seemed out of the question. The standard for an injunction was "irreparable harm," and as long as Gore could still file a contest, it seemed that no harm could be called irreparable. Waiting for certification and then filing a contest posed grave political risks. Gore feared that the public would see certification as the end of the election and that the pressure on him to withdraw would mount. Still, there seemed to be little choice, and Gore agreed to send Boies out to the Capitol in Tallahassee to say that the contest would begin as soon as Harris certified, presumably that evening. The Democrats would also file an appeal of Lewis II. Gore himself planned to deliver the same message, from the lawn in front of his home. The conference call ended just before four o'clock that afternoon.

Charles Wells, the chief justice of the Florida Supreme Court, had started his week by giving a speech down at Marco Island. But by the time Judge Middlebrooks ruled on Monday that the election disputes belonged in state court, Wells realized he had better hurry back to Tallahassee and prepare for the onslaught that was sure to follow.

Wells was silver-haired and sixty-one, a judge straight out of central casting. He had been appointed in 1994 by Lawton Chiles and named chief justice in 2000. (Unlike most appeals courts, the Florida Supreme Court rotates the position of chief among the seven justices.) For years, the Florida house and senate, both dominated by Republicans, had been looking for reasons to strip the state supreme court of its authority and its justices of their independence. Wells knew that the election would place the high court under a level of scrutiny unlike anything the justices had ever seen.

So on Tuesday afternoon, Wells rounded up the people who managed the day-to-day activities of the court and told them to get ready. The technology people had to enhance the security of the court's internal data network and prepare the public website to accommodate a dramatic increase in visits. The clerk's office had to get ready for a volley of fast-paced litigation. The marshals would have to deal with the greatest security challenge in the history of the court. The press officer, Craig Waters, had to make plans to distribute opinions to a voracious—national and international—audience. No court could fully prepare for the weight of a disputed presidential election falling on its collective shoulders, but Wells wanted to have the mechanics in place.

The substantive work began on Wednesday, November 15. Rejecting Klock's motion, on Harris's behalf, to stop the hand counts and consolidate all the cases in Tallahassee was an easy start. The justices wanted to send the signal that the process should continue—the votes should be counted—and then decide if there was any reason to intervene. The next day offered a similar challenge. On Thursday, Bruce Rogow's folly—his attempt to persuade the court to permit the hand count in Palm Beach—reached the justices. Again, the justices quickly, almost impatiently, brushed off the invitation to become involved. A court in Palm Beach had already approved the hand count, so the justices said Rogow's client should be counting votes, not filing lawsuits.

By Friday morning, when they received word of the decision in Lewis II, the justices had worked themselves into a rhythm of sorts, and they agreed immediately with one another that they would hear oral argument on the following Monday, November 20. Around the time they were preparing to release that order, James Baker's image flashed across the televisions in their chambers. Baker was at the Capitol, holding a press conference to celebrate Bush's victory before Judge Lewis. From Baker and from other reports on the news, the justices learned that Katherine Harris really was going to certify the election on Friday night or Saturday morning—even before the argument of the case on Monday. The seven justices quickly convened to consider what to do.

They were primarily concerned with preserving the status quo. If Harris were to certify the election, the counties would stop counting—and the court's previous two orders in the case would have been for naught. There was no mistaking that the justices were irritated with Harris. All week long, it seemed, she had been trying to shut down the recount process that was authorized under Florida law. True, no one had asked the supreme court to stop Harris from certifying, but if the court was going to keep its options in the case open, that was what the court was going to have to do. Collaboratively, the justices prepared a stay order, to go with the scheduling order they had written earlier in the day. Shortly before four o'clock on Friday afternoon, they gave both decisions to their spokesman, Craig Waters, who spoke at a podium set up on the steps of the supreme court building.

The scheduling order was not completely unexpected. The court would hear a consolidated appeal of all the cases on Monday, November 20.

But Waters had more to say: "The court has also entered the following order."

> In order to maintain the status quo, the Court, on its own motion, enjoins the . . . Secretary of State . . . from certifying the results of the November 7, 2000, presidential election, until further order of the Court. It is NOT the intent of this Order to stop the counting and conveying to the Secretary of State the results of absentee ballots or any other ballots.

Harris was barred from certifying the election. This order was a thunderbolt, reflecting great contempt for the secretary of state. As if addressing a child, the justices used all capital letters to say that they did NOT want to stop the counting of ballots—which was precisely what the secretary of state had spent the previous week trying to do.

In the Berger Davis & Singerman law offices, Boies, Klain, and the other lawyers were exchanging high fives. They had just told their client, the vice president, that it would be impossible to get an injunction against Harris from the Florida Supreme Court, but now the court had gone ahead and done it—without even being asked. Never had a group of lawyers been happier to be wrong.

Three blocks away, in Republican headquarters, Baker and company absorbed the news with steely rage. No one, not even Baker, with his vast experience, had been involved in events that had such vertiginous swings in momentum in a single day. But Baker promptly returned to the Capitol, where a few hours earlier he had been celebrating Judge Lewis for vindicating "the rule of law." He issued an icy dismissal of the Florida Supreme Court, noting that "the court issued an order that neither side requested" and reiterating his intention "to present our Constitutional challenges to the selective and subjective manual recount process at an appropriate time in the future." Politically, and legally, Baker was still laying the groundwork for getting the election out of the hands of the Florida Supreme Court altogether.

Suddenly, the picture looked so good for Gore's side. The vice president was behind by less than 1,000 votes, and Palm Beach, Miami-Dade, and Broward were still counting ballots. The Democrats were heading to the Florida Supreme Court, which had ruled in their favor three times in the past three days. A quiet weekend awaited them, devoted mostly to brief writing, with a break on Saturday night to watch the Florida–Florida State football game—the transcendent event of the Tallahassee social, political, and athletic seasons. (The competition for hotel rooms was so fierce that even James Baker was forced out of the Doubletree Hotel.)

Chief Justice Wells, a devoted "double Gator" (that is, a graduate of both the University of Florida college and its law school), decided not to go to the game in light of the political tension in the air. He was apparently the only one who felt that way. His fellow justices Major Harding and Leander Shaw showed up at the skybox belonging to FSU president D'Alemberte, and so did Jeb Bush. Ben Ginsberg paid his respects, as did Bob Butterworth, the attorney general. A constant stream of reporters filed through as well, but the real star that evening was Katherine Harris.

It had been more than a week since Harris had held her first press conference and emerged as a major national figure. There had been some mockery, mostly of her makeup, and Harris reveled in her victimhood in the wake of the unfair criticism. With her staff, Harris had taken to comparing herself, without irony, to Queen Esther, the Old Testament heroine who risked her life for her people. (As Harris replied to one of the 250,000 e-mails she received during the recount, "QUEEN ESTHER HAS BEEN A WONDERFUL ROLL [sic] MODEL. PLEASE PRAY FOR OUR NATION AND FOR ME.") The hard-right wing of the national Republican Party had embraced her, and the foyer in the Capitol was filled with bouquets of flowers from around the country. By that first weekend, there were so many flowers that the staff had to stack them in the basement. To all outward appearances, Harris loved the attention.

It was certainly true at the ball game, where she glided into the president's box trailed by her husband and two bodyguards. (She had received threats.) Harris made the rounds of the reporters present. She approached Dan Abrams, of NBC, and told him how much she enjoyed his reports on the case. "You know, there are times when my lawyer will discuss some legal issue with me and I won't really understand what he's talking about until I hear you explain it on television," she said.

"You know what I dreamed of today?" Harris said to a different group of reporters, which included Chris Vlasto and Eric Avram of ABC. "I dreamed that I would ride into this stadium on a horse, carrying the FSU flag in one hand and the certification in the other—while everyone around me cheered."

There was only one blemish on the resurgent Gore optimism that weekend, a small thing at first, but it triggered a chain of events that would change the tone of the battle. It was, in many ways, the paradigmatic conflict between Bush and Gore during the post-election period—one that best illustrated the differences in temperament and tactics between the two sides. It began when Dorrance Smith's cell phone rang on Friday night, November 17, at Republican headquarters in Tallahassee, which had more or less emptied out for the first time since Election Day.

Smith had served as the communications director in the first

Bush White House and had gone on to become executive producer of the ABC News program *This Week*. After leaving ABC, Smith had returned to part-time political work, and now he was assisting Baker in crafting a public-relations strategy. In light of the Florida Supreme Court's stay, Smith was thinking that things looked pretty bleak, when he heard from one of his former colleagues on *This Week*, the conservative editor Bill Kristol.

At this point, virtually all of the overseas absentee ballots had been counted, but Kristol had heard that the Democrats had circulated a memorandum to their lawyers advising them how to exclude ballots cast by Florida voters who were overseas. (Copies of the memo were leaked to several Bush operatives by friendly Democrats.) Bill Kristol thought this was political dynamite, because many of the absentee voters were in the military. The issue could be cast as Democrats so desperate to win that they were willing to exclude the votes of courageous fighting men and women overseas. Dorrance Smith agreed, and he wandered over to the bar at the Doubletree, which had become the unofficial after-hours headquarters for the national news media. There, Smith tried to gin up interest in the story. Bush headquarters in Austin did the same.

By Saturday morning, the entire Republican political apparatus had mobilized. Karen Hughes, the communications director for the Bush campaign, went before the press in Austin in full attack mode. "No one who aspires to be commander in chief should seek to unfairly deny the votes of the men and women he would seek to lead," she said. Retired general Norman Schwarzkopf, a Florida resident and longtime Bush supporter, was recruited to issue a similarly indignant statement: "It is a very sad day in our country when the men and women [who] are serving abroad and facing danger . . . are denied the right to vote [because] of some technicality out of their control."

It was not until Saturday afternoon that Gore, Klain, and the others even figured out what the Republicans were talking about. Earlier in the week, as they were preparing for the counting of the overseas ballots, both sides had arranged for lawyers to be present in all the Florida counties. On Wednesday, a Tallahassee lawyer named Mark Herron sent a memo to all the Democratic observers of the count, explaining how the process should work. At several points in the memo, Herron said the ballot must be "postmarked" to be valid. This was incomplete legal advice, at best. The Florida administrative code said ballots could be accepted if they were "postmarked *or* signed and dated no later than the date of the election." The Herron memo suggested that Gore lawyers should challenge all ballots that lacked postmarks. (No one in the Republican camp had leaked David Aufhauser's legal instructions that suggested rejection of civilian ballots lacking postmarks and acceptance of military ballots with the same defect.)

Thanks to the relentless prodding of the Bush camp, the overseas-absentee-ballot story blew up on Saturday, November 18, and the Gore campaign planned to send Lieberman to *Meet the Press* the following morning to deal with the controversy. By then, Lieberman had established himself as a strong, partisan voice in the Gore team's private deliberations, someone who was willing to file lawsuits and fight for every vote. The issue was teed up for him. On Sunday morning, NBC's Tim Russert brandished the Herron memo and asked the senator right away whether Gore was trying to invalidate military ballots because of "technicalities."

"Let me just say that the vice president and I would never authorize, and would not tolerate, a campaign that was aimed specifically at invalidating absentee ballots from members of our armed services," Lieberman said. "I would give the benefit of the doubt to ballots coming in from military personnel generally . . ."

Lieberman capitulated completely, ignoring several arguments that he might have made to defend the campaign's people in the field. First, the rules either mattered or they didn't. At the same time that the Bush operatives were fighting to prevent manual recounts to uncover validly cast votes, they were arguing that the rules should be stretched to allow overseas ballots to be counted. The Bush campaign shouldn't have been allowed to pick and choose which rules applied and which votes counted. Second, the Herron memo dealt with all overseas ballots, not just those from members of the military—and the Bush campaign itself had tried to exclude civilian absentee ballots because they lacked post-marks. Third, the Herron memo was right on the law (or at least more right than wrong). Here again the Gore campaign (repre-sented this time by Lieberman) backed down from a confronta-tion.

In theory, the matter of the absentee ballots should have been finished by that weekend, as the deadline for counting them was Friday, November 17. But Baker and others in the Bush camp noted the panic in Lieberman's remarks and decided that the Bush campaign would have much, much more to say about the overseas absentee ballots. The argument in the Florida Supreme Court may have been just a day away, but Baker's thoughts, as always, were on the future.

By tradition, all government buildings in Tallahassee are painted white. When the current headquarters of the state supreme court were constructed, in 1948, the walls were painted in dutiful con-formity with the rest of the city. But in the late 1980s, when the court was asserting its newly discovered power, the building re-ceived a thorough renovation that included an aesthetic declara-tion of independence, too. Just across Duval Street, the Capitol remained institutional white, but the justices of the supreme court wanted their building light beige, with red trim around the win-dows.

The renovation inside was just as dramatic. The justices subtly but unmistakably turned their courtroom into an elegant television studio. By 1990, when the changes were completed, Florida al-ready had the broadest rules in the nation for public access to gov-ernment, including cameras in the courtroom. Four camera bays were recessed into the walls, and a state-of-the-art sound system made sure that all the justices could be heard, both inside the courtroom and by the viewing public. In all, the building became a physical manifestation of the supreme court: It strutted.

The justices began the most dramatic day in the court's history with another kind of power play. In preparation for the arguments on Monday, November 20, the court directed that all lawyers and spectators take their places in the courtroom a full ninety minutes before the argument was to start at 2 P.M. So, like obedient schoolchildren, both teams were obliged to sit in relative silence for a very long hour and a half. David Boies sat at counsel table, opening and closing a file of papers without really looking at it. Mostly, he fidgeted and chatted with Dexter Douglass, who was seated next to him. Michael Carvin and Barry Richard, teammates on the Bush team but sartorial opposites, were at the opposite table. Carvin could untuck a shirttail sitting still, while Richard's white hair remained as immobile as the creases in his designer suits.

In the first row of spectators, Warren Christopher and James Baker sat as far as possible from each other. They never shook hands. The battle in Florida had taken a heavy toll on Christopher. He was cradling a day-old copy of *The New York Times* Week in Review section, reading it with methodical care to fill the long wait. On occasion, his head jerked as he fought sleep. James Baker talked quietly with Ben Ginsberg until the younger man was tapped on the shoulder by a court officer. Someone on the front steps of the courthouse needed to speak to him, urgently.

Someone Ginsberg knew—he would not subsequently identify him—was serving as an intermediary for a law clerk for one of the justices. Ginsberg's acquaintance handed him a typewritten note, which said that the justices had already decided the case and that Gore would win unanimously. A draft opinion had already been prepared. Most important, the note said, the court had decided to extend the deadlines for the counties to complete their hand counts—to Sunday, November 26. (It is ethical, even common, for judges to reach informal decisions on cases before they are argued, and the preparation of draft opinions is not unusual, either. But any disclosure of this process before the opinion is rendered is highly inappropriate.)

His worst fears about the Florida Supreme Court apparently confirmed, Ginsberg shuffled back to his seat and showed the letter to Baker. Together, they grappled with whether to tell Michael Carvin about it. Was it better to know that you have no chance of winning, or was ignorance, in this case, bliss? They decided to show it to Carvin, whose eyes widened. Baker whispered the only advice he could: "Just answer their questions, and let's get out of here."

At the appointed hour, the court crier boomed an introduction of the justices. "Ladies and gentlemen," he said. "The Florida Supreme Court."

Chief Justice Wells did not even try to pretend that this was just another case. "The court is certainly aware of the historic nature of this session," he said, "and is aware that this is a matter of utmost and vital importance to our nation, our state, and our world."

Almost as soon as the first argument began—it was presented by a lawyer for the Democratic state attorney general—the justices signaled that they thought the vote counting should continue. Wells stated that Florida's votes needed to be counted in the Electoral College. "What's the date—the outside date that we're looking at which puts Florida's votes in jeopardy?" he asked.

Paul Hancock, of the attorney general's staff, offered a tentative reply. "December 12, your honor, is my understanding. The Electoral College meets on December 18. The issue—and we have constitutional-law professors here who can address this. But my understanding is it's December 12 . . ." This brief, almost off-hand mention of the two dates would turn out to have enormous significance for the resolution of the election.

The questions to David Boies focused heavily on scheduling. Wells also pinned him down on the question of when "all the controversies and contests in the state have to be finally determined." Boies agreed—December 12. The Republicans regarded Wells as their best hope, but his emphasis on deadlines showed how strongly the court was leaning in Gore's favor. Bush's argument was that the election was already over and Harris should be allowed to certify immediately. Based on their questions, the justices seemed not to agree.

Michael Carvin was allowed to complete exactly three sentences before he was set upon by politely indignant justices. Justice Barbara Pariente, probably the best writer and the biggest liberal on the court, all but taunted Carvin with the law in Texas, which allowed for manual recounts and the counting of dimpled ballots. Other justices reflected profound misgivings about how the election had unfolded. As Justice Peggy Quince put it, "On a machine-counted ballot, where someone has gone to the polls and they have punched the hole properly but, for whatever reason, the chad didn't fall out, are you saying . . . that there is nothing that can be done?" In other words, were the thousands of people who cast undervotes to be disenfranchised?

Carvin answered, in effect, yes. Selective hand counts were unlawful, and furthermore, the counties had missed the deadline for recounts. It was all too late now, Carvin said. The election was over, and Bush had won.

Not so fast, said the seven justices staring back at him.

The note from Ben Ginsberg's mysterious informant was mostly correct. A draft in Gore's favor *had* circulated among the justices before the argument, and all were agreed that Harris had erred repeatedly during the previous week. First, she was wrong about the meaning of "error in vote tabulation." Florida law allowed the counties to use manual recounts as "a human check on both the malfunction of tabulation equipment and error in failing to accurately count the ballots." Second, Harris was wrong in her enforcement of the seven-day deadline, that is, on "shall" versus "may." Strict enforcement of the deadline did not punish the canvassing boards, the justices agreed, but rather "the county's [voters], for it in effect disenfranchises them." Harris's action was "unreasonable, unnecessary, and violates longstanding law."

So Harris had repeatedly violated Florida law, but what was the court to do about it? As the justices sat around the table in their conference room, they did some arithmetic. Harris had issued her incorrect legal opinions on November 13; if she had given the correct advice to the canvassing boards, they would have had until November 18 to submit their returns. The error had cost the counties five days. The justices were getting ready to release their opinion on Tuesday, November 21. They wanted to give the counties the five days Harris had taken from them, so they established a new deadline of Sunday, November 26, for the recounts.

All of this made a certain amount of sense. But as the opinion was being finalized on Tuesday, the justices didn't get around to explaining their reasoning for the new date. On the second-to-last page of the forty-one-page opinion, the justices simply announced the new deadline of Sunday afternoon, "provided that the office of the Secretary of State is open." If the office was not open on Sunday, the deadline was Monday, November 27, at 9 A.M. It was long after nightfall on the day after the argument when the chief justice called court spokesman Craig Waters and said the decision was ready.

Visitors to Tallahassee misjudged the weather at their peril. Even by the wintry standards of the late fall, the capital was unusually cold. During the week before Thanksgiving, as the nation awaited word from the Florida Supreme Court, the weather turned downright bizarre. Temperatures fell to the twenties, and a cruel wind swept the plaza that separated the secretary of state's office from the supreme court—a barren strip of cement that had become a tent city of video technicians and reporters. As their vigil stretched into the night on Tuesday, November 21, it seemed like every space heater in North Florida was combating the frigid gusts.

At ten o'clock, the lawyers for all sides received the court's decision by e-mail, just before Craig Waters announced the result to the television cameras. The unsigned, unanimous opinion was a complete victory for Gore, a total reversal of the previous day's decision in Lewis II. The hand counts were lawful in Broward, Miami-Dade, and Palm Beach, and the counties had five more days to complete them. Even though the opinion nominally reversed a ruling by Judge Lewis, the real target of the justices' ire was clearly Katherine Harris. Her decisions over the previous week were dismissed as "unreasonable," "unnecessary," "arbitrary," "contrary to law," and "contrary to the plain meaning of the statute."

Given the tenor of the hearing the previous day, the result surprised no one, but the sweeping nature of the decision left everyone stunned. Back in her office, Harris said, "This is a personal attack. Is this normal? Is this the way they do things?" No, her lawyers replied. It was an unusually ornery opinion. They consoled themselves with the thought that even though the opinion identified no individual author, "this thing had fingernail polish all over it"—that is, the mark of Justice Barbara Pariente.

The first reaction in Republican headquarters was hushed rage, an anger so profound that any words would be inadequate. Ben Ginsberg recalled a kind of existential dread, a feeling that the Republicans would never get a fair shake. The decision physically transformed James Baker. He lost the jaunty confidence of his earlier appearances before the press and instead appeared, just before midnight, in a state of coiled fury. "Two weeks after the election, that court has changed the rules and has invented a new system for counting the election results," he said. "All of this is unfair and unacceptable. . . . It is simply not fair, ladies and gentlemen, to change the rules, either in the middle of the game, or after the game has been played." Few major national figures had spoken as disrespectfully of a court since Southern governors during the civil-rights era.

But Baker had more to say: "One should not be surprised if the Florida legislature seeks to affirm the original rules." Article II of the Constitution appears to invest state legislatures with the power to instruct its electors how to vote in the Electoral College, regardless of the results of the popular vote. In other words, Florida's Republican-controlled house and senate could simply vote to give the election to Bush. Earlier on Tuesday, in one of his rare public comments on the election, Jeb Bush had suggested that he would sign such a bill. No such maneuver had ever been attempted in American history. It would have been profoundly—almost unbelievably—undemocratic to pre-empt the votes of the millions of Floridians who went to the polls, as well as the centuries-old system of judicial review. But here, on this Tuesday night, Baker was signaling that he wanted the Florida legislature to step in and remove this election from the grasp of the Florida Supreme Court. Baker's brief remark was the clearest sign yet that the Republicans would do anything.

In the Berger Davis & Singerman law offices, two weeks after Election Day, two days before Thanksgiving, Ron Klain said something that he had not allowed himself to utter during all his time in Florida: *Al Gore was going to win this election.* Broward was counting votes. Palm Beach was counting votes. Miami-Dade was going to start the following day. Once Miami-Dade started, nothing would stop them. *Al Gore was going to win Florida and become the president of the United States.*

CHAPTER NINE

MAYOR LOCO, CRAZY JOE, AND THE BATTLE OF MIAMI

WHEN KLAIN'S TEAM asked the Miami lawyer Kendall Coffey to come to Tallahassee on the first Thursday after the election—for the meeting with Daley and Christopher about whether and where to ask for recounts—Coffey agreed, on one condition: He had to return to Miami that same day. Coffey was going to be honored at a long-planned ceremony that night, and he didn't want to miss it. In the crush of events, no one paid much attention to his request. But if anyone had bothered to tease out this small thread in the tapestry of the Florida recount, the story of the November 9 tribute to Kendall Coffey might have helped explain why Al Gore's hopes for the presidency unraveled.

Coffey's life in the decade before the 2000 election served as a kind of petri dish of Miami eccentricity—not that you would know it from looking at him. He resembled the Scarecrow in *The Wizard of Oz* more than Don Johnson in *Miami Vice*. Tall, gangly, with a straw-colored combover and a sun-starved complexion, Coffey projected awkward intensity rather than tropical charm. He played the banjo, of all things. Still, Coffey loved the city where he had spent virtually all of his forty-seven years—"the excitement, the nuttiness, the sense of adventure that Miami represents," he once said. He had a special appreciation for what Latinos had done for the city. "Without them," he explained, "we would be Jacksonville on Biscayne Bay—that dull."

The year Bill Clinton was elected president, Coffey lost his only race for public office, a contest for a seat in the state senate. His foray into Democratic politics raised his profile just enough that he received a splendid consolation prize—the job of United States attorney for the Southern District of Florida. As a longtime civil litigator, he had little training for the job of chief federal prosecutor, but Coffey's zeal and intelligence quickly won over the nearly two hundred lawyers in the office. At the same time, his own grinding intensity wore him down—and led to one of the more spectacular fiascoes in the history of Florida law enforcement.

In February 1996, the U.S. attorney's office lost the biggest case of Coffey's two-and-a-half-year tenure. A jury acquitted Willie Falcon and Sal Magluta, known as Los Muchachos, on charges that they had smuggled $2.1 billion of cocaine into the United States over thirteen years. Mourning the verdict, Coffey went to the Lipstik Adult Entertainment Club, located on a seedy stretch of the South Dixie Highway, where he ordered a $900 magnum of Dom Pérignon and a "private dance" with one of the strippers. There was a dispute of some sort, which ended when Coffey bit the stripper on the arm. The incident made its way into the press, and Coffey was forced to submit his resignation to Attorney General Janet Reno. (In the freewheeling atmosphere of Miami, some saw Coffey's punishment as excessive. The stripper's husband, for example, said he and his wife did not want to see Coffey lose his job. "He bit her, but not like a crazy man," the husband said. "But he did break the skin." Coffey's travail served as inspiration for the characters Congressman Dilbeck and stripper Urbana Sprawl in Carl Hiaasen's novel *Strip Tease.* And in a suitably bizarre postscript, the foreman of the jury in the Los Muchachos case, Miguel Moya, was later convicted of taking a $400,000 bribe to throw the case for the defense.)

But Miami has always been generous with second chances, and Coffey shook off the humiliation, quit drinking, and resumed the practice of law. In November 1997, the city of Miami held a raucous mayoral race between Xavier Suarez and Joe Carollo. (Both men were colorful veterans of the Miami political scene, the former nicknamed Mayor Loco and the latter known as Crazy Joe.) As the votes were counted in the runoff, Suarez defeated Carollo 53 to 47 percent. But Carollo decided to challenge the results, and hired Coffey as his lawyer. A first court found such extensive fraud in absentee voting that it ordered a new election to be held. But the court of appeals decided to throw out all the absentee ballots—which was enough to swing the election to Carollo. (Later, the victorious Carollo was arrested for hitting his wife on the head with a tea container.)

The victory helped restore Coffey's reputation and earned him a great deal of attention and gratitude in Miami's Cuban community. (Both candidates were Cuban-American.) So it wasn't entirely surprising that shortly after Thanksgiving 1999, Kendall Coffey received a phone call from a man named Armando Gutierrez, who wanted to talk about a little boy named Elián.

More than forty years after Fidel Castro took power in Cuba, expatriates still refer to their stay in Miami as *el exilio,* the exile. The Cubans are here but they are not here; they are Americans, many native born, but they are Cuban too, and it is their homeland that drives the political passion in their city. Few ethnic groups dominate an American city the way Cubans dominate Miami, and no issue galvanizes such a group the way the struggle against Fidel—*la lucha*—does the Miami Cubans.

In the opera of Cuban life in Miami, children occupy an honored place. In 1961, just two years after Castro's revolution, the Department of State gave a Miami priest the right to waive the visa requirement for any Cuban child between six and sixteen who wished to immigrate to the United States. This program—one

without parallel in American history—became known as Operation
Pedro Pan, and more than fourteen thousand youngsters made
the journey to Florida under its auspices. Their successful escape
from Castro is a much-treasured part of Miami history. The passion of the anti-Castro struggle, with children at its core, quickly
turned the story of Elián González from an immigration issue to an
obsession.

Elián, then five years old, was found floating off the Florida
coast on November 25, 1999. He was one of three survivors of a
trip that took nine lives, including that of his mother. Back in
Cuba, Elián's father, Juan Miguel González, demanded that his
son be returned, and the U.S. Immigration and Naturalization
Service supported his claim. After Elián was released from the
hospital, he was turned over to the custody of Lázaro González, his
great-uncle, who lived in Miami and decided that the boy should
remain with him. In the days after Elián moved in with his Miami
relatives, their home in Miami's Little Havana was besieged by
the international news media. Unfamiliar with such situations,
Lázaro turned to Armando Gutierrez, a pillar of the Cuban exile
community and a veteran political consultant and public-relations
man. Gutierrez first found legal representation for his clients
among family-law practitioners but soon recognized that he
needed an expert in federal-court litigation, too—so he called
Kendall Coffey.

Coffey devoted four months to trying to keep Elián in the
United States. He argued in court, made the Miami relatives' case
in countless television appearances, and negotiated at length with
the American government. On the night of April 21, 2000, Coffey
was at the González home, serving as the principal intermediary
between the Justice Department and the Miami family. He was up
all night, and thought they had reached a deal at about 4 A.M. the
following morning. But shortly before dawn, as Coffey was trying
to catch a few hours of sleep in a back room of the tiny house, he
heard a rustling . . . and then he smelled pepper spray. The next
few minutes were a jumble as federal agents in body armor swept
in and took Elián into a waiting van.

Two months later, after more legal wrangling, Elián returned with his father to Cuba. Coffey had devoted a major chunk of his life to the case, and he had developed a special bond with the González family and their spokesman, Gutierrez. As a gesture of thanks to Coffey and the other lawyers, Gutierrez decided to hold a ceremony in their honor at the Dade County Auditorium. Lincoln Diaz-Balart, a fervently anti-Castro Republican congressman from the Miami area, would be the guest speaker. Gutierrez set the date for November 9, and he distributed two thousand tickets throughout the Cuban-American community. This was the event that Coffey rushed back from Tallahassee to attend.

It was early morning when Armando Gutierrez heard the first rumors that Coffey was going to work for Gore. Coffey's cell phone did not provide service outside the Miami area, so he was essentially unreachable in Tallahassee on Thursday. Over and over, Gutierrez dialed Coffey's number into his phone, but he kept getting a recording. What was Kendall thinking? Gutierrez asked Coffey's law partner, Manny Diaz.

To Gutierrez's mind, support for Gore was anathema. On Election Day, Gutierrez had traveled from polling place to polling place in Little Havana carrying a sign that read REMEMBER ELIÁN—VOTE FOR BUSH. This hostility was a bitter irony. All through the campaign, Gore had been ridiculed for his alleged pandering to the Cuban community on the issue of Elián González. Gore had argued that the case should be decided in family court, with a guardian appointed to decide whether staying in Miami or returning to Cuba was in the best interests of the child. (The Clinton administration took a contrary view, which prevailed, that the case was an immigration matter, in which Elián's father had the right to speak for his son.) A classic demonstration of Gore's inept political skills, the Elián case wound up as the worst of all possible worlds for him. He was simultaneously dismissed as a craven opportunist and rejected as a Clinton lackey.

Enraged by Coffey's defection to the Clinton-Gore cause—and

worried about the ceremony that evening at the Dade County Auditorium—Gutierrez decided to call a luncheon summit meeting. He invited Lazáro González, Lázaro's brother Delphin, and Manny Diaz to meet at Monty's, a big political hangout in Miami. There, the group quickly reached a consensus. Anyone who was working to elect Gore was a traitor to Elián's cause. By comparison, Coffey's months of work for the Miami relatives counted for nothing. What was more, as a further punishment for this apostasy, Manny Diaz promised to break off his law partnership with Coffey. In light of Coffey's defection, Gutierrez decided to cancel the ceremony altogether.

Coffey, of course, did not know about their reactions or the decision to cancel the ceremony. He had borrowed the private plane that Daley and Christopher had used to go from Nashville to Tallahassee in order to rush back to Miami. In the early evening, the plane pulled up to the executive terminal at Miami's international airport, where Coffey's wife was waiting for him. In her car, she told him that his trip to Miami had been for naught. The ceremony was off. Later, when Coffey found a Miami Cuban who would still talk to him, he defended his conduct. Coffey maintained that he had always been a loyal Democrat, and asserted that Gore and Bush's positions on the Elián case were substantively identical. This was all true but irrelevant. What Coffey learned that Thursday night was that his former friends in the Cuban exile community had chosen their side in the recount controversy, and they intended to pursue this new cause with the same intensity that they had brought to the struggle over Elián González.

The Republicans, too, recognized the importance of Elián's legacy in the Miami recount, and James Baker reached into the depths of his extraordinary memory to find the right person to exploit it.

In 1981, the first test of the political strength of the new president, Ronald Reagan, had come in the New Jersey governor's race.

Baker, who was then the White House chief of staff, threw all the resources available to him behind the Republican, Tom Kean. But the contest between Kean and Democrat Jim Florio had come down to a recount, and in the course of that bitter controversy, the work of a young political operative named Roger Stone drew Baker's attention. Kean ultimately won the race, and two decades later, Baker wanted Stone to repeat his recount heroics on a larger stage. Shortly after Election Day, Stone received a call from Baker aide Margaret Tutwiler, who said, "Mr. Baker would like you to go to Florida."

Following the win in New Jersey, Stone went on to a successful if often tumultuous career as a Republican political consultant. He specialized in the quixotic, short-lived presidential campaigns of people such as Senator Arlen Specter and developer Donald Trump, but also played a prominent role in Senator Bob Dole's race in 1996. However, that post came to an end when *The National Enquirer* found a personal ad in a magazine called *Swing Fever* that included a photograph of Stone and his wife, Nydia. The advertisement said the well-muscled pair wanted to find couples or single men to join them for group sex. ("Prefer military, body-builders, jocks. No smokers or fat please.") Stone claimed he had been set up by a "sick individual," but nonetheless he resigned from Dole's campaign.

Turning to other endeavors, Stone led the fight to defeat a statewide referendum in Florida in 1996 that would have levied a two-cents-per-pound tax on sugar and used the proceeds to help clean up the Everglades. Stone brought the vote-no forces from well behind in the polls to victory in November. In that race, he learned some important lessons about the power of the Cuban vote in Miami—and now he tried to put that information to work for George W. Bush.

Like many of the toughest conservative operatives, Stone had a surprising admiration for the left-wing protesters of the 1960s. They knew the power of protests, and Stone, following their lead, never hesitated to include noisy public demonstrations in his own political calculations. When it came to the battle of Florida, Stone left the legal niceties to the attorneys and the grand strategy to Baker. He wanted to control the streets, which was why he and his wife paid their first visit in Miami to a man named Armando Perez-Roura.

Radio has unique power in Miami's Cuban-American community. Several Spanish-language stations devote themselves entirely to talk about politics, and play a critical role in shaping the agenda of the city, region, and state. No print or television outlet can match radio's influence. (Notably, Miami doesn't even have one English-language station devoted to politics.) The most powerful station is Radio Mambi, a 50,000-watt behemoth that pulsates with anti-Castro invective twenty-four hours a day. The station's office is located in the biggest building on Calle Ocho, the legendary artery of Cuban Miami, and is decorated with pictures of pre-revolutionary Havana and posters saluting the veterans of the Bay of Pigs.

The principal owner and on-air voice of Radio Mambi is Armando Perez-Roura, a seventy-year-old Cuban exile and major political figure in Florida. On the Sunday before the 2000 election, Perez-Roura introduced George W. Bush to a rally of five thousand people. There Perez-Roura inveighed the crowd to remember Elián González when they went to the polls. "We must punish the enemy with our votes," he vowed. Perez-Roura had played this kind of role many times for the Bush family. His autobiography includes photographs of him on *Air Force One* and in the Oval Office with the first President Bush. Jeb Bush, who is fluent in Spanish, makes frequent on-air appearances with Perez-Roura. At the last rally before the election, Al Cardenas, the chairman of the state Republican Party, saluted Perez-Roura as "the Cuban-American community's Rush Limbaugh." (Miami can often seem like a small town. For example, Armando Perez-Roura, Jr., the broadcaster's son, was convicted of being a major cocaine importer in Miami during the

1980s. He testified as a witness for the prosecution in the case against Los Muchachos—whose acquittal led to Coffey's implosion at the Lipstik.)

But Armando Perez-Roura, Sr., was more than just a fiery partisan like Limbaugh. He was known for his ability to bring his listeners into the streets, and Miami political protests had a history of violence—threats, beatings, and even bombings. Perez-Roura had never been known to incite specific acts of violence, but his word unquestionably carried an edge of menace.

It was because of Perez-Roura's authority over the streets that Roger Stone and his wife, Nydia (also from a Cuban exile family, and her husband's translator), came to pay homage when the recount in Miami began. The visit to Radio Mambi kicked off a series of visits by the Stones to exile-radio broadcasters in Miami to make sure that the Cuban community could be counted on in the days ahead. Reassured, Stone left the rest of the battle to the lawyers, for the time being.

It was against this backdrop of political intrigue that the Gore campaign asked, on Thursday, November 9, for manual recounts in the four counties, including Miami-Dade. As in the other counties, the three-member canvassing board would determine whether the recount would take place. But as was often the case in Florida, Miami operated by its own rules, and a tropical haze quickly enveloped the board's deliberations.

In the first week after the election, Harris was still threatening to certify all the votes by Tuesday, November 14, so the other canvassing boards snapped to attention when they received the manual-recount requests. Palm Beach met on Saturday; Broward convened on Monday; Volusia *completed* its entire manual recount by Tuesday. By contrast, the Miami-Dade canvassing board didn't even schedule a first meeting to consider the recount until November 14—the supposed deadline to finish.

The reason for this languid pace can be traced to the structure of the Miami-Dade board. Every other county in Florida elects its supervisor of elections, in order to give this official a measure of political independence. According to a long-standing state law, however, the supervisor in Miami-Dade is appointed by the city manager, who is in turn selected by the mayor. The elections supervisor in Miami-Dade was an owlish fifty-four-year-old veteran bureaucrat named David Leahy, who had held the post since 1981. Through any number of election controversies, Leahy had impressed partisans on all sides with his integrity and honesty. But during his long tenure, Leahy had also developed the cautious instincts of a survivor. He avoided giving offense to his ultimate patron, Mayor Alex Penelas. In his office, Leahy kept a revealing sign about his philosophy: MY DECISION IS FINAL. THE ANSWER IS MAYBE.

Penelas, a Democrat, was first elected in 1996, when he was only thirty-five years old, and the victory marked an early capstone to a political career that looked limitless at the time. (Penelas held the post of mayor of Miami-Dade County, which is a more important job than Joe Carollo's position as mayor of the city of Miami, which is part of the county.) Unlike Mayor Loco and Crazy Joe, Penelas was a cool, intelligent technocrat whose appeal crossed ethnic lines. Vice President Gore, who recognized Penelas as an ideological soul mate as well as a useful ally in the swing state of Florida, had cultivated a relationship with the mayor for years. Penelas, too, saw the advantage in having a friend in the White House, particularly when it came to his pet project, the conversion of the former Homestead Air Force Base into a civilian airport in the southern part of the county. The relationship between the two men blossomed in part because Tad Devine, the Washington consultant, was an important campaign adviser to both men. As the 2000 campaign began, Gore looked to Penelas as his anchor in the always roiling political waters of Miami-Dade County.

But the Elián González case changed everything. Suddenly, Penelas's constituency was enraged at the Clinton administration, and the mayor had to choose sides. Not surprisingly, because 2000 was an election year for him, too, Penelas sided with the Miami relatives, even going so far as to prohibit the Miami-Dade police from assisting the federal government in its efforts to seize the boy. Penelas paid a price for his intransigence. His support in the Anglo community withered. He responded by turning even harder to the right—so much so that he won the endorsement of Miami's two Republican anti-Castro stalwarts in Congress, Lincoln Diaz-Balart and Ileana Ros-Lehtinen. In the September primary, Penelas just barely avoided a runoff, winning a sliver more than a majority of the vote. Then, with his own election behind him and Gore still counting on him in the home stretch in Florida, Penelas left for a twelve-day vacation in Spain.

The wily Penelas never formally withdrew his endorsement of Gore but, rather, retreated into political silence, especially when it came to the recount. A word, a hint, a gesture to the canvassing board might well have shifted this critical battleground to Gore's favor. This being Miami, however, there was no shortage of others willing to do the talking in Penelas's place.

When the three Miami-Dade canvassing board members finally did get around to meeting on November 14, they began by conducting the manual recount of the initial 1 percent of the ballots, to which the Democrats were entitled by law. Gore only carried Miami-Dade by 6 percentage points, whereas he won Broward and Palm Beach by nearly two to one. (The political price Gore paid for Elián was high: In 1996, Clinton won Miami-Dade by about 107,000 votes, but Gore's margin was just 39,000.) The narrowness of the race in Miami-Dade meant that the county was never likely to be a mother lode of new votes for the Democrats. Still, as in the other counties, the Democrats picked their best precincts to include in the 1-percent count, and the hand tally generated a net of 6 new votes for the Gore-Lieberman ticket.

Was this change substantial enough for the board to vote for a full manual recount? In addition to the supervisor of elections, David Leahy, the Miami-Dade canvassing board included two judges—Lawrence D. King and Myriam Lehr. Both enjoyed modest reputations. King was known chiefly as the son of James Lawrence King, the longtime chief judge of the federal court in Miami and a revered figure in the Florida legal community. (The federal courthouse was named after King while he was still alive.) Lehr was a little-known local lawyer until she was elected in 1996, largely, it seemed, because her name sounded both Latino and Jewish. (She is Belgian.) Both judges were Democrats, but Judge Lehr had employed the political-consulting services of Armando Gutierrez.

At the meeting of the canvassing board on Tuesday, November 14, Kendall Coffey argued that the 6-vote change in the 1-percent recount of the totals could translate into 600 votes in a recount of all the votes. (This was a dubious assertion, because Gore had won the test precincts by much wider margins than he had had in the rest of the county.) Leahy voted for no recount; King voted yes. Lehr broke the tie by voting no. It appeared that the Democrats would not get their recount in Miami-Dade County.

Coffey, however, kept fighting. He and Joe Geller, the combative Bronx-born head of the Miami-Dade Democratic Party, undertook a frantic search for statisticians who could use the data in the 1-percent recount to prove that a manual recount was justified. On Wednesday morning, Geller returned to the canvassing board, which was by then considering a recount in a congressional race, and asked them to reconsider their decision on the presidential contest. The board members agreed to hear the motion for reconsideration on Friday, November 17. Again, the process was moving in slow motion, seeming to fulfill Penelas's wish that the matter would somehow just go away without his having to take sides.

All through that week, Penelas was speaking frequently to the consultant Tad Devine, his intermediary with Gore, and a Miami lawyer named Chris Korge, a prominent fund-raiser for both the mayor and the vice president. Penelas found artful ways to explain his inaction, saying that he thought a recount in Miami-Dade probably wouldn't net votes for Gore anyway. Besides, Penelas said, he had no influence over David Leahy. Gore himself called Penelas during this period and heard the mayor promise that if the canvassing board voted for a recount, he would make sure it had the resources to complete the task. Notably, Penelas did not say that he thought the board *should* order a recount. (Penelas also called Leahy with the same careful message—yes to resources, but no opinion on the recount.) In a departure from his usual stoic demeanor, Gore became progressively angrier at Penelas for his cowardice. "I thought he was my friend," Gore told Devine, "but he's not."

In Miami-Dade, as in the rest of the state, Friday, November 17, had shaped up to be the most critical day of the post-election period so far. The morning began with bad news for Gore—Judge Lewis's order in Tallahassee that he wouldn't stop Harris from certifying the election that evening. Harris had said she was going to certify once she received the results of the overseas absentee ballots from each county that afternoon. (Consequently, Bush's lead grew from 300 to 930 votes.) Then, in an abrupt turn of fortune so characteristic of events in Tallahassee, the Florida Supreme Court issued an order prohibiting Harris from certifying the election and setting the case down for argument the next Monday. At around the same time, the Miami-Dade canvassing board reconvened to decide again whether to conduct a full manual recount.

A conference room on the eighteenth floor of the Stephen P. Clark Center (also known as the Metro-Dade Government Center) was set up as a sort of amphitheater for the canvassing-board showdown. Nearly every prominent politician, lobbyist, and hanger-on in South Florida wedged into the room to hear the debate. Republicans, led by the lawyers Miguel DeGrandy and Tom Spencer, wrote out the board members' prior comments on big poster boards, reminding Leahy and Lehr that they had already voted against a recount. Kendall Coffey argued that the progress in Palm Beach and Broward counties showed that manual recounts were justified. In the end, the question came down to whether Myriam

Lehr would change her mind. Without saying why, she did. The re-count was back on.

Once again, Leahy proceeded at a stately pace. On Saturday, November 18, the board met to discuss procedures for the recount of the 653,963 votes in the county. Leahy said that with twenty-five pairs of county workers beginning on Monday, they would probably finish in two weeks, by December 1. On Sunday, Leahy's team ran the ballots through the machines to identify the 10,750 undervotes—the ballots on which no presidential preference had been recorded.

On Monday, at last, the vote counting began, with each of the twenty-five tables monitored by both Democratic and Republican lawyers. Later that day, a local judge rejected a Bush lawsuit to in-validate the hand count. The following day, Tuesday, November 21, the Florida Supreme Court gave Gore his smashing victory, order-ing the hand count to proceed and setting a new deadline of Sun-day, November 26, for certification of the vote. The supreme court's decision also set the stage for the most dramatic, and dis-puted, events of the post-election period—the scene at Miami's Clark Center on Wednesday, November 22.

After the Florida Supreme Court ruling, the Bush legal team in Miami held an outraged vigil deep into the night at its Wyndham Hotel headquarters. For the first time since Election Day, it now looked as if Gore might win the presidency. This news changed the political, and emotional, climate all over the state, but especially in Miami.

In the two weeks since the election, partisans from around the country had been converging on Florida. Generally, the migratory patterns reflected the candidates' priorities in the recount. Klain had said on the first flight to Tallahassee, "We need lawyers"—so the Democrats recruited many attorneys, who took time off from their jobs and volunteered to take affidavits, organize court cases, and do whatever was necessary. At Gore's express directive, however, the shock troops of the Democratic Party—civil-rights, union, and other activists—were instructed to stay away. The vice president saw the recount as a legal, not political, process.

Republicans had plenty of lawyers, too, of course, but they also had a pipeline of operatives heading south, conforming with the Bush strategy of using protests as well as litigation to send its message. Some of the people arriving in Florida were well known, like Roger Stone, but also in the group were many young and determined congressional aides who had come to Washington since the House went Republican in 1994. Nearly a hundred of them made their way to the Clark Center shortly after dawn on Wednesday. The Bush campaign also had a much better-organized stash of high-profile surrogates in Florida. Governor Marc Racicot of Montana and four members of Congress—Miami's own Diaz-Balart and Ros-Lehtinen, John Sweeney of upstate New York, and Rob Portman from Ohio—arrived shortly after their more-junior partners.

What really distinguished the scene on Wednesday, though, was the atmosphere in front of the Clark Center. Through the preliminary skirmishes over the recounts, this area on the fringe of downtown Miami had been quiet, with many reporters but no large demonstrations. From the start, Wednesday was different. Early that morning, Armando Perez-Roura of Radio Mambi had sent a local activist who sometimes worked for him as a reporter to broadcast from the plaza. Evilio Cepero urged Perez-Roura's listeners to join the protest, addressing the growing crowd with a megaphone and interviewing participants like Diaz-Balart and Ros-Lehtinen. Cepero's motives were straightforward. As he told *The New York Times,* "We were trying to stop the recount; Bush had already won." From a building across the street, Roger Stone communicated with his people on the ground by walkie-talkie. Many held signs that became familiar in Florida over these weeks: SORE/LOSERMAN, they said, in a parody of the blue-and-white Gore/Lieberman signs used in the Democratic campaign. They chanted, "Remember Elián!"

. . .

At around six-thirty on Wednesday morning, elections supervisor David Leahy arrived at his office to consider the ramifications of the Florida Supreme Court decision. The court had set a deadline of November 26, which was five days before Leahy thought the board could finish counting all 653,963 votes. When the full canvassing board reconvened at 8 A.M., Leahy had a proposal to deal with the problem.

Judge King called the session to order in the large room on the eighteenth floor where the twenty-five counting tables were set up before him. (On the Gore side, Jack Young, the recount specialist, had joined Kendall Coffey.) Leahy's idea was simple. Instead of re-counting all the votes by hand, the board should only look at the 10,750 undervotes. That would give the county a "good, clear count" by the Sunday deadline. "I think it's doable. I think we can accomplish it," Leahy said. The Bush lawyers objected, asserting that the board had to count all the votes or none of them. The Republican lawyer Miguel DeGrandy inflamed the situation even more by suggesting that a continuation of the recount would discriminate against Hispanic voters, on the ground that the 1-per-cent recount, which would be included in the final vote totals, covered areas where few Hispanics lived. It was a dubious asser-tion, but it was sure to motivate the throngs of Cuban-Americans gathering inside and outside the Clark Center.

Notwithstanding the Bush lawyers' arguments, the two judges joined Leahy and agreed to count just the undervotes. Because the number of votes at issue had declined so dramatically, Leahy said the twenty-five pairs of counters could be dismissed. The board it-self would count the votes. Almost in passing, Leahy suggested that the board move upstairs one flight to the nineteenth floor, where the counting machines and his own office were located. "My recommendation would be to move up to the tabulation room," he said, where observers from each party could be "behind us watching us make decisions." Again, there was no dissent—at first.

Several hundred spectators had assembled in the common area on the eighteenth floor, and as the board members moved upstairs, a sizable number—perhaps fifty—of Republican protesters followed them up on the elevators. There was far less room for the public on the nineteenth floor, only a T-shaped elevator vestibule facing a glass wall that looked out over the offices of the supervisor of elections. The tabulation room, where the counting would take place, was at the other end of the building, and it could barely be seen from behind the glass wall. As the vestibule filled with people, the atmosphere grew tense, then angry. The Republicans wanted to observe the vote counting on nineteen as they had on eighteen. But Leahy was allowing only a pair of observers from both sides in the tabulation room. "Hopefully, the mood out front will settle down," Leahy said.

But the mood didn't settle down. "Until the demonstration stops, nobody can do anything," Leahy said. Reporters, too, were demanding greater access to the tabulation room on the nineteenth floor. At about 10:30 A.M., in light of the protest, the board shut down again and decided to reconvene on the eighteenth floor, after a short recess.

Lawyers from both sides continued to move to and from the tabulation room, but the crowd around the elevator was not allowed inside. This group included the hard core of the Republican congressional aides, who were shouting in the hallway, "They're stealing the election!" "Let us in!" "We want to see the votes!" Several started banging on the doors.

Shortly before eleven, Joe Geller, the Democratic Party chair, arrived on the nineteenth floor, hoping to resolve a minor mystery in the election. On the Miami-Dade ballot, Bush's votes were punched into the fourth hole in the ballot and Gore's into the sixth. However, Geller and others had noticed an unusual number of votes in the seventh hole, which made no sense to him, because it corresponded to no candidate. Geller had a theory that the holes were punched because Gore voters had improperly inserted their cards into the machine. Geller went to the window on the nineteenth floor to get a sample ballot so he could make a test. A clerk slipped him a ballot through the bank teller–style opening in the glass wall.

A voice shot out: "He stole a ballot!" The crowd converged on Geller. "He's stealing a ballot!" "Thief!" Geller fought his way to the elevator, but a group of what would become known as the Brooks Brothers mob followed him downstairs. In the lobby, the group surrounded Geller and refused to allow him to return to the Democratic staging area. Finally, a group of police officers arrived and separated Geller from his pursuers. He explained that he only had a sample ballot, and a little while later, the officers walked Geller to his car. (Geller's theory about the ballot placement turned out to be a viable one, but even he didn't think that the number-seven-hole votes could be counted for Gore.)

Back upstairs, the crowd was still chanting, adopting such Old Left favorites as "No justice, no peace!" and "The whole world is watching!" Congressman Sweeney was overheard yelling, "Shut it down!" (Later, the congressman explained, rather implausibly, that he meant shut down the count until more people could watch, not shut it down for good.) After Geller had safely escaped, sometime after eleven, Jack Young went back up to the nineteenth floor, where he believed the canvassing board would be reconvening shortly. When he tried to make his way through the Republican protesters, he and his colleagues were jostled, held, and harassed. At the window, Young was told that the board had decided to reconvene back on the eighteenth floor.

It wasn't until 1:30 P.M.—by which time the protests inside and outside the building had been roiling for several hours—that the board members finally took their places back on the eighteenth floor. Judge King began by recognizing David Leahy, who, it turned out, had had a major change of heart since the morning. Earlier, the elections supervisor had said that a recount of the 10,750 undervotes was "doable." Now, Leahy reconsidered. "I can't sit here and tell you that if we begin the process it will be concluded," he said. "We simply cannot get it done." Judge King agreed. "After discussing with staff and the very people that would have to do this process," he said, "we were in a different situation . . . than we were this morning when we made that decision, a radically different situation."

Jack Young was allowed to sputter some objections, but to no avail. Within a half-hour, the board had voted three to nothing to count no more votes—neither the undervotes nor anything else.

Back in Tallahassee, on Wednesday morning, Ron Klain was enjoying a brief moment of contentment, thinking the recount was finally back on track in Miami-Dade and elsewhere. Shortly after noon, he walked into the kitchen of the Berger Davis & Singerman law firm to make himself some lunch, and he saw on television what he thought was a recap of an earlier Miami-Dade canvassing board meeting. He soon realized it was a *live* broadcast and that the board was again considering whether to stop the count. Klain frantically dialed Kendall Coffey's cell phone. That isn't possible, Coffey said. Miami-Dade was counting votes. *Turn on your television*, Klain insisted.

Coffey bolted out of his office and headed for the Clark Center to see what he could do. By the time he arrived there, the hearing was already over. The recount had been aborted, never to be resumed. Coffey's old friends from the Elián González case were drifting away from the plaza in front of the building. Their work for the day was done.

Before dawn on Wednesday, November 23, Dick Cheney was rushed to a Washington hospital. George W. Bush held a press briefing later in the morning and said the hospital visit was just a "precautionary measure." By afternoon, however, Cheney's doctors revealed that he had had his fourth heart attack. The story of Cheney's uncertain health, and the Bush campaign's haphazard handling of the day's disclosure, dominated the headlines, and the shutdown of the Miami recount faded into the background.

But the events in the Clark Center had enduring significance for the course of the recount. David Leahy was quoted in the following day's *New York Times* as saying that the crowd was a factor in his decision to vote to stop the counting. Afterward, however, he insisted that he was misquoted and that the protests did not influence his decision. Leahy even went so far as to say that he was unaware of the tumult in the building, because he was at the opposite end of the nineteenth floor. Judges King and Lehr have said little publicly since November 22, but both have made clear that they reached their decision on the merits of the situation, not because of any intimidation.

As Leahy's on-the-record comments at the board hearing demonstrated, he knew about the protests as they were happening. Moreover, the nineteenth floor of the Clark Center is not so vast that the board members could have missed the chanting, screaming, and door-banging that went on for several hours. Furthermore, it is unclear that anything happened between 8 A.M.—when the hand counts of the undervotes were approved—and just after twelve noon—when they were canceled—to justify reversing the earlier decision. Leahy knew better than his staff members what resources were available to the board, so it seems unlikely that they talked Leahy into giving up the undertaking. Most important, subsequent events—after the Miami-Dade ballots were transported to Tallahassee—demonstrated that the board could easily have hand-counted 10,750 ballots in five days. The only reasonable conclusion, then, appears to be that the board members stopped counting out of fear—for their personal safety and their political future.

The next day, the Bush campaign improvised a Thanksgiving dinner for the several hundred volunteers and staff who had come from Washington and elsewhere to work on the South Florida recounts. In a hotel ballroom in Fort Lauderdale, the protesters from the nineteenth floor of the Clark Center told their war stories to colleagues gathered around chafing dishes of turkey and fixings.

Bush and Cheney offered their thanks by telephone. The highlight of the evening came when a surprise guest appeared—the venerable Las Vegas crooner Wayne Newton. He serenaded the troops with his signature tune, "Danke Schoen," which means thank-you in German.

CHAPTER TEN

THANKSGIVING STUFFING

WITH THE RECOUNT HALTED in Miami-Dade on Wednesday, November 22, only Broward and Palm Beach were still counting ballots. If Gore was going to make up the 930-vote deficit before Harris certified the result, he would have to find the votes in those two counties by Sunday, November 26.

At first, the recount in Broward County roughly paralleled the developments in Palm Beach and Miami-Dade. The three members of the local canvassing board—a judge named Robert W. Lee, a Democratic county commissioner named Suzanne Gunzburger, and the Republican supervisor of elections, Jane Carroll—met on the first Monday after the election to weigh Gore's request for a countywide manual recount. For the 1-percent sample, the Democrats selected three precincts that had voted overwhelmingly for the vice president, but the manual recount of those ballots showed a net gain for him of only 4 votes. In light of this—and Katherine Harris's opinion letter stating that manual recounts in such circumstances were contrary to Florida law—Lee and Carroll voted not to conduct a manual recount of the 500,000 votes in the county.

The next day, in response to Attorney General Bob Butterworth's public repudiation of the Harris opinion, Judge Lee changed his mind. (Butterworth, a Democrat, who also happened to come from Broward County, issued a formal opinion letter stating that recounts were justified if there was evidence of errors in the initial count that could affect the outcome of the election.) Gunzburger, a fierce Democratic partisan as well as a longtime believer in the efficacy of manual recounts, had always wanted a recount in the presidential race, and now Judge Lee, a patient, easily amused Hispanic who had been appointed by a Democrat, agreed with her. So the manual recount of all the votes in Broward County began on Wednesday, November 15.

Like her counterparts in the other counties, the elections supervisor in Broward never wanted any part of a recount. Jane Carroll was one of the few Republicans in an overwhelmingly Democratic county, but she was also an exhausted and fed-up seventy-year-old woman who was in the process of stepping down after thirty-two years on the job. Still, after the board's vote, Carroll set up for the recount in the county's Emergency Operations Center. The scene looked like the one in Palm Beach. Teams of county workers, with Democratic and Republican observers hovering over them, examined each ballot. Any disputed ballots went to the three board members for a final determination. The overall pattern repeated itself: Democratic insistence on vote counting, Republican delay and obstruction, and a steady parade of Bush surrogates denouncing the recount process as unreliable and absurd.

At first, the Broward board operated by a very narrow standard, one that recognized votes only if two corners of a chad were dislodged. In one precinct, many ballots were just punctured through—they had no dislodged chads at all—and the mottled backs looked like pages of Braille. Obviously, a voting machine had been miscalibrated, and legitimate votes were not being counted, even though the voters' intent was easy to discern.

Jack Young, Al Gore's recount guru, believed that if you could just get vote counters to look at the ballots, they would begin to see the voters' intent. Amid all the hoopla about chads, pregnant and otherwise, Young recognized an important truth: These ballots were the only existing records of people trying to *vote,* and conscientious counters would have a hard time ignoring that profound truth.

Not surprisingly, in light of Gore's wide margin in the county, the existing standard limited the vice president's gains. After 40 percent of Broward County was recounted, Gore had netted only 79 new votes.

But it wasn't only Democrats who were bothered by all the discarded votes. Ed Dion was the chief lawyer for Broward County and a Republican. As the canvassing board kept reviewing ballots, he was troubled by the omission of what looked to him like clear votes. In addition, he saw that Judge Jorge LaBarga, in neighboring Palm Beach County, had ruled that canvassing boards should focus on the broad concept of voter intent rather than arbitrary rules like two detached corners of chads. After a couple of days of counting, Dion thought the only fair thing to do was loosen the standard and recognize more votes.

As the first week wore on and the board examined more ballots, Lee and the others began to regard the standard as too restrictive. Gore's lawyers picked up on this sentiment, of course, and tried to capitalize on it. On Sunday, November 19, the day before the Florida Supreme Court argument, Gore's lawyers went to the board members and asked them to relax the standard. Like everything in the Florida recount, the change in the Broward standard was strongly colored by the partisan affiliations of the players. Dion may have been a Republican, but one of his chief deputies on the recount was Andrew Meyers, whose wife happened to work at Mitchell Berger's law firm. Still, all three canvassing-board members (including the Republican, Carroll) approved the change in the standard on that Sunday and then began the laborious undertaking of re-examining all the ballots. This drove the Republicans to new extremes in stalling tactics. At one point, Bush lawyers subpoenaed all three board members to appear at a court hearing, so counting during that time would be physically impossible. When they left the courtroom, some on the Bush team incorrectly instructed the board members that they had to return to court, which delayed the counting even more. It was also around this time that the Bush forces in Broward accused Democratic observers of eating chads.

The board's job was complicated further when Carroll, the frail supervisor of elections, announced that she was quitting the recount and going to California to spend Thanksgiving with her son. Judge Lee believed it was important for a Republican to replace her, because otherwise the board would have consisted only of Democrats. So the chief circuit-court judge in the area selected a local judge, Robert Rosenberg, for the thankless assignment. (With his eyeglasses perched on his forehead and magnifying glass aimed at the ballots, the otherworldly Rosenberg became a symbol of the Florida recount in front-page photographs around the country.)

Even with all the distractions, the Broward board worked steadily, sometimes from 8 A.M. to 11 P.M. The counting teams, as well as the three board members, kept plowing forward—working on Thanksgiving Day and into the weekend. And even though Rosenberg kept his distance from the two Democrats, the three board members wound up agreeing most of the time. In their votes on whether to recognize voters' ballots, they were unanimous about 81 percent of the time. In the end, Judge Lee's group finished its review of the half-million ballots with nearly a full day to spare. (The board also had the foresight to hire a local accounting firm to monitor its work and make sure the numbers were reconciled correctly.) Gore netted 567 votes out of the recount. The bounty of Gore votes surprised many, but the number was just on the high side of the estimates Jack Young had made for Broward County on the day after the election.

That left only Palm Beach. Once again, it looked like the whole election was coming down to the dotty county by the sea.

. . .

Endless days, long nights, dueling press conferences, fevered courtroom debates, cranky canvassing-board hearings, and very few votes actually counted—that was the course of the Palm Beach tragicomedy. Nothing happened. Loudly.

Way back in the early-morning hours of November 12, the Palm Beach canvassing board had voted for a full manual recount. Then on Monday, Harris issued her incorrect legal opinion about the recount. On Tuesday, Bob Butterworth—and Judge LaBarga in Palm Beach—corrected her, but Bruce Rogow wanted to make sure by asking the Florida Supreme Court. Wednesday, they waited (as Broward started counting). Thursday, November 16, the Florida Supreme Court said to proceed, and the counting started, sort of. Everyone promptly began fighting over the standard.

In the beginning, the board used a standard that had been adopted by an earlier Palm Beach canvassing board, after the election in 1990, even though that rule had apparently never been used to count any votes in later elections. The standard established a bright line: One corner of the chad had to be detached or the vote would not be counted. But the Democrats challenged this standard in court and won—or so they thought. Judge LaBarga said the 1990 standard "of a per se exclusion" was clearly wrong. Rather, according to the judge, the board "has the discretion to utilize whatever methodology it deems proper to determine the true intention of the voter, and it should not be restricted in the task." In theory, Judge LaBarga's ruling made sense. He was simply trusting the board's good judgment to look at each ballot in context and make a decision. In practice, however, LaBarga's order meant that there was no change in how ballots were really counted in Palm Beach.

As was so often the case, the reason for the narrow standard in Palm Beach came down to the idiosyncrasies of the decision makers. Judge Charles Burton—the big, good-natured friend to all who was in charge—wanted to make the vote counting as simple and mechanical as possible. That meant a clear, articulable standard, like the 1990 one-corner rule. A corner was either attached or it wasn't. As the vote counters in Broward had discovered, a more searching examination of the ballots produced clear indications of other votes, even if no corners were torn. But Burton wanted to avoid that kind of difficult decision making. Likewise, poor Theresa LePore, the luckless sponsor of the butterfly ballot, didn't want to have to make any more tough calls, either. So the one-corner rule appealed to her, too.

If anything, the tension inside the counting room in Palm Beach was worse than that in Broward. For one thing, the stakes were higher. From Election Day forward, Palm Beach had been ground zero in Florida, with the biggest crowds, the most journalists, and the toughest partisans. Right after the election, Michael Whouley had set up shop here for Gore, and he promptly turned the place into Boston's most distant suburb. He plucked the wiliest Massachusetts operatives he could find—including Jack Corrigan, Dennis Newman, and David Sullivan—and set them loose. Their Bay State style rubbed even some people on their own team the wrong way, and not just because they said "fuck" a lot. (All Gore lawyers were supposed to check with Klain before they went to court about anything. In the best outlaw tradition, the Boston operatives filed first and asked permission later. "Fuck it," Whouley explained.) Jack Young (a Virginian) was fond of giving lengthy lectures about his "principled recount theory," which rested on the idea of increasing the number of votes for all candidates, including Bush. Corrigan et al. had little patience for theories in general, and they certainly weren't interested in anything that might give George Bush a single new vote. They had come to Palm Beach for a single reason: *to help Al Gore win the fucking election.*

For the Massachusetts wing of the Gore campaign, the recount in Palm Beach was an exercise in watching the election slip away. This was maddening because a) they hated to lose and b) they believed they were staring at ballots—real votes—that were not being counted. In Broward and Volusia counties, for example, the recount produced a yield rate of about 25 percent—that is, about a quarter of the re-examined ballots were recognized as votes. But in Palm Beach, the yield rate was about 5 percent. The disparity led the Gore forces to believe that they were being shafted in the Palm Beach counting room. Worse, even though the Democrats kept running to Judge LaBarga and *winning*, Burton and LePore still wouldn't recognize the votes. Nothing helped. "We are leaving votes on the table," Newman, Gore's top observer in the counting room, would say every day.

As Thanksgiving approached, the tension continued to build. The Democratic lawyers would object to the exclusion of any Gore ballot that had even the slightest indentation on the chad. Under Jack Young's theory, they should have objected to such uncounted Bush ballots too, but of course this team did no such thing. The Democratic oversights prompted the Republicans, as a defensive measure, to object to any Bush uncounted dimpled chads. As a general matter, the Bush lawyers didn't believe in counting dimpled chads, but if the board was going to count those for Gore, the Republicans wanted them to count those for Bush as well. This led to the invention of an ornery shorthand. Whenever the Republican lawyers thought a Bush vote hadn't been counted, they'd shout out, "Objection! DDP!" which was short for Democratic Dimple Principle.

The haggling was extremely effective in slowing the process down. All three canvassing-board members had to review all of the disputed ballots, and the stacks before them kept growing. When the Florida Supreme Court rendered its decision on the night of Tuesday, November 21, it quickly became apparent that the board would have to decide whether to work on Thanksgiving, two days later. Even though the entire recount had to be completed by November 26, the board treated this decision about whether or not to work on the holiday in its typical haphazard manner.

On Wednesday, the county's public-relations person, Denise Cote, told the board that county workers were reluctant to come in on Thanksgiving. "We can't work tomorrow," said Cote, who had no right to make this decision.

"How are we doing?" Burton asked her.

"Well, we're picking up the pace," said Cote. This was debatable; it was clear even then that the board might not meet the deadline.

"Great, let's take the day off," said Burton. "I could use it."

And so, without further debate, the Palm Beach board decided not to work on Thanksgiving. Even though everyone had been working hard and needed a break, taking the day off was a stunningly irresponsible—and fateful—decision. (Everyone was toiling just as hard—and accomplishing far more—in Broward County, and they worked on the holiday.) There is nothing to suggest that Burton had sinister motives in approving the day off, no evidence that he was trying to run out the clock on the Gore campaign. He was simply another bumbler in a county that, on the whole, couldn't count straight.

Indeed, by Thanksgiving Day, Burton and LePore had managed in effect to cost Gore the election in two different ways—the schedule and the standard. (Earlier, of course, LePore had cost Gore the election in still another way—by approving the butterfly ballot.) Though a well-organized final push might have made up for the day lost on Thanksgiving, the standard was the fatal blow. After the election, *The Palm Beach Post* reviewed all the undervotes in the county. Applying a standard similar to the one used in Broward County, the newspaper found that Gore would have netted 784 new votes in Palm Beach, compared to the 200 or so net votes for him uncovered in the official recount. Since Bush eventually won the state by 537 votes, the difference would have been enough to swing the election. While the county might not have exactly duplicated the newspaper's standard or its methods, this reexamination of the ballots demonstrates the profound importance of the pre–Thanksgiving Day decisions in Palm Beach.

Still, just because a more generous vote-counting standard would have helped Gore, that doesn't mean it was necessarily the right one. What standard was correct—the more inclusive Broward rule or the more restrictive Palm Beach test? Should indented, or dimpled, ballots have been counted as votes? The fundamental truth is that chads don't move by themselves: They are pushed in because voters push them. To be sure, some voters are incompetent, just as it is also true that some of the battered and miscalibrated machines made accurate voting all but impossible. But neither is a reason to discount citizens' votes. In most states that have considered the issue in recent years, courts have endorsed a generous, Broward-style standard in determining voter intent. Though rules among the states do vary, the supreme courts of three states—Illinois, Massachusetts, and South Dakota—have endorsed this kind of rule, and the Texas legislature passed a Broward-style law in 1993. None of this was good enough for the Palm Beach canvassing board—to Al Gore's ever-lasting detriment.

The carnivals in Broward and Palm Beach were the great public spectacles of the Florida recount. But in the days before the November 26 certification deadline, there was another, much quieter development that may have been almost as important as the chad-fests. This drama included many of the same themes that played out across the state: the brutal determination of the Bush forces, the home-field advantage of the Republican Party, and the gnarled uncertainty of the Gore operation. Also involved here, however, was the most vexing story in the Florida recount—the issue of race.

In the days since the 2000 election, a kind of folklore has emerged about the injustices allegedly perpetrated on African-Americans to keep them from voting in Florida. On close inspection, however, many of the more inflammatory allegations fall away. For example, much was made of alleged police roadblocks in African-American neighborhoods on Election Day. However, the United States Civil Rights Commission, in a report otherwise harshly critical of state procedures, could identify only one roadblock in the entire state. It was part of an existing traffic-enforcement program in Tallahassee, and it lasted only ninety minutes. No proof ever emerged of systemic mistreatment of black voters at the polls. To be sure, voting facilities are government services, and as such, they are generally worse in poor areas, where many minority citizens live. But there was no credible evidence of an organized attempt to discourage African-Americans from going to the polls.

One well-known accusation—concerning a purge of the voting lists—presents a more complex story. After the tainted Miami mayoral election in 1997, the Florida legislature passed a law intended to scrub the voting lists of ineligible voters. In 1998, Katherine Harris's predecessor as secretary of state hired a firm called Database Technologies (DBT) to check the rolls for the names of dead people and duplicate names, and for convicted felons, who are ineligible to vote in Florida unless formally reinstated. The $4 million project, which ultimately yielded about 100,000 names, was a failure, especially the felon check. Most big counties simply ignored the DBT lists, which were riddled with errors, but some counties used them to attempt to remove some eligible voters. Because the DBT list of "felons" included a disproportionate number of blacks, the mistakes had a greater impact on African-American voters. Likewise, the DBT program did not stop many felons from remaining on the voting rolls. (For example, in Duval County, at least 258 felons voted illegally in 2000.) In all, the voter-purge program was ineptly designed and poorly executed. But the commonly made accusation that DBT—or the state of Florida or Katherine Harris—disenfranchised "thousands" of black voters seems baseless.

But neither is it true that black and white voters were treated equally in Florida. The election of 2000 was a special one for black Floridians. Jeb Bush's "One Florida" initiative, which was intended to put an effective end to affirmative action in the state, succeeded in mobilizing many thousands of new African-American voters to register and vote against the governor's brother. Two state legislators—Kendrick Meek, of Miami, and Tony Hill, of Jacksonville—had staged a celebrated sit-in at Jeb's Tallahassee office, and they built on their momentum with a voter drive they called "Arrive with Five"—that is, bring five new voters to the polls. The effort worked, and about three thousand new black voters registered in Jacksonville alone. It was in the crucible of that city that the racial divisions within Florida were exposed.

James Baker wasn't content merely to enjoy a public-relations victory on the issue of the overseas absentee ballots. When those ballots were counted around the state on November 17, many were disqualified for the reasons stated in the Herron memo to the Gore operatives—that is, the lack of postmarks or signatures. But since Lieberman had publicly repudiated Herron's undertaking on November 19, Baker—with his typical determination to squeeze every advantage to the last drop—thought the Bush campaign might want to get some of the votes reinstated.

After a day or so of strategizing, the Republicans came up with the idea of filing a lawsuit in Tallahassee to force the various canvassing boards to count more of the overseas ballots. The defendants were fourteen Florida counties in which as many as five hundred absentee ballots had been rejected. The idea was to get the judge, Ralph "Bubba" Smith, to force the canvassing boards to include the ballots, whatever technical defects they might have had. If Joe Lieberman wanted to give these ballots the "benefit of the doubt," the Bush campaign was going to shovel in as many as possible, even if they didn't have postmarks, signatures, dates, or anything else that might establish their legitimacy.

The Republicans filed their case on the day before Thanksgiving, and Judge Smith agreed to hear it on the day after the holiday, Friday, November 24. (In keeping with their fear of extending their public drubbing on this issue, the Gore lawyers didn't even send a lawyer to court.) Judge Smith was skeptical of the Republican claims—so hostile, in fact, that the Bush team decided to revise its strategy on the fly.

Again, the Republicans' home-field advantage helped them immeasurably. Jeb Bush had essentially turned over his entire legal staff to his brother's campaign for the duration. Frank Jimenez had taken a formal leave and his deputy, Reg Brown, hadn't, but the fact was they spent virtually all their time working for the Republican ticket. Along with two more local lawyers, Jason Unger and George Meros, they realized that Judge Smith had raised an issue fraught with peril for their candidate. Smith was a longtime nemesis of the governor's and had earlier in the year thrown out Jeb Bush's school-choice initiative. Smith was also a stickler for state prerogatives, and he saw that no Florida law had ever formally sanctioned the ten-day extension to count the overseas votes. There was a substantial body of Florida law that said consent decrees did not have the same authority as actual laws passed by the legislature and signed by the governor.

We have to drop the case, the Tallahassee Republican team said, not just because Bubba might refuse to add some of the excluded absentee ballots. He could wind up throwing out *all* of the overseas ballots, including the ones that had already been counted, because there was no authority for the ten-day extension. Instead of gaining a handful of new votes, Smith could cost Bush hundreds of votes that were already in the bag.

Besides, the Tallahassee contingent said, we have a better idea. The best Republican lawyers in every county in Florida already served on Jeb Bush's judicial-selection committees. Instead of fighting a losing battle in front of Judge Smith, the Republicans should fan out and fight to restore the absentee ballots in one county at a time. So with the certification deadline just two days away, the Republicans dismissed the case before Judge Smith and sent Jeb's troops out to battle. They had their greatest hopes in Duval County.

Decades ago, the city of Jacksonville extended its borders to include virtually all of Duval County. It is among Florida's oldest cities, named for the young general who fought off Seminole warriors in the small garrison there, almost two decades before he became president of the United States.

Located near the northeastern tip of the state, just below the

Georgia border, hard on the Atlantic, haphazardly bisected by the winding St. Johns River, Jacksonville lies at virtually the same latitude as Mobile, Alabama, and has kept a Southern flavor even as immigrants and tourists rubbed up against the local ways.

In the 1960s, Duval County was convulsed by racial violence every bit as intense as the better-known struggles in the South. Martin Luther King, Jr., suffered one of his rare setbacks when, in 1964, he tried to intervene in a black economic boycott of white-owned businesses in St. Augustine, just south of Jacksonville. King's campaign to desegregate the beaches there was opposed with greater violence, from Klansmen and others, than he faced in nearly any other part of the country. After his retreat from North Florida, which included a stint in the Duval County jail, King observed that "the racists in St. Augustine were worse than those in Birmingham."

Much, of course, has changed. While blacks remain economically downtrodden and are concentrated in the low-income northern side of the city, their political gains have been real. They have won any number of local offices around Duval County, usually in districts where they are in the majority, but whites have occasionally voted across racial lines, too. One of the most popular elected officials in this heavily Republican county is the sheriff, Nat Glover, an African-American Democrat.

John Stafford had a problem much like Theresa LePore's. Stafford was a longtime employee of the Duval County supervisor of elections who eventually ascended to the top job. Unlike LePore, he was a Republican, but like his Palm Beach counterpart, the doughy and stolid Stafford had a reputation for being apolitical. As he sat down to design the 2000 presidential election ballot, he also thought there were too many names to fit comfortably on one page. So instead of a butterfly, Stafford came up with . . . a caterpillar.

Specifically, Stafford designed a ballot that required voters to turn a page to see all the candidates. His office also made a clear mistake. In a sample ballot, which was widely circulated and published in the newspaper the Sunday before the election, the instructions erroneously stated that voters should vote on "every page" of the ballot. But with the presidential ballot stretching out over two pages, a vote on "every page" would be invalid—an overvote. The Democratic Party compounded this mistake. Trying to educate the many new voters in the county on the mechanics of voting, local party workers took up the cry of "vote every page." As the returns from Duval were analyzed, it became clear that thousands of voters made this mistake in the race for president.

The ballot in Duval County was probably a greater fiasco than Palm Beach's more notorious butterfly. Overall, Bush defeated Gore in Duval by 58 to 41 percent, a marked improvement for the Democrats after Bill Clinton's 35 percent showing in 1996. However, a whopping 9 percent of all votes cast were rendered invalid—21,942 overvotes and 4,927 undervotes. Nearly 9,000 of the invalid votes were concentrated in African-American precincts, where Gore won about 90 percent of the vote. (A post-election analysis of the overvote ballots by USA *Today* and Knight Ridder suggested that the ballot design cost Gore 2,600 votes in Duval County alone.)

However, the realization that Gore had lost thousands of votes was fatefully slow in coming. On the day after the election, Mark Langton, Gore's campaign chair in the region, called elections supervisor Stafford and asked about any problems in the vote. This was critical, because Democrats were then in the process of deciding where to ask for recounts. Langton recalled Stafford telling him there were problems with only about 200 or 300 ballots; the correct figure was over 26,000. (Citing litigation concerns, Stafford declined to comment.) In any event, Democrats did not learn of the magnitude of the problem until after Jack Young and his associates selected the counties for recounts. A manual recount in Duval surely would have captured at least some of Gore's lost ballots, but the Democrats didn't ask for one in time.

In the meantime, both sides were gearing up for their duel over the overseas absentee ballots. On the ten-day-extension deadline, November 17, lawyers for both sides gathered in front of the Duval County canvassing board to haggle over the 618 ballot envelopes that had arrived since Election Day. In a classic demonstration of the kind of legal trench warfare that was going on around the state, the two sides fought over whether the ballots should be counted for more than sixteen hours, until dawn on Saturday. The Democrats, led by a lawyer named Leslie Goller, worked from the Herron-memo playbook, seeking to exclude ballots without postmarks or dates.

The concern of the Gore team about dates was not frivolous. A suspicious pattern had emerged in the arrival of overseas absentee ballots in counties around the state. According to figures compiled by the Gore campaign, approximately half of the 4,256 overseas ballots were received by the counties between November 7 and November 15. That means that the other half of the ballots were received on the last two eligible days—and the pattern certainly raised the possibility that some of the ballots were illegally cast after Election Day. But since postmarks were not required, no one would ever know for sure.

None of this was of interest to the Duval County canvassing board, which consisted of four white Republicans. (Apparently, none of the members shared Broward judge Lee's concern that one-party canvassing boards looked bad.) Jim Post, the impassioned Bush lawyer before the board, dismissed the Gore concerns as nitpicky, or downright unpatriotic. "Strict compliance is not some sacred formula," Post said. "Isn't it ironic that the party of the man who wants to be commander in chief is trying to throw out the votes of the men and women he will be commanding." (This, of course, was at the same time that Bush lawyers in South Florida were arguing that strict compliance with the voting laws *was* a sacred formula.) Not surprisingly, the Republican-dominated board appreciated Post's argument and rejected most of the Democrats' challenges to the ballots. The Gore lawyers objected to 191 of the 618 overseas ballots, and the board sustained only 71 of these challenges. In all, the Duval overseas votes were a bonanza for Bush.

Even though an all-Republican board had already rejected 71 ballots, Post vowed to fight on, especially after Lieberman made his public repudiation of the Democratic efforts in this area. "We are not going to leave those 71 men behind!" This, of course, was a county where the votes of thousands of black citizens had not been counted. But rather than undertake any examination of that problem, much less do anything about it, the Republican establishment of the county aggressively mobilized to save those 71 votes. In Florida, one often heard Republicans asserting that if people (usually black people) were too dumb to follow simple directions, it was only fair to exclude their ballots. Apparently, though, if soldiers and sailors were too dumb to follow the rules, it was a patriotic duty to count their votes anyway. For the Duval County canvassing board, this wasn't a question of racism, just . . . priorities.

As Jeb Bush's lawyers knew, by withdrawing the Bubba Smith lawsuit, they would only increase the ardor of local party stalwarts like Jim Post. So, on Friday, November 24, the board reconvened to hear Post's claims on behalf of his 71 fallen soldiers. Wayne Hogan, the Gore lawyer, tried to make a simple point: Rules were rules. This very board had already rejected these ballots. And the board had done nothing at all about the thousands of black votes that remained uncounted. But board member Rick Mullaney, the general counsel to the city of Jacksonville, had a simple response: What about what Lieberman said? Didn't your vice presidential candidate say that these military voters should get the benefit of the doubt? Hogan tap-danced around the issue, but he was losing the battle. So late on Friday, just two days before the certification deadline, the canvassing board reinstated 68 of the 71 overseas votes. The votes of Duval's black citizens remained undisturbed in their boxes.

· · ·

Scenes like this went on all over Florida in the last days before certification. Emboldened by Lieberman's concession, Republicans returned to canvassing boards in counties that Bush had carried and asked that previously excluded overseas ballots be recognized as valid. There was no pretense of adhering to the rules. As a July 2001 *New York Times* report disclosed, Republican-dominated boards allowed not only ballots without postmarks, but ballots with domestic postmarks, faxed ballots, and ballots without the signatures of witnesses. According to the *Times*, canvassing boards included a total of 680 questionable overseas ballots, more than enough to change the final result of the election. In a curious twist, the Bush and Gore camps came up with the same nickname for this surge of questionable votes. As these newly added overseas absentee ballots were sent to Tallahassee on November 24 and 25, these votes padded Bush's lead by a critical 123 net votes—and they became known as "Thanksgiving stuffing."

As the week ended, it looked as if Bush might just survive the blow he had received on Tuesday from the Florida Supreme Court. Broward had delivered a windfall for Gore, but Miami-Dade had come up with nothing and Palm Beach was staggering to the finish line. Thanks to Jeb's private army, the Thanksgiving stuffing had delivered a precious, and unexpected, infusion of votes. Best of all, though, a surprising new player had emerged. On Friday, November 24, true to the prediction James Baker had made early on, the United States Supreme Court announced that it would review the judgment of the Republicans' seven enemies on the Florida Supreme Court.

CHAPTER ELEVEN

RSTONE@ GOAMERICA.NET

Throughout Al Gore's tenure as vice president, his staff used to joke about the "Bad Gore"—sullen, demanding, taking an almost sadistic pleasure in cross-examining ill-prepared underlings—and the "Good Gore"—upbeat, curious, displaying a childlike glee in the discovery of new things. During the campaign, the ratio had been about 80–20 in favor of the Bad; during the recount, it flipped completely despite the heightened tension. Gore wasn't just tolerating the recount; he was reveling in it. He was energetic, sympathetic, and grateful to all those who were working on his behalf. With Klain and others, he'd often sign off his phone calls with a cheerful "We're gonna win!"

The recount catered to Gore's distinctive vision of the life of a politician. He never seemed motivated by the usual things that seemed to inspire candidates for elective office—personal acclaim, the creation of great public works, or big public legacies like tax cuts or new laws. Rather, Gore thrived on learning, on collecting information. Some people around the vice president believed that he had never stopped seeing himself as the reporter he once was for the Nashville *Tennessean,* more interested in rooting out problems than solving them. For much of the recount period, Gore was joined at his home by Wendell Rawls, a retired reporter for *The Tennessean* and *The New York Times*. Though the two men had had little contact for years, Rawls volunteered to call reporters and editors to spur investigative reporting about the voting in Florida. While Republicans were mobilizing protesters, Gore was imploring journalists.

Early in the recount period, Gore was genuinely disappointed to have missed the "family reunion" conference that he and Tipper had sponsored for nine straight years at Vanderbilt University, in Nashville. The conference featured academics and other policy analysts talking about issues related to family life. It was all very earnest—and well removed from the lives of actual families—but Gore thrived on this scholarly if detached approach to government.

The recount gave Gore the chance to bring his analytic skills to bear on a problem of enormous complexity. Early in the recount, he found a copy of a twenty-thousand-word article that had been published in *The New Yorker* in 1986 about the then-new technology of punch-card ballots. The article, by Ronnie Dugger, prompted Gore to make a string of requests of David Ginsberg, the chief of research for the Democratic National Committee. A wild-haired twenty-five-year-old, Ginsberg operated out of what might have been the most cluttered office in Washington, where he had won renown in the political community for his ability to locate the most obscure information—fast. Still, Ginsberg could scarcely keep up with Gore's questions. Who owned the voting machines? What company manufactured them? Who was the largest shareholder? Did that company have a Texas connection? Who controlled the parent company? Dugger's article had raised questions about the reliability of the software used in the vote-counting process. Could the campaign subpoena the software? How about the source codes for the software?

Gore insisted that his campaign avoid making unproved allegations about the conduct of the recount, but in private he displayed a conspiratorial turn of mind. He saw the hidden hand of the Republican congressional leadership, especially House majority whip Tom DeLay, in all kinds of sinister activity. When Al Kamen, a columnist for *The Washington Post,* held a lighthearted contest to identify the congressional aides who were photographed during "the Brooks Brothers riot" in Miami, Gore did more than just follow the results obsessively. With the help of reader e-mails, Kamen ultimately identified seventeen of the protesters; the reporter had no way of knowing that David Ginsberg had pinpointed thirteen of those and then sent in their names through others to the *Post.*

Gore's e-mail address was Rstone@goamerica.net, which had a useful double meaning. (The address has since been disabled.) Gore had adopted the "handle" after a staffer named Robert Stone left the government; the vice president thought his abandoned address would offer a secure, anonymous way to communicate. But Gore also admired a novelist by the same name, the author of *Dog Soldiers* and *Damascus Gate,* who, like the vice president, saw the world with a decidedly jaundiced eye. (To amuse themselves during the recount, Gore's spokesmen Mark Fabiani and Chris Lehane held a secret punning contest. In interviews, they would try to get into print descriptions of the vice president as a "rock," a "pillar," or a "tower of strength"—all synonyms for his e-mail address.)

For sending e-mail, Gore used his BlackBerry, which allows users to type out messages with their thumbs. Because the vice president had one, the small, wireless device became a fashionable accessory during the campaign, even though most people had trouble with the awkward typing mechanism. Unlike everyone else, the meticulous vice president seemed never to make a spelling error on his. On one level, Gore's proficiency amazed his subordinates, but at the same time, it contributed to the distance between the vice president and the people around him. His fastidiousness was just a little . . . weird.

As the recount progressed, no subject occupied more of Gore's time than following the legal developments in the sprawling case, and the way he received his information had an important impact on the course of the litigation. Klain spoke to Gore several times a day, and his conspicuous skill at juggling the many pieces before him impressed the vice president as it did everyone else. But Klain was ultimately staff, not anything like a peer, so Gore looked elsewhere for the seasoned judgment he wanted. The vice president had no pre-existing relationship with David Boies. Before Florida, the two men had only met once, at a dinner party in New York, but it turned out that Gore and Boies had perfectly complementary temperaments: They were both cerebral without being intellectual, and dispassionate, almost bloodless; neither had any interest in small talk.

Boies's victory in the Florida Supreme Court two days before Thanksgiving gave Gore an almost unlimited faith in the lawyer's abilities. At the time, Boies thought the decision had more or less completed his involvement in the recount controversy, and he flew home to the Westchester suburbs on the night before the holiday. But when he arrived, his wife, Mary, told him the vice president was looking for him and he should call immediately. Gore patched in Michael Whouley, who said that it looked like Bush would be leading when Harris certified the election on Sunday night, November 26. With the Miami recount scuttled, there didn't seem to be any chance for Gore to pull ahead. What should they do now?

Gore, as always, was worried that the Washington establishment would see certification as the end of the process and that calls for his withdrawal would mount. In light of this, Boies suggested that the campaign make an immediate public statement that a contest would be filed as soon as the certification took place. That preemptive strike would avoid any stories suggesting that this would be the last weekend of the election. Rather, the press would spend the weekend looking ahead to the next chapter in the saga—the contest, starting on Monday. Exactly my thoughts, said Gore. And one more thing: The vice president wanted Boies to turn around, return to Florida, and conduct the recount trial himself. A conference call with the full campaign leadership on Thanksgiving Day sealed Boies's assignment. As he prepared to return to Tallahassee, his wife, feeling sorry for him, made him a turkey lunch before he left. On the way to the airport, they stopped to see some friends, who presented him with another turkey meal for the road.

The next morning, Gore had a new question for him. The Supreme Court—the *real* Supreme Court. How did they get into the act?

Of the many surprising events that marked the post-election period, there was probably no greater shock than the leading, and ultimately dispositive, role played by the Supreme Court of the United States. In general, the Court avoided immediate political controversies, deferred to states to run their own affairs, and steered clear of the gritty mechanics of election law. Almost no one—except James Baker and a handful of former law clerks—anticipated that the Supreme Court would enter this fray. But there was, it turns out, a clue to the real reason for the Court's activism.

In the strict division of labor that characterized the Bush post-election effort, the United States Supreme Court belonged to Ted Olson. He had been ready for the defeat in the Florida Supreme Court on Tuesday, November 21, and he filed the campaign's petition for a writ of certiorari in the United States Supreme Court the following morning, which was the day before Thanksgiving. The petition repeated several of the arguments the Bush forces had been raising since the beginning of the recount. Olson and company told the justices that there were three "questions presented" by the case:

> Did the Florida court change the election rules after the voting had taken place, in violation of federal law?
>
> Did the Florida court violate Article II of the Constitution, which suggests that state legislatures, not state courts, make the rules for presidential elections?

Did the chaotic recount process violate the equal-protection and due-process clauses of the Constitution?

In the petition, the Bush lawyers went on to argue that the Florida court had opened the door to "an electoral catastrophe" and that the United States Supreme Court needed to step in to prevent "the ascension of a President of questionable legitimacy, or a constitutional crisis." In a second filing, submitted to the Court the same day, the Bush team asked for expedited consideration of the case. Of course, the election had to be resolved quickly—although the precise deadline would become a matter of controversy—so Olson believed that the Court's usual deadlines for the submission of briefs would have to be shortened considerably. He suggested that Gore be required to answer on Friday, November 24, that the Court receive briefs on the merits the following week and then set oral argument in the case for Tuesday, December 5. It would have been as fast a schedule as any case in the Court's recent history.

What happened next was noticed only by those with detailed knowledge of the Supreme Court's arcane procedures. Two critical things took place on Friday, November 24. First, the Court granted certiorari in the case, and second, it granted the motion for expedited consideration—and then some. An even faster schedule was set up than the extremely abbreviated one Olson had sought. Oral argument would not be on December 5 but rather on Friday, December 1, just one week from the day after the Court granted review.

William H. Rehnquist had been chief justice of the United States for fourteen years, and a justice for twenty-eight, when the election cases arrived on the Supreme Court's doorstep. In his early years on the Court, shortly after Warren Burger became chief justice, Rehnquist's extremely conservative views made him almost an outcast, an afterthought among the nine justices. But as Republican appointments reshaped the Court and Rehnquist himself was promoted, he watched the Court come around to his position on any number of issues, including states' rights, the death penalty, and criminal procedure. Not all of his views had prevailed—most notably those on the incendiary topic of abortion—but time had been his ally, and the chief justice could rightly regard the Supreme Court in 2000 as his own.

Rehnquist's perpetually aching back gave him a slight stoop and his vaguely distracted air made him look more like a professor than a judge, but he savored the perquisites of his position. He corrected those who called him *justice;* he was *chief* justice. It wasn't chief justice of the *Supreme Court,* either; the correct title was chief justice of the *United States.* When he put gold stripes on each sleeve of his judicial robe—an inspiration he received from a Gilbert-and-Sullivan production—it was more than clear to the other justices that they shouldn't get the same idea. Rehnquist took his procedural responsibilities seriously, too. The chief had the unwritten authority to control things like scheduling and deadlines, even if such matters technically required a majority vote. The Court's order of November 24 thus meant that the chief—and not just the majority of the Court—wanted to hear Bush's appeal on a fast track.

This was by no means to be expected. Like the Bush lawsuit in federal court before Judge Middlebrooks in Miami, the appeal of the Florida Supreme Court ruling stood several conservative legal values on their heads. The first was federalism. If there was one touchstone of Rehnquist's jurisprudence, it was the primacy of states' rights under the Constitution. The election dispute concerned a state court interpreting a state law under the state constitution on a matter—presidential elections—that the Constitution expressly delegated to the states to decide. Rehnquist and his colleagues had been especially reluctant to invoke the broad commands of the Bill of Rights—the clauses requiring due process and equal protection of the laws—to discipline state courts' interpretations of their own laws. Moreover, there was a practical reason for the Supreme Court to appear ill-disposed to enter the case at this moment. The recounts were still ongoing, and the election hadn't even been certified by the Florida secretary of state. Under normal circumstances, the Rehnquist Court insisted on a final judgment—a really final judgment—before it would even consider taking a case. Here, there was certain to be a contest, and that case would surely be appealed as well. For all of these reasons, the Gore legal team—led by Laurence Tribe—had a high degree of confidence that the Supreme Court would stay out of the action, at least for the time being.

But it turned out that Olson's troops—especially their core of recent Supreme Court clerks—knew better. Law clerks for the conservative justices had created a powerful network for themselves in recent years; at times, some of them referred to themselves, half-jokingly, as the Cabal. They had met and mingled at organizations such as the Federalist Society (in which Olson was a prominent member), and they circulated among the same law firms and government agencies. In Tallahassee and Washington, the Bush team abounded in such former clerks, including Ted Cruz (Rehnquist), Tim Flanigan (Burger), John Manning (Scalia), Noel Francisco (Scalia), Alex Azar (Scalia), Helgi Walker (Thomas), Rick Garnett (Rehnquist), Bill Kelley (Scalia), Glen Summers (Scalia), Shawn Fagan (Rehnquist), Sean Gallagher (O'Connor), Matt Stowe (O'Connor), Andrew McBride (O'Connor), John G. Roberts, Jr. (Rehnquist), Miguel Estrada (Kennedy), and Tom Hungar (Kennedy). There was nothing improper about this kind of networking; liberal clerks did it, too, but they had less of an impact, because their numbers were smaller.

These former clerks now said, Trust us—the justices will want this case. Sure, Scalia usually insisted on all the procedural niceties being observed, and Justice Sandra Day O'Connor often made a point of deferring to state courts and legislatures, as she herself had served in both. But this case was different. The former clerks knew that the justices read the papers, listened to the radio, and had strong feelings about Bush and Gore. The drumbeat Baker had been orchestrating for almost a month—that the election was being stolen—would reverberate with the justices, too. Rehnquist and company would simply not sit out an event of this magnitude.

In its cryptic order granting certiorari, the Court offered one clue about its thinking. Speaking in one voice, the justices said that they wanted the parties to brief only the first two questions the Bush team had presented, which related primarily to federal law, and not the third question, which invoked the Bill of Rights. In other words, even though the Republicans had argued that the Florida court had violated the equal-protection clause, the Court didn't find that point persuasive enough to merit further briefing.

With the minutes dwindling until certification on Sunday night, November 26, the two sides had no choice but to continue working on parallel tracks. They went ahead with their brief writing and other preparations for the battle in the United States Supreme Court, but they also fought and clawed for every last vote. The Republicans tended to the Thanksgiving stuffing—the late overseas absentee ballots, which were arriving at Harris's office over the weekend. The Democrats sat an increasingly forlorn vigil before the Palm Beach canvassing board.

From his first day on the job, Mac Stipanovich had preached the gospel of setting and enforcing deadlines, and he used the Florida Supreme Court opinion to persuade Harris to set another one. In the oddly phrased conclusion to their opinion, the justices said the final returns had to be submitted by "5 P.M. on Sunday, November 26, 2000, provided that the office of the Secretary of State, Division of Elections is open to allow receipt thereof. If the office is not open for this special purpose on Sunday, November 26, 2000, then any amended certifications shall be accepted until 9 A.M. on Monday, November 27, 2000." The court could have simply set a clear deadline; instead, it gave Harris a choice—Sunday afternoon or Monday morning.

Harris and her husband, whom Stipanovich jokingly called the King of Sweden, took a brief trip to Georgia for Thanksgiving, and they stopped by Mac's home when they returned to Tallahassee. "We're gonna hoist the court by its own petard," Stipanovich told her. If the court was going to force them to extend their deadline, they were going to extend it as little as the Florida justices would permit. Since we have the choice, we're going to cut it off on Sunday. Of course, Stipanovich's plan was contrary to the spirit of the Florida Supreme Court opinion, which was principally concerned with including as many votes as possible. So, well before the weekend, Harris's office announced that she would be open for business over the weekend and the deadline—the *final* deadline—for submitting votes was Sunday afternoon, November 26, at 5 P.M.

At the Emergency Operations Center in Palm Beach, the sense of crisis built slowly. By that Friday, county workers had separated out all the contested ballots. The only people left were the canvassing-board members, the representatives of each side, and the dozens of journalists who were monitoring every move. Burton enjoyed bantering with the visiting Republican dignitaries, most of whom promptly went out and trashed what the judge was doing. The judge even collected autographs from the senators, governors, and congressmen who came in to watch. By and large, Burton maintained a sunny disposition, fueled by a diet of cigarettes and M&M's. The judge said of the candies, "Melts in your mouth, not on your ballot."

By Friday, however, Burton began to worry that the board was going to miss the deadline. As he closed the operation down shortly before midnight, he said, "We're going to make some tracks tomorrow, though. That's for sure." But they didn't. The Republican objections, often expressed at length, continued to slow things down. A combative young lawyer named Mark Wallace particularly drew Burton's ire. "Mark, no more," he said at one point. "I'm sick of this. We've got a long night. If you can't shut up, we'll get somebody else here."

Panic set in on Saturday morning. Burton was losing his sense of humor, saying, "Let's go. Next. Time's running. The clock is our enemy." In keeping with the strange atmosphere, Palm Beach was hit by thunderstorms and blackouts as the vote counting continued, and at times the ever-more-fitting setting of the Emergency Operations Center was operating with backup generators.

By noon on Sunday, Burton realized there was no way the board was going to finish by five, so he thought he'd try to persuade Harris to delay the deadline until Monday morning. He asked the county attorney to write a letter to her, requesting the extension, but then the judge remembered that he had live television cameras at his disposal. So Burton just read the letter out loud, knowing that Harris would hear it, which she did.

In the Harris bunker at the Capitol in Tallahassee, Stipanovich was steeling his client. No extensions! In for a landing! At about 3:30 P.M., Judge Burton called Clay Roberts, director of the Division of Elections, to ask for more time. "I've got people busting their asses here," Burton said. Anyway, the judge added, "I don't think there's a big vote swing here, if that's what you're worried about." For a judge who claimed to be removed from the political passions of the case, it was a blunt appeal to Harris's partisan agenda. Still, Roberts said no. What about seven-thirty? Burton asked. No, said Roberts. Five o'clock was the deadline.

Burton had no way of knowing it, but Clay Roberts was fighting his own battle in Tallahassee—with Mac Stipanovich. Most everyone in the secretary of state's office believed that if Palm Beach did not finish its recount, the canvassing board would submit the work that had been thus far completed. Roberts said he would have accepted figures from a partial recount. But Stipanovich wanted a hard line: All the votes recounted, or back to the original numbers. Of course, this served the Republicans' interest, because a partial recount would have eaten into Bush's margin, if only by a little. Roberts and Stipanovich were shouting at each other when Burton appeared before the cameras in Palm Beach.

"So the secretary of state has decided to shut us down with approximately two hours left to go," Burton said. "We believe there are approximately 800 to 1,000 ballots left to count. So, unfortunately, at this time we have no other choice but to shut down. The supervisor of elections needs to hurriedly gather all the paperwork and prepare to file the returns that we have. We certainly don't want to get anything in there at 5:01." Burton went on to say that the board would take the couple of hours to complete its recount that evening, even if the results would never be included in the official totals.

Five days after his triumph in the Florida Supreme Court, Gore's victory had turned to ashes. Miami-Dade had aborted its recount; Palm Beach had missed its deadline. Only Broward had completed its obligations. The Palm Beach story had a suitably bizarre postscript. Just before the five o'clock deadline, Theresa LePore faxed a document to Tallahassee that purportedly gave the Palm Beach County results, but it was presented in a nearly incomprehensible manner—page after page of columns of numbers. Eventually, Roberts and Stipanovich decoded LePore's letter to see that she had submitted the partial numbers, but Stipanovich triumphed once more: Harris did not accept the partial recount. She used the original Palm Beach votes in the totals she planned to certify that evening.

The actual counting of votes by the canvassing board ended shortly after seven that evening, but LePore still had a lot of work ahead of her. (Unlike Broward County, Palm Beach had not hired accountants to help with the record keeping.) LePore had to reconcile the counts and recounts in all the precincts. As it turned out, she didn't finish a complete retabulation of the votes until Wednesday, November 29. And even then there was confusion. The Gore monitors insisted that the final totals showed that the vice president had netted 215 votes in the Palm Beach recount, but LePore's final numbers showed a net gain to Gore of only 176 votes. To this day, it remains unclear which figure is correct—an uncertainty that seems fitting for the hopelessly botched election in Palm Beach County.

Ben McKay, Harris's chief of staff, had spent most of the past week planning the certification ceremony. As always with the secretary of state's office in this period, the goal was to persuade the public that the election had come to a dignified (and final) conclusion—and that Gore's attempts to extend the recount amounted to bad sportsmanship. There was no need for any ceremony, because Harris, Roberts, and Bob Crawford, the Florida commissioner of agriculture, merely had to sign a handful of documents. But McKay took over the state cabinet room, with its raised stage and high-backed leather chairs, and allowed admission only by printed tickets, which said "Admit one (1) to the convening of the Florida Election Canvassing Commission."

The commission had no responsibilities other than the ministerial act of certifying the vote. According to state law, the governor was a member, but Jeb Bush had recused himself on the day after the election and appointed Bob Crawford in his place. A nominal Democrat, Crawford had been a loyal ally of the Bush family for years, and now, on live television, broadcast around the country, he urged Gore to accept the result. "After all the jokes, after all of the anguish, we've just got a close election," Crawford said. "But I think it's over. It should be over. And Yogi Berra once said, 'It's not over till it's over.' Well, it's over. And we have a winner, and it's time to move on."

The three officials signed multiple copies of the document: "The certified result in the presidential race in Florida is as follows— Governor George W. Bush, 2,912,790; Vice President Al Gore, 2,912,253"—a margin of 537 votes.

The minutes passed in near silence; the only sound was that of pens scratching on paper. No one had stapled the documents together, so McKay simply tossed them into folders. Soon the papers were slipping out of order, and he was getting nervous about the dead airtime. Finally, in something close to panic, he signaled Harris to call the ceremony to a close, even though Roberts had not finished signing. In the front row of the audience, Mac's wife, Mary, and daughter, Heather, watched with pride. Stipanovich himself remained where he had been for the preceding seventeen days—just steps away in the Capitol but out of public view, in Katherine Harris's conference room. He watched the certification on television, thinking what a fine way it was to celebrate his fifty-second birthday.

The cameras were turned off at the conclusion of the ceremony, but there was another step to be completed. Jeb Bush's legal staff had spent the previous several weeks researching the precise measures to be taken after certification to ensure that Florida's votes would be cast for the Texas governor in the Electoral College. So, while the public ceremony was going forward, the Florida governor's staff was putting the final touches on a document called the certificate of ascertainment, which was to be filed with the National Archives in Washington. Jeb's lawyers worried that the Gore lawyers were going to subpoena the certificate to keep it from being filed there. They had heard, too, that the Gore team was going to file its contest at 10 A.M. on Monday. So they devised an elaborate subterfuge to keep the document out of the enemy's hands and get it to Washington by the time the next chapter in the struggle began.

Frank Jimenez arranged for the certificate to be whisked from the Capitol to the governor's mansion on Sunday night, just after the certification. Three of the governor's staffers—deputy counsel Reg Brown, press secretary Katie Baur, and another lawyer—hand-carried the documents in an unmarked police car, hoping to avoid notice from the press or Gore lawyers. After Jeb affixed his signature to the required three copies, the second lawyer, a woman who had had nothing to do with the electoral fight, took the package home for the night. The Bush lawyers gave the precious cargo to her because she was someone the Democrats would never think to track down and subpoena. The following morning, Monday, November 27, the documents would be mailed to Washington as soon as the post office opened.

At eight o'clock on Monday, the woman made her way to a branch of the post office on the outskirts of Tallahassee. (She was instructed to go there because Jeb's staffers worried that the

Democrats might stake out the downtown post office.) The woman handed the envelope to the clerk and, as had been done in previous elections, asked that it be sent by certified mail. The clerk filled out the appropriate paperwork, and the messenger returned to the Capitol.

The woman promptly delivered the receipt to Reg Brown, who was waiting anxiously at his desk in the Capitol. Brown carefully checked the postal receipt and the relevant federal law. With mounting discomfort, he realized that the law called for the certificate to be sent by registered mail and the woman had used certified mail, which had not existed when the law was passed. After a hurried consultation with Jimenez, Brown raced back to the post office with the woman and implored the clerk to give him back the envelope. Displaying his identification to prove that he really did work for the governor, Brown redid the paperwork so that the package would be "registered."

It had been a more chaotic morning than anticipated, but Reg Brown slipped the newly addressed envelope back to the clerk at 9:59 A.M. Once again in Florida, the Republicans had backed up a boast with action.

CHAPTER TWELVE

LOSE SLOW, LOSE FAST

Bill Daley telephoned John Podesta first thing in the morning. "The president woke me up in the middle of the night last night, and he said there were three things we had to do to win this thing in Florida," Daley told Bill Clinton's chief of staff. "But I was asleep when he called and I don't remember anything he said, so do you think you could go in and ask him what he meant?"

To the Gore campaign, Bill Clinton was like a crazy uncle in the attic—an eccentric voice to be appeased rather than heeded. By Election Day, the relationship between the president and vice president had reached a tense standoff. Clinton had stewed through the final weeks of the campaign, frustrated that Gore was neither letting the president campaign for him nor embracing their shared legacy of peace and prosperity. For his part, the vice president and his staff regarded the stain of impeachment and Monica Lewinsky as a continuing burden on their efforts, and Gore was determined to win his race on his own terms. During the recount, both Gore and Clinton wanted to see a Democratic victory, but once more they saw different routes to the same goal.

In public, President Clinton did his former running mate an unquestionable service. Before the pardons that marred his departure from office, Clinton was riding a great wave of public support. His calm presence during the recount in Florida—which included important, albeit overshadowed, trips to Vietnam and Ireland—reminded the country that the machinery of government continued to function. Clinton limited his public remarks to bland but useful reminders that the United States had both a sitting president and an orderly process for a constitutional transition of power.

Clinton in private was another story altogether. Probably more than anyone, he saw the recount in Florida as the final chapter of a long siege. He regarded the plague of investigations he had endured as a fundamental challenge to his legitimacy in office. Whether it was in the Paula Jones lawsuit, the ever-mutating Whitewater investigation, or the impeachment crisis, Clinton believed that his critics had engaged in an extended struggle to destroy him as a political force. Florida, as he viewed it, was simply the next step—an attempt to inflict the same punishment on his rightful successor.

In the modus vivendi between their camps, Clinton's deputy chief of staff, Steve Ricchetti, was the designated point of contact with the Gore campaign. Ricchetti had worked closely with Bill Daley earlier in the Clinton years, and the two men got along well. Daley spoke on occasion to both Podesta and Clinton, but he and Ricchetti talked almost every day. Under this arrangement, it was Ricchetti's job to listen to Clinton talk—and rage—about the recount all day long. "Tell Daley this. . . . Make sure Daley sees this story in the paper. . . . Why isn't Daley doing that?"

"You are going to win this thing," Clinton told Gore in a phone call just after the vice president rescinded his concession on election night. But Clinton's philosophy about how to win posed a dramatic contrast to Gore's. "I would never have conceded to Bush"—this was only the first of the many ways Clinton told people around him that he would have fought the recount differently. Whereas Gore regarded the battle as primarily legal, Clinton saw it as political—and fierce. Gore wanted no demonstrators in the streets; Clinton wanted lots of them. Gore worried about pressing his case in court; Clinton thought the vice president should have sued everybody over everything. Gore believed in muting racial animosities about the election; Clinton thought that Democrats should have been screaming about the treatment of black voters. Gore believed in offering concessions, making gestures of good faith; Clinton thought the Republicans should be given nothing at all but should rather be fought for every single vote. "He's being screwed," Clinton would say of Gore. "He got more votes—more people wanted to vote for him. This is the essence of democracy. But the fix is in. This thing stinks."

As always, Clinton reflected the id of the Democratic Party. The recount allowed him to indulge some of his pet obsessions from the previous eight years. Clinton loathed the media in general and *The Washington Post* in particular, which he thought was out to get Gore because of his association with Clinton. "The salon crowd in Georgetown," as Clinton put it, wanted to see them both humbled. Clinton especially distrusted Chief Justice Rehnquist, who, he thought, had stacked his Senate impeachment trial against him. "These are not apolitical people," Clinton said of the Supreme Court. There was some irony in the Florida setting of this final battle of the Clinton years, because out of all the Republican governors in the country, Clinton may have liked Jeb Bush the most, regarding him as the smarter and savvier of the Bush brothers.

By Thanksgiving, Clinton despaired over what he saw as Gore's timid performance in the recount. Why weren't blacks in the streets? Jesse Jackson was calling Clinton to complain about being muzzled. Where was labor? Why was Gore so worried about stretching out the fight? There was plenty of time—just get the right result. Why hadn't Gore asked for a recount of the whole state? Why such a timid public-relations message? Count all the votes—not good enough. What about *We won and they're stealing the election?*

Podesta never found out what exactly was on the president's magic list of three things for Bill Daley. But he passed the gist of Clinton's comments to Daley, who, along with Al Gore, promptly buried them.

.   .   .

In Mitchell Berger's law offices in Tallahassee, David Boies was vowing to eat only the red M&Ms. The food options in North Florida demoralized even a confirmed junk-food addict like Boies, and he periodically made short-lived vows to clean up his act. So did Klain, who was fighting an even less successful battle against weight gain and, as a consequence, was coming to resemble the actor Jon Lovitz more closely every day. But November 26 was no time to start a diet. After Harris certified the result that Sunday evening, Boies and Klain—and their client—had to make their final decisions about the contest. What parts of the election would they challenge in court?

By then, Gore had an even greater adversary than the Republicans: time. Here again the caution and hesitancy of the Democrats returned to haunt them. The new president would be inaugurated on January 20, 2001. According to federal law, Congress would meet on January 6, 2001, to hear any challenges to the electoral votes of any state. The electors, meanwhile, would cast their votes at meetings in each of the state capitals on the first Monday after the second Wednesday in December. Accordingly, that date— December 18—was the true final deadline for the recount. But during the first argument to the Florida Supreme Court, Boies had said that the election would be over on December 12, because of an obscure provision of federal law.

In an effort to avoid the chaos that followed the 1876 Hayes-Tilden race, Congress in 1887 passed a complex set of new rules for presidential elections. Since then, they had mostly been forgotten, because all subsequent elections had been long resolved by the time the Electoral College came into play. But they remained on the books, and among them was one that said if a state designated its electors at least six days before the Electoral College deadline, those electors could not later be challenged in Congress. States could still designate their electors during the following six days, but they would lose the benefit of this so-called safe-harbor provision if they did so. Feeling the pressure to wrap up the election as quickly as possible, Boies committed himself to the safe-harbor deadline rather than the real deadline. His caution, on Gore's behalf, meant that the Democrats might have lost the precious days.

As of the night Harris certified, Boies and Klain knew they only had sixteen days until their self-imposed deadline. In that period, they would have to 1) try and win their case in the contest, 2) survive any appeals of that verdict, 3) conduct the actual vote counting that they had been seeking for so long, and then 4) protect the results of the vote counting in subsequent appeals. Was it possible to do so much so quickly? Boies and Klain pulled out their calculators.

Their primary goal was to construct a contest that would require only a legal conclusion by the judge—no time-consuming testimony from witnesses or recounting of ballots. Klain made a list to show how they could make up the 537-vote deficit.

- 215 net votes in Palm Beach: Harris's cutoff of the recount was arbitrary, so those ballots should be included.
- 157 net votes in Miami-Dade: The canvassing board had examined these ballots before it voted to cease its recount.
- 51 net votes in Nassau: In this small county, just north of Jacksonville, the automatic recount had produced fewer votes than the election-night totals. The local canvassing board had voted to return to the original numbers, which cost Gore votes. The recounted numbers should stand.
- 123 net votes in "Thanksgiving stuffing": These last-minute additions to the total of overseas absentee ballots should be disallowed, because they had arrived late and in violation of state law.
- So: 215 + 157 + 51 + 123 = 546. Gore wins by 9 votes!

At one level—at several levels—the Gore lawyers' caffeine-fueled conclusions that Sunday night were implausible. Why 215 votes in Palm Beach and not the 176 from Theresa LePore's official totals? How could they include the 157 from Miami when those votes came from heavily Democratic precincts and the Republican areas had not even been recounted? Who was to say which count was more accurate in Nassau? Finally, were Gore and Lieberman willing to wade into the political disaster area of the "military" ballots once more and try to get those votes excluded? And finally—9 votes? Sure, 537 was small enough, but did anyone think that the courts would let a presidential election come down to this preposterously minuscule margin?

In a larger sense, Boies and Klain's arithmetic exercise showed the costs of Gore's approach during the previous nineteen days. The tiny circuitry of their lawyerly analysis obscured many of the larger truths about the recount. Gore had been reduced to parsing partial counts in the handful of counties where his campaign had asked for reviews of the ballots. He would have been in a much stronger moral, political, and perhaps even legal position if he had asked for recounts in all sixty-seven counties: That was the way to "count all the votes." The racial issue had been abandoned and was invisible except in a handful of press reports. Boies and Klain were probably right that there was no time to raise these complex subjects. But as Bill Clinton and James Baker had recognized, this was a political street fight from day one, requiring the full arsenal of contemporary weapons. Gore had seen his recount as a logic puzzle, to be solved after judicious reflection. But while the vice president and his aides were hunched over their calculators, the Republicans were breaking bar stools over their heads.

The final conference call to determine the shape of Gore's contest was scheduled for early Monday morning, November 28. As for the toughest decision of all—what to do about Seminole and Martin counties, where another absentee-ballot issue had emerged—the lawyers were going to leave that one up to the vice president.

. . .

For more than a decade, the national Republican Party had worked hard to expand the use of absentee ballots. Many wealthy voters welcomed the chance to avoid a journey to their polling places on Election Day, and Republican organizers sought to make absentee voting as convenient as possible. In Florida's Seminole and Martin counties, as in many other places around the country, the local Republican organization had hired a contractor to send out preprinted absentee-ballot applications to local party members. But as the Republicans realized to their dismay in the fall of 2000, the contractor made a mistake. He had omitted a place on the form for including voter-identification numbers, which were required before local election officials would process the applications.

There was never any real dispute about how this situation came about. However, to address the problem, local Republican Party volunteers asked for and received permission to "fix" the applications. In Seminole County, a heavily Republican area just north of Orlando, the Republican supervisor of elections let local party people set up shop in her office for ten days while they added the voter-identification numbers to thousands of applications. In Martin County, which was on the Atlantic coast north of Palm Beach, Republican officials simply gave the applications back to Republican Party workers, who added the identification numbers and then returned the corrected forms. The privileged treatment for the Republican voters may well have violated state election law. From the time that the Seminole and Martin schemes were uncovered a few days after the election, local Democratic officials said they wanted to throw out all the absentee ballots in both counties.

By the standards of this election, the stakes were enormous. In absentee voting alone, Bush netted 4,700 votes in Seminole and 2,815 in Martin. Eliminating them would have wiped out Bush's margin more than ten times over. But the issue posed a political, and moral, dilemma for Gore. His campaign had organized its recount effort around the slogan "count all the votes." A fight in these counties would mean the Democrats were trying to disenfranchise thousands of voters who had done nothing wrong—indeed, to penalize voters who didn't even know that their ballot applications had been amended by Republican officials.

In characteristic fashion, Gore agonized about what to do. Earlier the previous week, he had asked Klain to explore the possibility of a limited revote in Seminole and Martin counties. Everyone who had asked for an absentee ballot would be sent another one, and then they could vote again. But Klain discovered that such a procedure would take far too long. Moreover, after the fact, there was no way to separate out the ballots whose applications had been amended by party workers. Because the actual ballots were secret, without the voters' names attached, the counties presented Gore with an all-or-nothing proposition: try to throw out thousands of ballots in both counties—or accept them all. Gore wanted to think about it for one more night.

It was eight o'clock in the morning on Monday, November 27, when Boies and Klain convened the largest and most important conference call of the post-election period. As Jeb Bush's lawyers were trying to mail the certificate of ascertainment to Washington, the Gore team had one final discussion of the contest. (The Republicans' machinations about hiding the certificate from process servers turned out to be unnecessary; the Democrats never considered subpoenaing the papers.) The participants in the phone call included Gore, his brother-in-law Frank Hunger, Daley, Lieberman, his top aide Tom Nides, Warren Christopher (calling from Los Angeles), Boies, Klain, Mitchell Berger in Tallahassee, and Michael Whouley in Palm Beach. The roll call alone demonstrated Gore's priorities. For this most important decision, nearly every seat at the table went to a lawyer.

As the conference call began, the first subjects were dispensed with easily. Gore would ask for 1) 215 net votes in the late Palm Beach recount, 2) 157 net votes from the partial recount in Miami-Dade, and 3) 51 net votes from Nassau. But with a 537-vote deficit, Gore needed something more. The lawyers quickly agreed that they had to add some "counting claims," as they referred to them. These issues might drag out the trial, but the potential bounty was simply too great to ignore. So the lawyers would ask that the court 4) instruct Miami-Dade to complete its aborted recount and 5) direct Palm Beach to re-examine its contested ballots with a more liberal intent-of-the-voter standard. Another issue on the table was easy to abandon—Palm Beach's butterfly ballot. There was simply no reasonable solution to the problem of Theresa LePore's benighted progeny, so they decided not to pursue the matter.

Boies took the lead on Seminole and Martin. "There is an elegant solution here," he said. "In Miami and Palm Beach, the Republicans are saying you have to observe the letter of the law. They say if the ballots don't comply with every technical requirement, then they should be thrown out. But in Seminole and Martin, they say they want to respect the intent of the voter, even if they break some rules along the way. But they can't have it both ways. If we include Seminole and Martin, we flush them out. And if we get a consistent opinion from the judge, we win either way. A hard line gets rid of all the absentee ballots in Seminole and Martin. And a soft intent-of-the-voter standard gets us our votes in Miami and Palm Beach." Klain enthusiastically endorsed Boies's view.

Gore was intrigued, but ultimately he said Boies's approach was "too clever by half." No one would focus on the subtle inconsistencies in the Republican position; they would only see that the Democrats were trying to get thousands of ballots thrown out. Instead, the vice president approved a kind of half-measure. A group of Democrats in Florida would file separate lawsuits challenging the Seminole and Martin votes, and Gore would officially stay neutral in those cases. But if they won, the votes might be thrown out anyway, and Gore would win the election.

That left only one issue—the Thanksgiving stuffing. In many respects, this was the best legal case. It would not have been difficult to prove that many of the last-minute overseas absentee ballots had been improper.

"We can win the election without any more counting in Miami and Palm Beach," Klain said. "If we don't go after the military-ballot thing, you have to have counting, and that may take time."

"We have good claims," Boies said, "and we should bring them."

Gore quietly ended the discussion. "Even accepting that Ron is right and there is a theoretical way that I could win by nine votes, I couldn't be president of the United States that way. It's not right," he said. "If we knock out thousands of votes of military people, I couldn't govern. I could win, but I couldn't govern." Gore opted to ask for more counting.

For all his inconstancy, his diffidence, his undue regard for the self-appointed mandarins of Washington, his surfeit of analysis and his paucity of warmth, Al Gore did care about doing the right thing. This was not the only occasion when he raised the issue of the morality of his actions. He spoke of this concern often, even obsessively, as the recount stretched on. Throughout the recount he behaved as if there were higher values than winning. That, too, is part of his legacy in this election.

Klain listened to Gore's decision about the grounds for the contest and understood—sort of. As a lawyer, he could see why Gore gave up on Seminole and Martin, on Thanksgiving stuffing, on the possible civil-rights claims, on the outrage in Duval, on the statewide recount, and all the rest. As Klain was stewing about all this, the strangest thought popped into his head—about Clarence Thomas and Anita Hill. In the first great political battle of Klain's life, he had seen how the Republicans never hesitated, and attacked at full bore from the first moment. To Klain's eyes, Orrin Hatch, Arlen Specter, Alan Simpson, and the others didn't agonize about whether they were being unfair to Anita Hill. They had a job to do, and they did it. But the Democrats—like Klain's old boss Joe Biden—worried about how they would look. Where did this institutional self-censorship come from? If we're supposed to be advocates, why don't we advocate? Here in Florida, there were *judges* who were supposed to be the neutral parties. Why are we doing their jobs for them? Why don't we Democrats know how to fight? Ron Klain had arrived in Florida as Warren Christopher's son— and he left as Michael Whouley's brother.

After the conference call, Klain joined his fellow lawyers to adjust the complaint in the contest case in accordance with Gore's wishes. Prolonged exposure to Tallahassee had radicalized Klain's troops there, and no one was too pleased to hear the way the vice president had pared down their work. John Newton added the last touches to the document and pushed the print button. Standing nearby, Jeremy Bash, the youngest member of the Gore team, said the complaint had been in the works for so long that it seemed like they were giving birth. He called over to Dexter Douglass, the wizened old Florida hand, who had watched the hesitant, public relations–obsessed Gore effort with mounting disdain. Seeing Douglass hold the newly printed pages of the contest complaint in front of him, Bash said, "Dexter, is it a boy or a girl?"

"Let's take a look at this thing," Douglass said, scowling. He paused, then responded, "It's a boy. It's got very small balls, but it's a boy."

A veteran Tallahassee lawyer, Douglass served as the in-house Gore expert on local judges. In the normal practice of the Leon County Circuit Court, Douglass believed, there were three judges likely to be assigned to the contest case: Terry Lewis, who had ruled against Gore on the matter of Harris's discretion to certify the election; Bubba Smith, who had given the Republicans such a hard time in the overseas-absentee-ballots case; and Nikki Clark, who was the only African-American woman on the bench. When filing the complaint on Monday morning, the Gore lawyers could have related the matter to Judge Lewis's earlier case, virtually guaranteeing that he would handle it. But Douglass thought Smith and Clark were slightly better choices—and he didn't want to be accused of judge shopping—so he said they should simply leave the choice up to the computer's random selection.

Douglass, Mitchell Berger, and Jeremy Bash made the trip across the street to the courthouse, passing a throng of reporters. At the window of the clerk's office, at 12:14 P.M., Douglass handed the papers to David Lang, the clerk of the court, who entered the new case into the computer system.

"Who'd we get?" Douglass asked.

"The wheel gave you Sauls," the clerk said.

Douglass dropped his voice to a whisper so Lang could hear but the reporters around him could not. "This is a bad office," Douglass said. "This is a bad office."

Douglass, Berger, and Bash hustled off to take a freight elevator to the courthouse exit. When they were alone, their local expert said only one thing: "Redneck."

In the curious lottery that is American judicial selection, it was not surprising that a medium-sized city like Tallahassee would have some judges as good as Terry Lewis and others as bad as N. Sanders Sauls. He had lived all of his fifty-nine years in the North Florida political and legal world. His mother had run the Democratic Party in Jefferson County, and his father had been county clerk. The safe cocoon in the old-boys' network served Sandy Sauls well, for he won appointment to the federal bankruptcy court when he was just thirty-seven years old. He left after one term to make some money in private practice, but then in 1989, Florida's Republican governor, Bob Martinez, put him on the Leon County Circuit Court.

On the bench, Sauls earned a reputation for a knee-jerk conservatism, an imperious demeanor, and, above all, a consuming laziness. He was petty—he fought his first wife in court over a $50 saddle. He was inept—he was often reversed by appellate courts. And he was vindictive—as chief judge of the circuit court, he tried to fire the court administrator who dared challenge his choice for a patronage position on the court. After that controversy, in 1998, the Florida Supreme Court threatened to demote him from chief judge, because of "the continuing disruption in the administration of justice" on his watch. He later resigned as chief. Afterward, Sauls spent most of his time riding circuit among the courthouses in the little counties outside Tallahassee. Douglass thought the judge was out of town so much that he was unavailable for new cases, but to his enduring chagrin, he was wrong.

In his first act as judge in the contest case, Sauls lived up to his reputation. Knowing that he would soon be receiving a great deal of press attention, he had his secretary distribute to reporters a list of references, complete with phone numbers. The second name on the list was none other than Dexter Douglass, who was, of course, one of the lawyers in the case before him. It was bizarre and it was ethically dubious; but it was also poignant. Sauls knew that this assignment would prompt stories about his humiliation at the hands of the Florida Supreme Court, so he wanted to attempt a preemptive strike at the press. But Sauls had so few friends that he listed Douglass among them—even though the lawyer had nothing but contempt for the judge. On this inauspicious note began the most important trial in the history of American presidential elections.

It was four o'clock that Monday afternoon when the lawyers assembled for the first time in front of Judge Sauls. The courtroom was almost comically overrun with people—the jury box was full of video- and still-camera operators, more than two dozen lawyers crowded the well, and spectators spilled out of the double doors. All the chairs were occupied by the time Boies and Douglass arrived, so they stood awkwardly through the hour-long hearing.

There was no mystery about either side's strategy. Florida law said that the defendants, who included Katherine Harris and George W. Bush, could have no more than ten days to respond to the complaint. In truth this response, called an answer, was a pro forma document that the defendants could easily have produced overnight, especially when only sixteen days remained until the meeting of the Electoral College. But just as the Democrats wanted to move quickly, Bush and his allies wanted to stall. Joe Klock, representing Harris, suggested that he didn't even have the authority to agree to less than the full ten days. Barry Richard, for the Bush campaign, put on a somewhat more reasonable front, but he too was pressing for a languorous pace of litigation, under the circumstances.

Douglass and Boies tried to play good cop/bad cop with Judge

Sauls—the Southerner oozing cooperation and the New Yorker pushing for speed. Neither made much difference, because Sauls was already wending his way along the path of least resistance. Richard said the Bush team might be able to answer in three days and then spend several more on discovery. Sauls embraced this proposal and then, near the end of the hearing, listened as two lawyers for purported "intervenors" in the case stood up. The lawyers represented a pair of extreme-right-wing organizations that had no business at all in the courtroom, but Sauls welcomed them to the case. "Now, we can't get too many cooks in the stew," he said—and then, after Boies objected, said he would revisit their participation later on. The judge appeared incapable of deciding much.

The Bush lawyers marched sharply out of the courtroom and pronounced themselves well satisfied with their first day in court. The Gore team looked more dispirited than they had in weeks. The torpid pace of life before Judge Sauls seemed to drain the energy from them. Their mood did not improve when they made it back to their office and watched Al Gore's brief televised remarks explaining why he was filing the contest.

The speech was set at the Naval Observatory, in a room that had never before been used for this kind of event. There was no procedure in place for the taking of flash photographs during Gore's address, and no one thought to address the issue in advance. In his remarks, the vice president rehearsed his familiar themes—pre-eminently the need to count every vote—but the message was lost in the non-stop explosions from the cameras. Watching the spectacle from the next room, Bob Shrum could only shake his head and ask Carter Eskew, "What the fuck is going on?" The flashes rendered the speech nearly unwatchable.

Down in Tallahassee that night, Boies tried to rally the troops, after a fashion. "Here's what we're going to do," he said. "We're going to lose—quickly."

CHAPTER THIRTEEN

GREAT
AMERICANS

Around Republican headquarters in Tallahassee, they sometimes used to talk about the battleships. As Gore lurched from one potentially fatal crisis to another, with the justices of the Florida Supreme Court his only apparent allies in town, James Baker lined up one ship after another that could sink the vice president's hopes once and for all. For starters, there was an almost-forgotten case. Ted Olson and company had appealed Judge Middlebrooks's dismissal of their federal case to the United States Court of Appeals for the Eleventh Circuit. That famously conservative court had decided to hear the case on an expedited basis and could, at any moment, shut down all recount activity. Then there was the state legislature, especially the house, which was preparing to vote to award Florida's electoral votes to Bush, regardless of what the vote totals showed—and growing more serious about it with each passing day. There was also the hovering presence of the United States Supreme Court. Then, in the distance, should it be necessary, the Republicans apparently had the votes in the United States Congress to settle the election once and for all. To put it another way, Bush had to win just once, in any of these places—and Gore had to run the table.

Baker knew, however, that for all the legal machinations, it was the vote count that mattered. Bush had good days and bad days in court, but as long as he had more votes than Gore in Florida, the Texas governor was going to win the election. That was why Baker had called in reinforcements to prepare for the contest case— almost a dozen lawyers had been working full-time since Thanksgiving. (Baker's first choice to try the contest was Brendan V. Sullivan, Jr., who had defended Oliver North during the Iran-contra scandal. But Sullivan turned Baker down, because he was scheduled to represent the Warnaco company in a civil trial against Calvin Klein in January. Sullivan's opposing counsel in that case, David Boies, had no similar worries about managing his workload. In any event, the Warnaco case settled on the eve of jury selection.)

The obsession with the vote totals also fed Baker's concerns about Seminole and Martin counties. Instead of the quibbles over dozens of votes in Nassau or Palm Beach, there were thousands of votes at stake in these controversies. Once more, the word went out from Republican headquarters in Tallahassee: The case simply must not be lost. (Of course, at the same time, Gore was taking a predictably half-baked position on the absentee-ballot-application issue in Seminole and Martin. The vice president avoided formal involvement in the lawsuits, but his campaign gave plenty of unofficial assistance to the Democratic fund-raisers who were running the case.) To handle Seminole and Martin, Baker summoned his Baker Botts law partner Daryl Bristow. "I need some white hair on this case," Baker told Bristow. "This is one with no upside. On the facts and the law, we ought to win it, but I don't know if we will. If we lose it, it may be the presidency."

Throughout the litigation and politics of the Florida recount, Baker had stuck with a pattern: unlimited resources, unparalleled talent, tightly coordinated legal and media messages, and advocacy in streets as well as in courtrooms. But in *Harry N. Jacobs v. the Seminole County Canvassing Board,* the machine kicked into high gear, and the result was something new—and ugly.

. . .

By 2000, forty-eight-year-old Nikki Ann Clark had lived the law-school version of the American dream. As a young African-American girl Clark, the sixth of seven children, had watched her hometown, Detroit, burn in the riots of the 1960s. She went to college near home, but started a new life when she enrolled in the law school at Florida State. After graduating in 1977, she made a dogged march through the state legal establishment, with brief tenures as a prosecutor and a legal-services defense lawyer, and then spent a decade as an assistant attorney general. In 1993, Governor Lawton Chiles made her the first black woman on the Leon County Circuit Court, where she quietly built an enviable reputation. (In her colleague Terry Lewis's novel, a character based on Clark was a heroine.)

On the same day that the contest began before Judge Sauls, the Seminole case was assigned to Judge Clark, and Baker's high command panicked. When Jesse Jackson, who was in town for one of his periodic visits, sat in on part of the first court session in the case, that panic turned to terror. Anyone who knew anything about Nikki Clark recognized that the Republicans were overreacting. To be sure, she was a Democrat, but through years of toil on the bench and as a lawyer, she had proved herself no radical. (In fact, her sister Kristin Clark Taylor had been director of media relations in the first Bush White House.) Barry Richard, the lead Tallahassee-based lawyer for the Bush campaign, assured both Ben Ginsberg and Baker that they had nothing to fear from Clark.

But Bristow, who was running the case, had his instructions from Baker, and he wasn't going to take a risk on Nikki Clark. On November 29, the Bush forces asked the judge to disqualify herself from the case. As the pretext, they cited Governor Jeb Bush's recent decision not to appoint Judge Clark to a seat on the district court of appeals. According to the Bush lawyers' brief, the governor's rejection of Clark created a fear that "the Republican Party will not receive a fair trial in this Court on account of the perceived bias of Your Honor." This was plainly absurd. Trial judges apply for appellate court positions all the time, and they continue ruling on cases that affect the governor, as this one did. In their brief, the Republicans did not cite one case where a judge had recused himself or herself in such circumstances.

As some Bush lawyers later more or less admitted, they moved to recuse Nikki Clark because she was black—period. "I had a very clear view that Judge Clark would have her own pressures coming from her own constituencies that would be partisan in nature," Bristow said. "There was too much at stake to ignore the issue." Clark had said nothing to prompt this suspicion; the Bush campaign simply believed that no black judge could preside over a case that might decide the presidency. This overt racism was too much for Barry Richard, who refused to sign his name to the recusal motion. So Bristow hired a Tallahassee firm especially for this motion, and Al Cardenas, the chairman of the state Republican Party, filed an affidavit in support. Just minutes after the Bush team submitted the motion, Judge Clark rejected it.

Most lawyers are loath to file recusal motions. After all, such requests suggest that a judge lacks the integrity to evaluate her own suitability to preside fairly. If a recusal motion fails, it may poison a lawyer's relationship with a judge from the beginning of a case. Ironically, at just this time, the Gore campaign had a strong case for recusal against Judge Sauls. John Newton, Mitchell Berger's law partner, had helped lead several earlier efforts to force Sauls from the bench; relations between the judge and lawyer were dismal. But the Gore lawyers, as ever, declined to force a confrontation; instead, they proceeded into the judicial abyss that fate had sent them. Not so the Bush team. When Judge Clark declined to withdraw, Bush appealed to the district court of appeals. Clark's participation, the lawyers wrote, "creates at least the strong appearance and possibility of unfairness, if not actual bias. Therefore, to avoid the appearance of impropriety, to preserve the integrity of the judicial process . . . Judge Clark must be recused from this case."

The following day, the court of appeals issued a one-word answer to the Republicans' appeal: DENIED. As a strictly legal matter, then, the motion to recuse Judge Clark had no effect, because she remained the trial judge in the Seminole County case. In a broader sense, though, this legal skirmish left a stain on the case. The Bush operatives smeared a distinguished judge and, in doing so, demonstrated the kind of crude attitude about race that has, fortunately, largely disappeared from public discourse in America. Most of all, though, James Baker's team proved once more how far it would go to make sure its candidate was elected.

The Republicans prepared with their usual thoroughness for the contest litigation before Judge Sauls. The Bush campaign stashed a team of visiting all-stars—including law partners Fred Bartlit and Phil Beck, from Chicago, and Irv Terrell, also from Baker Botts— in the office of a law firm that had not previously been involved in the recount, so the attorneys worked undisturbed by the press. They had almost a week, working around the clock, to prepare their case. There was one person handling Palm Beach issues, another for Miami-Dade, one more to prepare and cross-examine experts, along with as many young attorneys and paralegals as necessary to draft the briefs, prepare the depositions, and make the charts that were indispensable to the litigation.

As usual, the Democrats prepared in more ragtag fashion, though at least not in the confines of Mitchell Berger's overcrowded Tallahassee office. Dexter Douglass owned a vacant storefront a few blocks away, and he rented it to the Gore recount operation as a contest war room. Unlike the Republicans' site, there was nothing secret about the Douglass office. Boies moved his continuous floating press conference to the sidewalk out in front, so the cameras always knew where to find him.

Several days behind the Republicans, the Democrats beefed up their trial team. They brought Kendall Coffey back from Miami, as well as another trial lawyer and activist named Stephen Zack. At Dexter Douglass's suggestion, Gore hired a Tallahassee attorney with the mellifluous name E. C. Deeno Kitchen. Kitchen had worked with Sauls many years earlier, but more important, he was a well-established local and would help insulate the Gore team from the taint of the interloper. On a separate agenda, Klain and company recruited Jeffrey Robinson, a successful Washington lawyer, to the contest team. The presence of Robinson, an African-American, underscored the extraordinary whiteness and maleness of the sprawling legal fight over the recount in Florida. Dozens of lawyers appeared for each side, and Robinson was the first—and only—black face. The Democrats had only two women on their legal team. Lisa Brown, who was on leave from Gore's White House staff, helped write briefs, and an Atlanta lawyer named Teresa Roseborough handled their case in the Eleventh Circuit. The Republicans had none—no women of any prominence and no blacks at all.

Thinking on the fly, as was his custom, Boies came up with a simple premise for his work on the contest. It was a return to the theme that had served Gore best in the early days of the recount. Boies wanted Sauls to count all the votes. Of course, in light of Sauls's reputation and the disastrous first day in court, Boies had little hope of persuading Sauls to do that. But Boies believed that focusing on the ballots would serve him well in his real priority— teeing up the case for the Florida Supreme Court. When Boies told his colleagues that he wanted to "lose quickly" in front of Sauls, he meant that he wanted to get the case to the Florida Supreme Court before it was too late.

So, on Tuesday, November 28, Boies sought an emergency hearing in front of Sauls and the vast squadron of lawyers once again filed into the small courtroom. "Here, the witnesses are primarily the ballots," Boies told Sauls. "The issue is whether particular ballots do or do not express a voter's intent." Boies cut through the fog of details and asked the judge to do only one thing: bring the almost 14,000 disputed ballots to Tallahassee and start counting them. This was a legal argument, of course, but Boies also recognized that the ballots from Palm Beach and Miami-Dade had an almost totemic significance—that it would be difficult for any court, when faced with the actual ballots, to decide not to examine them.

Not surprisingly, Boies's idea struck fear into the Bush forces. Barry Richard wisely decided to try to shift the focus away from the ballots—to the county canvassing boards. "Counsel is trying to put the cart before the horse," Richard told Sauls. "I would suggest to Your Honor that the first thing we need to do is schedule a hearing for Your Honor to determine whether or not the canvassing boards . . . abused their discretion in some fashion. If they didn't, there is nothing more to do." Unless the Democrats could prove that the boards had erred in some way, Richard asserted, there was no reason to examine the ballots. Then came his pitch for delay: "I would urge Your Honor that that hearing ought not to begin Friday [December 1], which is not sufficient time. We need to get witnesses here, we need to get documents here . . . and that needs to start next week"—that is, December 4 or later. Richard was calling on Sauls's innate conservatism, and on his respect for other judges. As the Bush lawyer posed the issue, it wasn't whether to examine the ballots—it was whether to second-guess the judges who served on the canvassing boards.

In the end, Judge Sauls split the difference. He ordered the disputed ballots brought to Tallahassee, but he wouldn't commit to when, or whether, he would examine them. On Wednesday, to keep the pressure on, Boies appealed this decision. He knew that mid-trial appeals such as this almost never succeed, but he thought that the very act of appealing might light a fire under Sauls and remind the Florida Supreme Court justices how hard Gore was fighting to get the votes counted. (The Democrats retained the right to appeal any final judgment by Sauls at a later time.) Also on that Wednesday, the Bush lawyers laid a clever trump card on top of the Gore request to have the disputed South Florida ballots shipped to Tallahassee. If Gore wanted the nearly 14,000 undervotes moved to Tallahassee, the Republicans asked Sauls to order *all* of the 1.16 million votes from Palm Beach and

Miami-Dade sent with them. The Bush team figured Judge Sauls would find the magnitude of such a delivery so overwhelming that he wouldn't be tempted to examine the ballots.

In all, then, the contest was shaping up just as Dexter Douglass thought it would when he heard Sauls's name called out from the wheel. After the better part of a week, the case was on a slow boat to nowhere, with a trial of some sort scheduled for the weekend of December 2 and 3, but with no one clear on what exactly would happen during those two days. Boies had reached the end of November without figuring out how to lose quickly. His only success had been to persuade Judge Sauls to order the ballots brought north to Tallahassee—and thus create one of the more memorable tableaux of the recount period. On Thursday, November 30, the ballots were hauled by Ryder truck to the capital city, and their progress was marked by breathless live coverage from news choppers. O. J. Simpson, who had moved to Florida six months before the election, pronounced this visual echo of his own strange journey in a Ford Bronco "boring."

In Austin, meanwhile, the Bush operation sought to build an aura of inevitability. After several days of silence, Governor Bush met on Thursday at his ranch with retired general Colin L. Powell, his all-but-official choice for secretary of state. "I've won three counts, and I think it's time to get some finality to the process," Bush told reporters. The Republicans stayed on message: The election was over, and Bush had won.

Then, on Friday, December 1, the twenty-fourth day since the election, there was at last a stillness in Tallahassee, indeed in all of Florida. The justices of the United States Supreme Court were stepping from behind their ruby curtains and, for the first time in American history, hearing a case to determine the presidency of the United States.

Bill Daley had never seen an argument in the Supreme Court. The clerk's office had allowed Daley, along with Warren Christopher, to avoid the long lines where even the invited guests were waiting, and they were ushered into a silent and empty chamber on that Friday morning. Christopher, who had just returned from Los Angeles for the first time since before Thanksgiving, had served as a law clerk to Justice William O. Douglas in 1949 and argued his first case before the court in 1957. The two men paused to savor the moment, and then noticed they were not alone. George F. Will, the conservative columnist, was sitting on a spectator bench. Justice Clarence Thomas had invited Will to the argument, and he had arrived early to secure his seat. It was, in all, an unusual day.

As the chamber quickly filled to bursting, there was a strange feeling of good spirits in the air. For one thing, everyone was just so happy to get a ticket. People had started lining up for the handful of public seats more than a day earlier. Nearly a dozen senators sat lined up in the front row. Al Gore's children sat near the back with Goody Marshall—the son of the late Justice Thurgood Marshall—who had worked for their father. Judge Charles Burton, extending his brief moment of fame in Palm Beach, had claimed a seat, as did Barbara Olson, the fierce Clinton critic who had come to watch her husband represent George W. Bush. In the chair closest to the bench was the stooped figure of Byron White, who had retired from the court in 1993. The former football star was wizened and unwell, but he, like everyone else who had the chance, didn't want to miss this (apparently) once-in-a-lifetime event.

The election controversy had, by this point, sullied every American institution it had touched—including the press, the voting public, and the machinery of democracy. In the hour or so before the argument began, the great chamber was filled with the hopeful sense that the Supreme Court might set matters right. Senators Orrin Hatch and Patrick Leahy, respectively, chairman of and ranking Democrat on the Judiciary Committee, arrived together, as a kind of bipartisan show of faith in the justices. Even the chief justice gave a hint that the Court wanted to show off a little. For those unable to attend, Rehnquist had decided to allow, for the first time in the Court's history, an audiotape of the proceeding to be released immediately after arguments were completed.

After the justices appeared from behind the curtains, the chief justice intoned, in his usual phlegmatic cadences, "We'll hear argument in number 00-836, *George W. Bush v. the Palm Beach County Canvassing Board.* Mr. Olson?"

As is customary in arguments before the Court, Olson had scarcely said more than a sentence before he was interrupted with questions. They came, at first, from Sandra Day O'Connor and Anthony Kennedy, and the gist was the same: What are we doing here? Isn't this a state matter? As O'Connor put it, "If it were purely a matter of state law, I suppose we normally would leave it alone, where the state supreme court found it, and so you probably have to persuade us there's some issue of federal law here, otherwise why are we acting?" In the week since the Court had granted certiorari, a measure of buyer's remorse had set in with several justices. The contest wasn't even over. Florida looked like it was on the way to settling the election on its own. Why, they wondered, had they taken the case at all?

But when Tribe stood up, it turned out things were not so simple. The chief justice saw a federal interest in the case, and he plainly had little use for the Florida Supreme Court. Neither did Justice Antonin Scalia. (In the experience of veteran Supreme Court watchers, the stated views of the chief and Justice Scalia invariably meant that Justice Clarence Thomas was in accord, even though he, as was his custom, did not say anything during oral argument.) Given the stakes, the justices seemed to go out of their way to show how narrow the issues before them were. The world may have seen this case as *Bush v. Gore,* but the justices were trying to send the message that they were weighing a less politically charged choice. For the most part, this was a Court of technicians, not philosophers, so their comments hewed to esoteric details. Did the Florida Supreme Court interpret state election law on the basis of the state constitution (which would be impermissible) or in light of laws passed by the state legislatures (which would be appropriate)? Should the U.S. Supreme Court or the Congress interpret the "safe-harbor" provision of federal election law?

By the end of the allotted ninety minutes, the mood of chipper expectation had evaporated into one of baffled resignation. In the great milestone cases across its history, the Supreme Court had always sought to speak with one voice. In *Brown v. Board of Education* and the first round of modern desegregation decisions, just as in the momentous *United States v. Nixon*, the Court had burnished its authority by uniting around a single opinion. But what view could command a majority, much less unanimity, of this obviously fractured Court? None was apparent, and even if the Court could find a view to rally around, it was likely to be so complicated that most of the country probably wouldn't understand it, much less coalesce behind it. The tense, arcane, unresolved battle among the justices meant that it looked, once again, as if Florida was probably going to have to settle this election for itself.

Soon enough, the state would have its chance to try. The trial in the contest was to begin less than twenty-four hours later, on Saturday morning, December 2, before Judge Sauls in Tallahassee.

Mitchell Berger had a clear opinion about how many witnesses the Gore side should call during the contest—none. As Boies had prepared the case, the issue was simple. How many votes were in dispute? Was that number of votes enough to swing the election to Gore? They could prove the answer to both questions without calling any witnesses. If they were at all serious about losing quickly, a no-witness presentation was the quickest route to the Florida Supreme Court.

Boies was generally sympathetic to this idea. He didn't want to delay their trip to the Florida Supreme Court, but he did think they had to establish a couple of things in the record. First, they had to prove that the punch-card system was flawed—that in a significant number of instances, voters marked their ballots in such a way that the machines couldn't read them. Second, they had to prove that manual recounts worked—that hand counts of ballots were more accurate than machine counts. Boies chose two witnesses to make his two points, and afterward, the only question was which one was the bigger disaster.

The lawyers had prepared for a marathon on Saturday, December 2, and Judge Sauls didn't disappoint them. He opened the proceedings with uncharacteristic promptness at 9:03 A.M. and declared that they were going to sit as long as it took to get through the plaintiff's case. Once again, though, matters got off to a languorous start as Sauls allowed opening statements not only from Boies, Barry Richard, and Joe Klock but also a host of eccentric intervenors and publicity seekers who had attached themselves to the case. It was mid-morning before the Gore side turned to the evidence.

Deeno Kitchen made the first presentation, which involved no witnesses. He sought to introduce into evidence transcripts of virtually all the proceedings before the county canvassing boards, and, most important, he put the disputed ballots before the court. Kitchen's presentation looked like just a boring recitation of documents, but it was actually a critical part of the case. The ballots were now introduced as evidence in the contest. The challenge for Boies and his team was to persuade Judge Sauls—or his superiors at the Florida Supreme Court—to look at them.

With that, the Democrats turned to their first witness, Kimball Brace, who ran a company called Election Data Services, based in the Virginia suburbs of Washington. In the small world of election experts, Brace was known for testifying for Democrats in redistricting cases. The way Boies planned it, Brace had a limited purpose as a witness: to show that punch-card systems were flawed. But as often happens in high-profile trials, both the witness and the lawyer, Steve Zack, appeared determined to milk their moment in the spotlight. Squat and bearded, with an outgoing disposition, Brace gave long, rambling answers about all sorts of subjects, including the design and maintenance of voting machines, voter errors, dimpled ballots, and "chad buildup." Brace's direct testimony stretched past lunchtime during the supposedly stream-lined presentation, and it would be mid-afternoon before Phil Beck began his cross-examination.

Brace had some interesting theories about how voters created dimpled ballots rather than punching all the way through the chads. He testified that the rubber strips in the voting machines "may become old, brittle, hard . . . and you're not able to push through the chad." And in the most fanciful part of his presenta-tion, Brace said that dimpled ballots were more likely to occur on the left side of the ballot—where the Bush-Gore race was located—than anywhere else. "Because the left side gets more use, you have the better chance of the left side filling up with chad, or having larger deposits of chad, because that is the more frequently used area of the machine," he said.

When Beck finally began his cross-examination, he made a con-vincing case that the witness didn't know what he was talking about. Brace was a political scientist who had never studied rubber in voting machines or anywhere else; he had no idea whether rub-ber got harder or softer with repeated use. And as for the theory that, as Beck put it, "as all these little chads fall down, and they kind of stack up on one another, and then they stop somebody from pushing the stylus through the hole," this too was pure speculation. Brace had no idea how many people used these ma-chines or whether the machines were jostled enough to move the "big mountain of chad." Brace started with a simple point—that punch-card machines sometimes miss votes—but he built this small, useful insight into a vast structure of theories that Beck suc-cessfully toppled. And all of this took several hours.

Beck was anxious to get to the next witness. Nicolas Hengartner, an associate professor of statistics at Yale, had first surfaced as a Democratic expert on voting patterns in one of the many judicial hearings during the Palm Beach recount. He, too, had a simple point to make: that the rate of undervotes in punch-card ballots was far higher than that in optical-scan ballots. As part of the Palm Beach case, Hengartner had filed a sworn affidavit with the court outlining his conclusions. With the relative leisure of a few days to study Hengartner's paper trail, Beck found a rich vein to exploit during cross-examination. Indeed, Beck was confident enough that he told his younger colleagues, who were going to take Hengartner's deposition before his testimony, to ask no probing questions. Beck didn't want to tip his hand.

Hengartner, a Quebecois Canadian, had an ingratiating manner to go along with modest English-language skills. In his analysis of the data from South Florida, Hengartner found that the "recovery rate" of undervotes in Palm Beach was far lower than in Broward or Miami-Dade. This suggested that Palm Beach had used too restrictive a standard on its recount and excluded legitimate votes. Analyzing further, Hengartner found that the votes recovered in the recount generally mirrored the overall breakdown of votes in the county. Since Gore won South Florida handily, this meant, in sum, that hundreds of Gore votes had not been counted in Palm Beach.

Beck began by pointing out that Hengartner had not controlled all the possible variables in his conclusions. He was really warming up for the moment when he placed the witness's sworn statement on an overhead projector. In the statement, Hengartner had pointed out that more votes were cast in the 1998 governor's race than in the senatorial race of that year. "A closer inspection of the Palm Beach County ballot reveals that the senatorial race was recorded in the first column, and the gubernatorial race is the second," the statement went on. On this evidence, Hengartner concluded that it was harder to vote in the first column than in the second—the point that Brace had raised earlier in the day. In short, something about these machines made it difficult to vote in column one, where the Bush-Gore race was located in 2000.

"Now, Professor," Beck asked. "You've never inspected the ballot that was used in 1998 in Palm Beach County, closely or otherwise, have you?"

"I have not seen the ballot," Hengartner answered.

With a theatrical flourish, Beck displayed a copy of the actual

1998 ballot. The ballot showed that, contrary to Hengartner's statement, both the senator's and the governor's races were in column one on the ballot.

"You can see here that that sworn affidavit . . . just wasn't true, was it?"

"It contained a mistake," Hengartner replied softly.

"And as you said it, notwithstanding what your affidavit said about a closer inspection of the ballot, you never even looked at the ballot, right?"

"I've looked at the order in which the races were run, sir."

"And when you signed that sworn statement, you were relying on the Gore legal team to give you the straight facts, weren't you?"

"Well, I relied on the facts that I received, yes."

Beck lifted his head to Sauls. "That's all I have, Judge."

As the Gore lawyers would labor to point out, this error did not go to the heart of Hengartner's testimony. Still, it was too late—Beck had made the entire Democratic effort look foolish. This understaffed operation had accomplished a great deal, but their seat-of-the-pants style caught up with them. After only two witnesses, the Gore effort had actually lost ground with both the judge and the public.

As Hengartner absorbed his punishment on the witness stand, Barry Richard whispered to Boies, his friendly rival, "I hate it when this happens." And Boies murmured back, "Do you think anyone would notice if I left now?" When the young statistician left the courtroom, he burst into tears.

At one point, the Bush lawyers had raised the possibility of calling ninety-five witnesses. But Barry Richard and his colleagues decided not to run out the clock so transparently, and limited themselves to a relative handful. As the Saturday session drew to a close, Fred Bartlit put on Charles Burton, the Palm Beach judge who served as chair of the county canvassing board. As the Republican lawyers predicted, Burton's aw-shucks demeanor endeared him to Judge Sauls, who ushered him off the stand with the words "I'll have to salute you as a great American, as a matter of fact."

When the trial spilled over to Sunday, the Bush side unleashed its own expert, who could not have posed a greater contrast to the hapless Professor Hengartner. Laurentius Marais made his living in one of the more odious corners of the American legal industry—as an expert-for-hire. A statistician, Marais had an unremarkable point to make: that one could not necessarily tell that most of the undervotes in Palm Beach would have gone to Gore. A native of South Africa with an icy demeanor, Marais happened to be good at his work too, and Boies could only flail away at him during cross-examination. "For example," Boies asked him, "you testified that certain statistical analyses that linked lead paint with injuries in children didn't meet your standard for statistical scientific analysis, correct?"

Beck vaulted up and accused Boies of trying to tar the witness with his unpopular client. Beck asked Sauls to limit Boies to asking about Marais's methods. "Otherwise, all he's doing is grandstanding."

"Your Honor," Boies said, "I'm not grandstanding."

Boies, who was grandstanding, just hoped to escape at that point. For the first time during his sojourn in Florida, Boies had found a judge who was immune to his charms.

Steve Zack had a chance to do some preparation for Bush witness John Ahmann, a California rancher who had helped design punch-card machines in the 1970s. The Bush lawyers put Ahmann on the stand to say that Brace's chad-buildup theory was absurd (which it was) and that the punch-card machines generally worked pretty well. Zack knew that Ahmann had received several patents relating to voting technology in previous years, and he asked a lawyer from his firm to search Ahmann's applications for cross-examination material. Moments before Ahmann took the stand, Zack's colleague, Jennifer Altman, hit pay dirt back in Miami. She faxed the product of her research to Tallahassee, hoping it would reach Zack in time.

As it happened, someone slapped the folder marked URGENT! in front of Zack just as Ahmann was being sworn in as a witness. Zack found that in the early 1980s, Ahmann had applied for a patent on a new stylus for punch-card machines. He had done so for the precise reason the Gore side had been citing for the previous twenty-six days. As Ahmann had written nearly two decades earlier, punch-card machines can produce "potentially unreadable votes." Stunned that Zack had come up with the old document, the bolo-tied Ahmann was suddenly willing to agree with almost anything Zack had to say. So manual recounts were useful, correct?

"You need either reinspection or a manual recount if you have that situation, yes, you do," said Ahmann.

It was a full-fledged rout of the witness, every bit as bad as what had happened to Hengartner—and on a more significant subject. Zack's Perry Mason moment, as it became known, did not give the Gore lawyers any illusions that they might actually prevail before Sauls, but it did embolden them a little as the Sunday session dragged on and on. Kendall Coffey decided to liven things up with a bomb on his own.

Irv Terrell had put on a New York political activist named Tom Spargo to testify for the Republican side that the shutdown of the Miami-Dade recount had occurred in a peaceful environment.

"Good afternoon, Mr. Spargo. I'm Kendall Coffey," the Miami lawyer began the cross-examination. "Isn't it true," Coffey snarled, "that the last time you were on the witness stand on matters of reliability and integrity in an election scenario, you took the Fifth Amendment nineteen times?"

OBJECTION! Terrell cried. Coffey might not have had the right to raise the decade-old incident involving Spargo—Sauls threatened the lawyer with contempt charges if he brought up the issue again—but unlike so many on the Gore team, Coffey was a street fighter, and he liked the idea of going after Bush's witnesses.

It was after eleven o'clock on Sunday night, fourteen hours after the court day began, when the lawyers finally wrapped up their legal arguments to Sauls. Both sides had staggered through the contest, and the hodgepodge of witnesses did not give a full picture of this bedeviled election in Florida. But some truths did emerge. The Democrats were clearly wrong in asserting that the uncounted votes would fall in a predictable pattern for Gore; no one could say with certainty how the recount would turn out. But the Republicans were equally wrong in disparaging the accuracy of hand recounts; their own witness John Ahmann, as well as common sense, suggested that a manual recount of the Florida vote would certainly produce a more accurate result than the machine-counted status quo. The simple justice at the core of the Gore position—Count all the votes!—deserved to survive the scrutiny of the Honorable N. Sanders Sauls.

The judge said he would have a decision the first thing the next morning, Monday, December 4.

CHAPTER FOURTEEN

"FOURTH DOWN AND LONG"

Aʟ Gᴏʀᴇ turned into the Ancient Mariner of the Florida recount, the man who couldn't stop talking about his plight. There was an almost compulsive quality to his lobbying of the press. He called network anchormen, substitute network anchormen, and weekend network anchormen, not to mention cable personalities, newspaper columnists, and the editorial board of his beloved *New York Times*. Yet, as so often was the case, he never proved a very successful messenger. From Election Day forward, Gore had believed the Washington conventional wisdom that the public would quickly run out of patience with the recount. This turned out to be largely false. Throughout his effort to count the votes, Gore maintained remarkable popularity despite the many crises of the period—even through the "military"-absentee-voting controversy and the certification of the election by Katherine Harris. True, the numbers of people supporting Gore's efforts dropped in early December, falling to around 40 percent in most polls. But notwithstanding the predictions, there was never a hemorrhage of support. The recount cause inspired loyalty, even if Gore himself did not.

The vice president's neediness seemed to inspire a degree of contempt from those who interviewed him. On CBS's *60 Minutes*, on Sunday, December 3, Lesley Stahl practically baited Gore. "You're not really reaching the public with this argument," she informed him. "You've been making it over and over: 'Every vote has to be counted.' There is more of a sense that you're asking, you know, to change the rules of the game. Can you go on if you lose the public?" Gore responded in his by now familiar singsong style: "The public, I think, has shown a remarkable amount of patience and a determination to see that all the votes are counted. Of course, it is split . . ."

"But it's slipping. It's slipping," Stahl said.

"Well, you know, I—this isn't easy for—for any of us in this country," he replied. "And I know that the Bush family, same as my family, is wanting this to be over, and I—and I know the American family wants it to be over. But as strongly as people feel about that, they feel even more strongly that every legally cast vote should be counted." The "count all the votes" theme had less visceral impact than "we wuz robbed," but the cautious vice president would never allow the latter sentiment to pass his lips.

If Gore's mission looked like a lonely crusade, that's because it was. The vice president's political operation in Washington belatedly brought together surrogates to speak for him in Florida, but it was a halfhearted endeavor on both ends. Gore didn't have the kind of relationships with elected officials in which he felt comfortable asking them to go to Florida, and in turn, few Democratic politicians felt like putting themselves out for Gore. The Bush team, by contrast, ran its surrogates' program out of Tallahassee and came up with more than a dozen names to fill a white marker board every day. "*CBS Morning News*—Gov. Racicot," "*CNN Midday*—Gov. Whitman," and so on. The surrogates' operation also displayed the trademark Bush-team cockiness. Once the contest ended, Republican media adviser Dorrance Smith grew so confident about Gore hurting his own cause that he took to telling bookers, "We'd really like you to put Gore out again."

Donna Brazile, Gore's nominal campaign manager, who had

been edged into irrelevance during the recount, grew so frustrated that she started a freelance surrogate program on her own. In this way, she pushed a few urban liberals and members of the Congressional Black Caucus to visit Florida. As far as crowds were concerned, Gore remained steadfast in his objections to them—with one exception. He finally grew so irritated by the Republican chants outside his home at the Naval Observatory that he asked Brazile to arrange for some counterdemonstrators to drown them out. "These people don't want to go to your house," Brazile told him. "They want to go to Florida!"

By early December, even Joe Lieberman was leaving Gore to his own devices. Lieberman's private hawkishness in the early days of the recount—his advice to Gore to consider filing lawsuits, for example—had made its way into press reports. But like the vice president, Lieberman always had a keen nose for the conventional wisdom in Washington, and the senator didn't want to become known for being too aggressive. So Lieberman made a special effort to appear conciliatory in public, most notably when he undercut the Florida operation regarding the overseas absentee ballots on *Meet the Press*. Of course, when the Republicans were blistering Gore as a sore loser and putative thief, the last thing the Democrats needed was another voice of circumspection and moderation, but that was all that Lieberman was willing to be. Then, when the polls began their slight turn for the worse, Lieberman started to refuse to appear on morning shows, or on any program where he might be challenged. "I'm overexposed," the senator told the vice president's spokesman Mark Fabiani.

The Gore team had set up a separate office for the recount operation on Capitol Hill, not far from Democratic National Committee headquarters, but the high command of the campaign generally found reasons to be elsewhere. Eskew, Shrum, and Devine remained in their consulting offices in Georgetown, while Daley went back and forth between his home and the Naval Observatory. Fabiani came in now and then, as did Brazile and research director David Ginsberg, but for the most part people stayed in touch by cell phone, daily conference calls, or BlackBerry messages. Staffed mostly by volunteers, the recount office had the intensity of an accounting firm in late April. By the first Monday in December, the Democrats' recount operation really only existed in two places—the brain of Al Gore and the hearts of a dozen or so overworked lawyers in Tallahassee.

At 11:30 A.M. on Monday, December 4, the United States Supreme Court rendered its decision. It was as close to an absolute tie as the justices could craft.

The unanimous decision, which was signed not by a single justice but rather per curiam, a designation the Court usually uses for minor decisions, represented an artful compromise. In keeping with the chief's control over the process, it was Rehnquist's chambers that produced the brief opinion for the Court. The justices observed that "there was considerable uncertainty as to the precise grounds" for the Florida Supreme Court's decision. Because of the uncertainty, the Supreme Court asked the Florida court to clarify its ruling of November 21. "As a general rule, this court defers to a state court's interpretation of a state statute," the justices wrote, but went on to note that both the U.S. Constitution and federal law also governed the conduct of presidential elections. In light of this, they sent the case back to the Florida Supreme Court to allow those justices to explain whether they had considered the relevant portions of the federal Constitution and law.

The peculiar decision gave something to both sides. For Gore, the questions posed to the Florida court clearly allowed the seven justices to answer them in a way that would satisfy the United States Supreme Court. In other words, there was no realistic chance that the original Florida Supreme Court decision—Gore's victory on November 21—was going to be overturned. But the opinion of the United States Supreme Court may have offered the Bush forces something more important. It was a shot across the bow of the Florida Supreme Court—a warning that it was

treading on dangerous ground. All nine justices, not only the conservatives, were worried that the Florida court was stretching to
help Gore win the election, and they wanted their junior colleagues to know it. This message was especially important, because it came when the election was within hours of returning to
the Florida Supreme Court.

Notwithstanding Judge Sauls's promise to render his decision in
the morning, he took to the bench at four-thirty that afternoon to
deliver it, five hours after the Supreme Court had ruled. Sauls
could have simply issued a written opinion, but he summoned
all the lawyers (and the accompanying television cameras) so he
could deliver his verdict in person to a waiting nation.

In an opinion that took eighteen minutes to read, Sauls ruled for
Bush across the board. In the tradition of Katherine Harris, the
judge had not even thrown a bone to the Democrats—not even the
51 votes in Nassau County. The Republican team of Barry Richard
and the out-of-town all-stars had made a perfect pitch to Judge
Sauls's sensibility. (Joe Klock, representing the nominally independent Harris, had also made a persuasive presentation, and Sauls's
opinion drew heavily on Klock's submissions.) It was at best a
thinly reasoned effort by the judge. Sauls admitted that "the record
shows voter error, and/or less than total accuracy" in the Florida
voting machines, but he asserted that there was no "reasonable
probability that the statewide election result would be different" if
the votes were counted correctly. The "great Americans" like
Charles Burton who had counted the votes had done their best, or
at least had not "abused their discretion." The gist of Sauls's opinion was that the result may not have been accurate and the procedures may not have been fair, but the result certified by Harris
was . . . close enough.

Sauls had done the Democrats one favor: He had made up his
mind. If the judge had really wanted to destroy any hope for the
vice president, he could simply have run out the clock until De-

cember 12 (or December 18) without issuing an opinion. Sauls had not moved as fast as the Gore forces would have liked and he certainly didn't count any votes, but at least he gave Boies time for a final shot. Sauls was still talking in his courtroom when the Gore team delivered its notice of appeal to the Florida Supreme Court.

After Judge Sauls's decision, the recount turned into a full-fledged deathwatch for Al Gore. The Democrats were down to their last two chances, and neither one looked very promising. On Tuesday and Wednesday, the trials in the Seminole and Martin absentee-ballot cases would proceed in Tallahassee. Judge Nikki Clark had held on to the Seminole case, notwithstanding Republican protests, and Terry Lewis, the novel-writing judge who had earlier upheld Katherine Harris's authority to certify the election, was presiding over the Martin challenges. The two judges held staggered court sessions so that Barry Richard could represent Bush in both cases. The evidence in both trials produced few surprises. Republican officials had been allowed to add voter-identification numbers to absentee-ballot applications; Democrats had not been granted that privilege, but they hadn't asked for it, either. There was no clear evidence of the kind of invidious discrimination that might prompt a judge to take the extreme step of throwing out thousands of ballots. The cases were long shots for Gore.

That left only the appeal of the contest to the Florida Supreme Court. In Washington, only Gore himself seemed to think he had much of a chance. Back in Tallahassee, Klain was ever hopeful, and he called Larry Tribe at Harvard to tell him to expect to defend another favorable ruling from the Florida court in the United States Supreme Court. But after Gore and Klain, Democratic optimists were in short supply.

Through this first week in December, no prominent Democrat called on Gore to withdraw, but the general exhaustion with the recount had become palpable. Even Lieberman performed in public as if the game were almost over. When he spoke to a group of congressional Democrats on Tuesday, December 5, he said that he was "proud of the race we ran"—a sort of proto-concession. Washington is essentially a conservative city that favors stability, finality, and orderliness—in this case, an end to this extraordinary election. Gore clung to values that held less currency in the cynical capital city. Washington had heard more than enough talk about fairness and democracy. It was time to wrap things up.

The Florida justices set the argument for Thursday morning, December 7, and both sides kicked in with the last vestiges of their legal and political strategies. For the Republicans, the watchword was inevitability, the sense that these final machinations amounted to little more than a last gasp for Gore. James Baker didn't even show up for this second argument—not worth his time, apparently. The Democrats didn't bother to pretend that they had any chances but this one. Bill Daley bestirred himself to return to Tallahassee for the first time since before Thanksgiving. (He arrived by private plane just before the argument and departed immediately afterward.) In the hallway of the marble courthouse, just minutes before the argument was to begin, Boies was on his cell phone with Al Gore, who was offering some final words of advice and encouragement.

When the argument began, Charles Wells, the grandfatherly chief justice, barely let Boies say a word before he jumped in with the first question. More than any of his colleagues, Wells had felt the sting of the United States Supreme Court's rebuke earlier in the week, and he wanted to make sure it wouldn't happen again. He asked Boies about a case the justices in Washington had raised, *McPherson v. Blacker.* "I want to know from each counsel its importance here," Wells said.

Boies had to summon all of his sangfroid at this moment, for the simple reason that he hadn't read the case. He adroitly steered the question toward a point he wanted to make: that Article II of the Constitution did not prevent state courts from interpreting laws about presidential elections. As Boies put it, "I don't think that the Constitution of the United States in any way means that the legislature has to sit both as a legislative body and a judicial body just because an election of presidential electors is involved." Boies was artfully showing that the Republicans had based their legal position on leaden interpretations of federal law and the Constitution. Of course, it wasn't a violation of Article II or federal election statutes for a state court to do what state courts always do—interpret state law, even about a presidential election.

As the argument proceeded, it became clear that the justices—some of them, anyway—still felt that some real votes of Floridians had not been counted. Indeed, Justice Fred Lewis, a populist former trial lawyer originally from West Virginia, said, "If we have undervotes in one location and those are considered, then you've demonstrated that there's legal votes that have not been counted. Why would that not exist in other counties? And why would this not require . . . judicial relief that be applied in a statewide undervote?" Justice Barbara Pariente echoed the point: "Why wouldn't it be proper for any court, if they are going to order any relief, to count the undervotes in all of the counties . . . ?" A full statewide recount? Boies thought that would do nicely.

But for the first time in this courtroom, the Gore side faced some clear hostility as well, from both the chief justice and Justice Major Harding. Like Judge Sauls, Chief Justice Wells worried that all losing political candidates could make Gore's argument and get recounts. "Someone would say they lost by 130,000 votes in Dade County, and we'd have to have the court count those votes," said the chief justice.

Not so, said Boies. We have pinpointed 215 votes in Palm Beach and 168 in Miami-Dade, he went on, "so these are ballots where we know that if you look at the undervotes, you find ballots that can clearly have a discernible intent of the voter found from them. And yet they are not counted."

Barry Richard, the local Democrat who had proved his loyalty to the Bush cause through so many court hearings over the previous month, had earned the right to take over from Michael Carvin, the

Washingtonian who had received such rough treatment in the team's first outing here. Richard fenced as elegantly as Boies had. The Florida Supreme Court's two most liberal members, Harry Anstead and Barbara Pariente, fired away at Richard. Why didn't Sauls examine the ballots? Might such a review "place in doubt" the results of the election, which is what the contest statute required? No, said Richard; the Gore team had failed to prove that the canvassing boards had abused their discretion, so there was no need to examine any ballots. Pariente was particularly dogged, pressing Richard to explain why undervotes should be examined in one county but not in another. Richard said that each county should have the right to choose for itself, but his answers left Pariente plainly unimpressed. (In Bush headquarters, the lawyers dubbed Justice Pariente the Ambassador, because they believed she was angling for a job in a Gore administration. There was no evidence of this, but it demonstrated the Republicans' fear of her.)

As the questioning closed, this case was far more difficult to call than the first Florida Supreme Court decision. Two votes, Wells and Harding, appeared safe for Bush; two others, Anstead and Pariente, looked clear for Gore, and Lewis and Quince seemed to be leaning his way as well. The views of Leander Shaw, Jr., the court's senior member and the first African-American to serve as chief justice, were difficult to discern.

The most striking aspect of the argument was that the stakes appeared to have grown even as the attorneys were speaking. Boies had asked for recounts to proceed in only two counties, Palm Beach and Miami-Dade, but three justices raised the possibility of a recount of all the undervotes in the state, even at this late date. With a margin that remained at just 537 votes, any sort of statewide approach would throw the election into a new realm of uncertainty. Notwithstanding these clear hints from the court, the lawyers on both sides tended to discount this possibility. On this Thursday night, December 7, the one-month anniversary of Election Day, it was as if their minds could not even process the possibility of an upheaval of this magnitude.

. . .

When Ron Klain opened the door to his room at the Governor's Inn on Friday morning, December 8, he saw the all-too-apt headline on the *Tallahassee Democrat*: FOURTH DOWN AND LONG FOR GORE. Klain couldn't quarrel. All flights out of Tallahassee the next morning were booked. Today, it seemed, the election would finally come to a close.

Judges Lewis and Clark had announced that they would issue the rulings in the Seminole and Martin cases at the same time, probably in the early afternoon. The Florida Supreme Court made no formal announcement of when its ruling would appear, but everyone expected that it would also come on Friday. Making his way over to the contest-litigation office, Klain found a last-day-of-school atmosphere. Lawyers were trading T-shirts and hand-signed copies of the briefs. Steve Zack had ordered lunch flown up from Joe's Stone Crab, in Miami's South Beach, for a celebration of all their hard work. Klain didn't object to good food, but he hated the valedictory air to the occasion. "This is absurd. Stop doing this," he told his colleagues. "It's not over." Thinking ahead to an expected victory, Klain put in a call to the Washington recount headquarters. He wanted to tell them to get ready to send reinforcements to Florida for the new vote count he expected the Florida Supreme Court to order.

Monica Dixon, his former colleague from the Nashville "kitchen," returned the call with a question. She wanted a list of all the lawyers who had worked on the recount in Florida so that Gore could thank them when it was over.

"Fuck, no!" Klain said. "You people should be ready for us to fucking win, not to lose!" (He was even starting to talk like Whouley.) Klain didn't blame Dixon, who was just doing as she had been asked and generally agreed with Klain's disdain for the defeatist attitude of the Gore operation in Washington. Given the choice between planning for a victory or preparing for a defeat, Daley's troops chose the latter every time.

Still, the pessimism seemed understandable. At 2:23 P.M., Judges Lewis and Clark threw out the challenges to the Seminole and Martin absentee ballots. Nikki Clark noted the "faulty" judgment of the election officials in Seminole, but still found that the election represented a "full and fair expression of the will of the voters." (By making this manifestly correct ruling, Clark provided an elegant rebuke to the Bush lawyers who had tried to disqualify her.) Terry Lewis ruled likewise for Martin County. By midafternoon, Al Gore's fraying hopes for the presidency rested entirely with the seven justices of the Florida Supreme Court.

On the day of the argument in the contest case, Chief Justice Charles Wells made his customary 7 A.M. arrival at the supreme court with his mind on two men, neither of whom was named Bush or Gore. Edward Castro was scheduled to die by lethal injection that evening at the Florida state prison in Starke. A drifter from California who in 1987 had confessed to three murders, Castro had dropped all his appeals, but he could still change his mind and ask for a last-minute stay. Robert Glock was scheduled to be executed the next day, Friday, December 8. He had been convicted of kidnapping and murdering a young schoolteacher in 1983, but his attorneys were still fighting to save him.

The month after the election had stretched the Florida Supreme Court nearly to the breaking point. Three of the justices—Lewis, Quince, and Pariente—had been on the ballot themselves on November 7. The governor appoints supreme court justices in Florida, but continued service on the bench requires an up-or-down verdict from the voters every six years. None of the three faced a serious challenge in 2000, but the state election was on their minds. The justices had also heard a full slate of cases during the first week in November, just before they started issuing stays and orders regarding Katherine Harris's attempts to certify the election. They also rejected a challenge to the butterfly ballot, ruling unanimously on December 1 that there could be no new voting or reallocation of votes in Palm Beach County. They heard arguments in their regularly scheduled cases during the first week in December. Then there was the contest appeal. And Castro and Glock.

As the justices met in conference on Thursday afternoon after hearing the arguments from Boies, Richard, and Klock, there was still another matter—the biggest of all—hovering over their deliberations. On Monday, the United States Supreme Court had asked the Florida justices to clarify their ruling from November 21. Now they had to decide the contest appeal. The question before them was which one to decide first.

Prudence would have dictated a simple response. When the United States Supreme Court asks a question, it deserves an answer—pronto. The Florida justices had actually started drafting an answer. Chief Justice Wells said he planned to dissent, but he had not yet started writing that dissenting opinion, leaving the majority opinion floating in a kind of netherworld. And now suddenly there was the contest ruling to address, with time clearly running out for any more votes to be counted. Inertia took hold. The justices never really made a conscious decision to ignore the remand order from the United States Supreme Court; instead, they shifted their attention to what seemed like the more immediate task, the contest appeal.

In that case, the votes fell into place fairly quickly. Anstead, Pariente, Lewis, and Quince all wanted to reverse Judge Sauls. Wells, Shaw, and Harding wanted to affirm. Chief Justice Wells was especially heartsick to be in the minority. He showed his colleagues in the majority the holiday decorations in the journalists' tent city in the plaza across the street. *Christmas trees!* It was time—past time, the chief pleaded—to put an end to this election. But by a vote of four to three, the Florida Supreme Court was starting—or trying to start—a whole new chapter.

The majority easily agreed on several specifics. Gore should have received the 215 (or 176) net votes that were submitted late from Palm Beach. (The justices left it up to Judge Sauls to decide which of these two figures was correct.) The court also gave Gore the 168 net votes from the partial recount in Miami-Dade. On the other hand, the justices found that Gore was not entitled to the 51 net votes from Nassau County and that there was no need to re-examine the dimpled ballots from Palm Beach. In light of the ruling Bush's lead in the state fell from 537 to 154 votes (or the lead may have been 193, depending on which figure from Palm Beach was correct). Dramatic as these changes were, Bush was still the winner of the election.

Since the first Thursday after the election, the Republicans had been berating Gore for his "selective" approach to the recount process—the way he had cherry-picked heavily Democratic counties where he could expect to pick up votes. Now, with a kind of mordant sense of humor, the majority said, "We agree with the [Republicans] that the ultimate relief would require a counting of the legal votes contained within the undervotes in all counties where the undervote has not been subjected to a manual retabulation." It was an epic of bluff calling. The Florida Supreme Court simultaneously echoed the Republican complaints about Gore's strategy and handed the vice president the greatest—and most surprising—judicial victory in the history of this or any other election. There were approximately 60,000 undervotes statewide, and the majority wanted them all examined.

For an appellate court, the justices then went into considerable detail about how they wanted the recount to take place. Since the undervotes had already been counted in Broward, Volusia, and Palm Beach counties, the justices ordered Judge Sauls to direct the remaining sixty-four counties "that have not conducted a manual recount or tabulation of the undervotes in this election to do so forthwith, said tabulation to take place in the individual counties where the ballots are located." In what the court knew was an understatement, the justices added, "We are mindful of the fact that due to the time constraints, the count of the undervotes places demands on the public servants throughout the State to work over the weekend. However, we are confident that with the cooperation of the officials in all the counties, the remaining undervotes in these counties can be accomplished within the required time frame." At least one justice in the majority had wanted to include a footnote acknowledging that the court planned to respond promptly to the questions posed by the United States Supreme Court, but in the rush of events, that task was forgotten.

The legal basis for the Florida Supreme Court's decision would become the subject of immediate challenge, but there was another, less-noted dimension to the opinion: It established a process that would surely have produced a more accurate vote count than anything the Democrats or Republicans had proposed during the previous month. Gore wanted some undervotes counted; Bush wanted none. Only the Florida Supreme Court saw that a statewide recount would come closest, or closer, to achieving a true measure of the intent of the voters.

At 3:50 P.M., the court spokesman returned to the makeshift podium on the steps of the supreme court building. "Hello. I'm Craig Waters," he said in the affectless tone that was becoming familiar to a national television audience. "The court has authorized the following statement: By a vote of four to three, the majority of the court has reversed the decision of the trial court. . . . The circuit court shall order a manual recount of all undervotes in any Florida county where such a recount has not yet occurred. Because time is of the essence, the recounts shall commence immediately." As Waters's words tumbled out, the media encampment seemed almost to vibrate with a collective sigh of astonishment.

With this bold stroke, the Florida Supreme Court had taken the election away from the lawyers on both sides and returned it to the streets, groves, and beaches of this complex state: People were going to be counting votes once more.

On Duval Street, the supreme court building was suddenly quiet. Edward Castro went to his death without complaint and virtually without public notice. In light of the election tumult that so distracted the justices, the court issued a thirty-day stay of execution in the case of Robert Glock. But after both the Florida and United States supreme courts rejected his final pleas, he was executed on January 11, 2001.

CHAPTER FIFTEEN

IRREPARABLE HARM

In Austin, at Republican headquarters and the governor's mansion, the people around George W. Bush picked up on his mood of serene confidence. From the first days after the election, Bush had decided to leave the mechanics of the recount operation to James Baker, and the Texas governor never second-guessed his Florida viceroy. "I don't want to be seen with two cell phones and a BlackBerry telling people what to do," Bush told an adviser. Instead, the governor spent most of his time planning his new administration, meeting with current and prospective advisers, and barely acknowledging the hubbub in Florida.

But even Bush saw the implications of the Florida Supreme Court's decision on Friday, December 8. It was, he told his chief political adviser, Karl Rove, a "solar punch," and it must not stand. Rove had spent the recount period in frustration—"You were useless if you weren't a lawyer," he said—but he saw that it was time to jump back into action. Given his prominence, Rove had worried that he might have been a distraction if he had gone to Florida at the beginning of the recount, but now he couldn't stay away.

Within hours of the court's decision on Friday afternoon, Joe

Allbaugh, the Bush campaign manager, who had been in Tallahassee since the day after the election, devised a plan to send 450 people to Florida for the sixty-four separate recounts that would begin the next morning. Campaign staffers frantically tried to book rooms, rent cars, and get ready to train the volunteers who would be arriving by nightfall from Texas in two chartered jets. In Austin, Don Evans, the campaign chairman, asked Rove if he wanted to go to Florida for the denouement. "I'd love to go," Rove said. "So would I," said Evans. It wasn't precisely clear what they would do in Florida, but given the magnitude of the events that were unfolding, they simply had to go. Karen Hughes, the chief communications aide on the campaign, agreed to stay behind in Austin, recruiting volunteers and handling the press that remained near the governor.

It was about nine-thirty on Friday night when Rove arrived in Tallahassee and called in to Hughes at campaign headquarters. He found his longtime colleague, herself a tested veteran of the political wars, in tears. At first, this worried Rove. "What's wrong?" he said. Nothing, Hughes replied. "It's just that not one person said no. There's no one here anymore. Just me. Nobody turned me down. People were going to the airport on their own. It was just so amazing."

My God, thought Gore media adviser Bob Shrum after the Florida Supreme Court ordered the new recount; we really are going to win. This called for a celebration.

So Shrum convened a dinner party at what might have been the unofficial headquarters of the vice president's campaign—the Palm restaurant, a Washington steak house whose walls are festooned with cartoons of the regulars. Bill Daley came, as did Shrum's fellow media adviser Carter Eskew, and so did a few friends like Mickey Kantor, the former commerce secretary, and Jim Johnson, another old Washington hand.

The Gore campaign chartered a plane that night, and a group of young Democrats, mostly Capitol Hill aides, flew south to work on the recount the next morning. But none of the leaders of the Gore effort—a group that included Daley, Shrum, Eskew, Tad Devine, Mark Fabiani, Chris Lehane, Donna Brazile, and Tom Nides, among others—went to Florida for the climactic day of the recount.

Just as the Bush Texas airlift was landing in Tallahassee on Friday night, Terry Lewis was convening one of the more unusual legal proceedings in American history.

Ruling that afternoon, the Florida Supreme Court had directed Sanders Sauls, the Leon County Circuit Court judge who had heard the contest case, to supervise the recount of the 60,000 or so undervotes. But when Sauls saw the decision, he decided to pull out. The opinion amounted to a direct public rebuke of his work, and Sauls already thought that the court had treated him poorly in the past. Seething, Sauls told the chief judge of his court that he wanted no more of the election controversy. The next judge in line was Nikki Clark, who had rejected the Democratic challenge to the Seminole County absentee ballots. But Clark was still bruised by the Republican effort to force her off that case, and she decided to withdraw as well.

That left the case in the hands of Terry Lewis, who would now begin his third major case of the post-election period: the sixty-four-county weekend recount. On Friday night, at 8 P.M., Judge Lewis summoned the lawyers on both sides to the Leon County Courthouse to help him accomplish the task the Florida Supreme Court had laid out. Events were moving so quickly that the only available court reporter monitored the hearing from home, listening to the broadcast on C-SPAN.

The day's happenings wrought a physical transformation in the Bush lawyers. Barry Richard was going to handle the session before Judge Lewis, but he was too exhausted, overwhelmed, and disappointed to appear in court. Richard asked Phil Beck to take over

for him, then got a bailiff to let him out a side door of the courthouse so that reporters wouldn't track him down. As for Beck, the
confident destroyer of Professor Hengartner suddenly had the
thousand-mile stare of a disaster survivor. His rambling presentation to Lewis resembled a filibuster more than a legal argument.
He tried to persuade the judge to turn the recounts into sixty-four
separate legal proceedings, with judges reviewing each ballot and
court reporters taking down every word. Later, Beck admitted that
his words had really been directed to the law clerks of the justices
of the United States Supreme Court, who he hoped were watching
on television.

Beck did succeed in zeroing in on one of the key vulnerabilities
of the Florida Supreme Court's opinion. The justices had ordered
a recount, but they hadn't identified the standard. Must the chads
be hanging? How many corners had to be detached? Should dimpled chads count? The Florida Supreme Court hadn't answered
those questions, because the justices were intimidated by the Bush
lawyers' invocation of federal law. The justices worried that if they
set a standard, they might run afoul of the notion that the legislature alone should determine election procedures or of the idea
that the recount rules should not be changed after Election Day.
So the Florida court simply reasserted state law—that a ballot
should be recognized if there was a "clear indication of the intent
of the voter." It was now Terry Lewis's job to turn that command
into practical directions for the people who would be counting the
votes. So Lewis asked Beck to define the standard.

"We have a wealth of evidence on that," Beck told the judge.
"And so we're frankly going to need to educate you." Beck said
they'd like to do a presentation about the standard . . . tomorrow.
Rarely had the Bush strategy of delay been more apparent.

No deal, said the judge. Tell me now. What's the statewide standard?

There is none, said Beck.

So what should the standard be? the judge asked.

You can't set one now because that would be changing the rules in the middle of the game, Beck replied. The Bush argument was a perfect circle: There must be a standard, but there can't be a standard.

"You're confusing me," Lewis said with his usual half-smile. Actually, he wasn't confused at all. He saw that the Bush lawyers were stalling, venting their anger at the Florida Supreme Court by creating impossible demands in his courtroom. In any event, Lewis said simply, "The standard is what the [Florida] supreme court says it is, because that is what I'm bound by."

As for Boies, his expression was as equable as it had been when Sauls was battering him in a courtroom a few doors down the hall. Boies knew that with every passing minute, more votes went uncounted, so he limited himself to urging Judge Lewis to get started. "We think the court meant immediately when it said immediately," Boies said. "Hours make a difference here."

At about 10 P.M., Judge Lewis announced he was taking a break, and he left a surreal scene behind him. Here it was, late on a Friday night in the otherwise empty courthouse, and this single room was packed with people weighing potentially the most important lawsuit in the history of the American presidency. There were more than a dozen lawyers for each side, close to fifty reporters, a handful of civilian spectators, and they had nothing to do but mill around. Thanks to the Sunshine law, Florida has almost no restrictions on where reporters can wander, so journalists were sitting at the counsel table, and lawyers were sprawled in the jury box. No one knew what to expect next. Lewis didn't say how long he'd be gone, so no one felt comfortable leaving the building, if only for a little fresh air. In keeping with the discombobulated nature of things in Tallahassee, the weather kept getting warmer as winter grew nearer. Christmas lights sparkled, and suddenly—meteorologically as well as politically—it was Election Day all over again.

Terry Lewis didn't tell the lawyers, but he had called his own secret meeting back at his chambers. He had asked about a half-dozen of his fellow judges in Leon County to join him to discuss a recount effort.

Lewis was exquisitely aware of the time pressure. The safe-harbor deadline was Tuesday, December 12, a little more than three days away. Still, to the extent it was possible, he wanted judges to supervise all the recounts. That was the only way, Lewis thought, to create a dignified and trustworthy process.

So, the judges wondered as they stirred their coffee, what is the standard for counting a vote? Lewis said that the Florida Supreme Court had now twice declined to set a single statewide standard. In light of this, he wasn't going to impose one, either; instead, he would rely on the words of the law—the "clear intent" of the voter. "Don't forget that first word, *clear* intent," Lewis told his colleagues. "If you've got some question about it, it's probably not a clear intent. I've got my Johnnie Cochran sound bite for you. 'If in doubt, throw it out.' "

It was past eleven-thirty on Friday night when Judge Lewis returned to the bench. He told the groggy crowd that he wanted the vote counting to start first thing on Saturday morning and be completed by 2 P.M. on Sunday. The biggest collection of undervotes, about 9,000 from Miami-Dade County, had already been gathered and sent to Tallahassee, and they would be counted at the Leon County public library, starting at 8 A.M. Though he would try to place judges in all the recount locations, Lewis said he would remain on call in his office to settle any disputes, including any controversies about whether to recognize individual ballots. All counties would be required to fax to Judge Lewis a statement of their plans for compliance by noon on Saturday. With that, Judge Lewis sent the lawyers into the restless Florida night.

"This is the last night in Vegas and you've got a hundred dollars in your pocket and no ticket home."

Jack Young, the redheaded recount expert, had reappeared in Tallahassee on Friday night and was holding an all-night training session for Democratic vote-counting volunteers. With the same confidence that he had while lecturing his young troops on Lieberman's plane on election night, he was now holding forth at a full march on a Tallahassee sidewalk on the way to the public library. Jack Corrigan, one of Whouley's Boston boys, had spent the night making sure the Gore team would have representatives in each of the sixty-four counties. (The Bush forces had done the same thing.) Remarkably, given the magnitude of the task and the scant time available, the whole thing was coming together.

"We're putting it all on the table," Young went on as about two dozen twentysomethings trailed behind him at seven-thirty on Saturday morning. "We've already done our best precincts in Miami-Dade. We're just trying to hang on." Suddenly, Young came to a stop and posed a question to no one in particular. "By the way, does anyone know where this library is?"

Young eventually found his way, only to discover that there had been a change in plans. As Judge Lewis initially planned the recount, workers from the local election board would go through all the ballots and one of Lewis's colleagues would supervise any disputes. But so many judges volunteered to participate that they replaced the county workers entirely. The judges represented the entire political spectrum, but they had all decided to participate in this once-in-a-lifetime civic obligation. At the Leon County public library—where even the book drop was closed in deference to the recount—David Leahy, the Miami-Dade supervisor of elections, arrived just after 8 A.M. Two weeks earlier, he had asserted that his own county couldn't manage to count all the ballots in time. Now he was going to see if the judges from the sleepy northern part of the state could do the job.

At 9:51 A.M., the chief judge administered an oath to all the vote counters in the library, and at 10:07 A.M., the counting began. There were four tables with two judges each, who were in turn surrounded by a pair of county workers and one observer from each campaign. Before the judges were a set of five old envelope boxes, each with a different marking: BUSH, GORE, OTHER, NO VOTE, CONTESTED VOTES. After examining a ballot, the judges placed it in the appropriate box. When the judges couldn't agree, they put it in the CONTESTED box, which Terry Lewis would review later.

After just a couple of hours at this pace, it became clear that the count of the Miami-Dade undervotes would be completed by Saturday night. The last attempted manual recount of the votes in Miami-Dade had ended after the "Brooks Brothers riot" in Miami on November 22. At the time, the members of the Miami-Dade canvassing board justified their decision to abandon the recount on the grounds that they couldn't possibly finish the job by November 26. But here a group of Tallahassee judges was going to accomplish the job in less than twelve hours, rendering that fateful decision in Miami even more suspicious.

As Saturday began, scenes similar to the one in the Tallahassee library were taking place across the state. The Republican talking points for the Florida Supreme Court's decision had promised chaos across the state, but the state's judges and civil servants— people of all parties and political inclinations—gave a convincing refutation. In his decent and careful way, Terry Lewis had created a structure that could work—and was working. Some counties had only had a handful of undervotes, and they finished the entire process in about an hour. Other counties took longer to get started, but Judge Lewis's deadline of Sunday at 2 P.M. began to look like a reasonable target.

This lightning-speed statewide recount also offered further proof of something Jack Young had said from the beginning: Once people of good faith actually started counting votes, they saw it was a meaningful undertaking that created a better, more accurate accounting than an exclusively machine-driven tally. Quietly, efficiently, to be sure imperfectly, hundreds of people were making a better presidential election across the state of Florida on the morning of Saturday, December 9.

In the immediate aftermath of the Florida Supreme Court's decision, Ron Klain organized his Florida operation into three teams. Corrigan made sure all the counties were covered; Boies handled everything before Judge Lewis in Tallahassee; and Klain supervised the filing of appellate briefs.

Of course, Klain had joined in the general euphoria over the Florida court's decision on Friday afternoon, but his joy was leavened with a dose of foreboding as well. First, the court's remedy—a full statewide recount—was almost too good to be true. The Democrats had not even dared ask for such a dramatic turnabout and yet the court had granted it, which was certain to draw the attention of the United States Supreme Court. Second, the Florida court's failure to articulate a standard was troubling. Klain thought the supposed federal constitutional and statutory obstacles to establishing a standard were bogus. Gore would have been better off with a single standard for the whole state. Third, and most important, the Florida Supreme Court had not even acknowledged the United States Supreme Court's decision of five days earlier. As a former Supreme Court clerk, Klain knew that that Court minded its prerogatives and required deference from lower courts; several justices were likely to be offended by this apparent slight. In addition, Chief Justice Wells had written a passionate dissenting opinion that practically begged the United States Supreme Court to reverse his colleagues. By predicting an "unprecedented and unnecessary constitutional crisis," Wells would surely find some receptive ears in Washington.

With all this in mind, Klain sat down on Friday night for a brief-writing marathon—four briefs were due within ten hours. By midnight, Gore had to submit a brief to the Florida Supreme Court in response to a Republican request that the justices stay their own judgment. Then on Saturday morning at 7 A.M., Klain's team had to oppose a request for a stay of the recount in the Eleventh Circuit, in Atlanta, a case that was part of the still-simmering appeal of Judge Middlebrooks's decision in Miami; two hours later, the brief on the merits was due in that case. Finally, at 10 A.M., the Gore brief was due in the United States Supreme Court, in opposition to the stay that the Bush lawyers had sought immediately after the Florida Supreme Court's decision.

At about 3 A.M. on Saturday, a few of the younger lawyers found
Klain asleep at his desk in Dexter Douglass's storefront, his feet
propped on a chair, his head tilted back, a high-volume snore
issuing skyward. At that moment, it was difficult not to draw the
contrast with Klain's Republican counterpart in Tallahassee—
James A. Baker III. To be sure, Baker made useful suggestions to
the lawyers in the various cases, but he was about three levels removed from the actual preparation of briefs. Several other Gore
lawyers worked on Klain's briefs, but he participated as a nuts-and-
bolts drafter on all of them. Klain did this in addition to his duties
as media strategist, press spokesman, personnel manager, and
minute-by-minute hand-holder to Al Gore. Klain did exceptionally
well under the circumstances, but the gap between Baker and him
spanned more than just three decades. True, no senior Democrat
could compete on equal terms with James Baker. But no one even
tried.

The news on Saturday morning remained good for Klain and his
colleagues. The briefs were filed, the recounts were started, and
the first court decision—in the case Klain may have feared most—
came out in Gore's favor. Shortly after noon on Saturday, by a vote
of eight to four, the full U.S. Court of Appeals for the Eleventh Circuit declined to stop the recount. The judges did rule that Katherine Harris could not change the certification of Bush as the winner
in Florida until the United States Supreme Court had weighed the
issue. For present purposes, however, the big news from the
Eleventh Circuit was its statement that "[n]othing in this order
should be construed to prevent, obstruct or impede the continuation of the manual recounts that are currently being conducted."

No stay . . . the Supreme Court quiet . . . votes being counted—
life was good. For the second time since he had arrived in
Florida—the first being the moments after the Florida Supreme
Court's decision of November 21—Klain started to believe that Al
Gore was going to win.

.   .   .

Within moments of the Florida Supreme Court's decision on Friday afternoon, Ted Olson's team in Washington was drafting a petition to the United States Supreme Court for a stay of the recount process and a reversal of the Florida court's judgment. At 9:18 P.M., the Bush lawyers submitted a compelling forty-two-page "emergency application for a stay of enforcement," but the most important part may have been the title page. The decision in the contest appeal on Friday had borne the heading *Gore v. Harris,* but Olson and company rejiggered the order and identity of the parties so that the stakes of this lawsuit could not be clearer. As of Friday night, the Republicans gave the case the name by which it would be known henceforth: *Bush v. Gore.*

Once again, Chief Justice Rehnquist took the initiative. He circulated his view that the stay should be imposed, certiorari granted, and oral argument set for Monday, December 11. In his bludgeoning fashion, Rehnquist had his clerks draft a one-paragraph opinion that didn't attempt to justify the stay but merely granted it. The chief's frequent allies Scalia and Thomas quickly joined his view. But in this case, the chief had an even more enthusiastic ally—Sandra Day O'Connor. The Gore forces had hoped that O'Connor's background as a state judge and legislator, as well as her strong federalist views, would lead her to sympathize with the Florida court. In this the Democrats were entirely mistaken.

As it turned out, in the tight whirl of the Republican social establishment in Washington, O'Connor's views on the election were already well known. On the previous Monday, December 4, the day of the Supreme Court's first opinion on the election, O'Connor and her husband had attended a party for about thirty people at the home of a wealthy couple named Lee and Julie Folger. When the subject of the election controversy came up, Justice O'Connor was livid. "You just don't know what those Gore people have been doing," she said. "They went into a nursing home and registered people that they shouldn't have. It was outrageous." It was unclear where the justice had picked up this unproved accusation, which had circulated only in the more eccentric right-wing outlets, but O'Connor recounted the story with fervor. Similarly, on election night Justice O'Connor and her husband had attended a party at the home of Mary Ann Stoessel, the widow of a prominent diplomat. When the states looked like they were falling into place for Gore, Justice O'Connor said, "This is terrible," and she hastened away from the television, which was located in a basement den. Her husband, John, explained her reaction to the partygoers, saying, "She's very disappointed because she was hoping to retire"—that is, with a Republican president to appoint her successor.

Of course, O'Connor's ultimate motivation—whether principled and judicial or craven and political—cannot be known, but from the start of the election cases, she displayed a thoroughgoing disgust with both Gore's tactics and those of the Florida Supreme Court. Late on Friday night, December 8, Anthony Kennedy joined her, making a majority of five for a stay.

In a peculiar way, the response of the remaining four justices recapitulated the overall reaction of Gore supporters since the beginning of the recount. This moderate-to-liberal quartet—John Paul Stevens, David Souter, Ruth Bader Ginsburg, and Stephen Breyer—were stunned, shell-shocked by the determination of their colleagues on the Court. They thought that the majority would never wade into such an intense political controversy; would never betray their federalist principles; would never leave themselves so open to the attack that they had manipulated the legal process to a political end. But these four justices—like the Gore campaign as a whole—misread the intensity of feelings that this election had prompted.

According to long-standing law, a party seeking a stay must show that he will suffer "irreparable harm" if the stay is not granted. The events of Saturday morning, December 9, made clear that the Bush campaign had no basis to show any irreparable harm. At that time, of course, the Eleventh Circuit had ruled that Katherine Harris could not certify Gore as the winner of the election. Florida could continue counting its votes, but the certification could not change. Thus, the only possible "harm" to Bush was the counting of Florida's votes. Of course, those new totals could later be undone by the Supreme Court, so the notion that the mere counting of votes constituted an irreparable harm seemed absurd on its face.

As noon approached on that Saturday, Justice Stevens wrote a brief dissenting opinion from the stay to make just this point. The eighty-year-old Chicagoan, the senior associate justice on the Court, wrote with restrained eloquence: "Counting every legally cast vote cannot constitute irreparable harm. Preventing the recount from being completed will inevitably cast a cloud on the legitimacy of the election. . . . The Florida court's ruling reflects the basic principle, inherent in our Constitution and our democracy, that every legal vote should be counted. Accordingly, I respectfully dissent." Souter, Ginsburg, and Breyer quickly joined the Stevens dissent.

In the final minutes before the stay was issued, Justice Scalia decided that he couldn't let Stevens go unanswered, so he sat down and drafted a three-paragraph opinion of his own. He began with the kind of swagger that was characteristic of the Republicans throughout the recount. "I will not address the merits of the case," Scalia said, but then added, "It suffices to say that the issuance of the stay suggests that a majority of the Court . . . believe that [George W. Bush] has a substantial probability of success." In other words, Scalia noted—correctly—that his side already had the game locked up.

But then Scalia did discuss the merits. He said the whole point of the case was to determine whether the votes had been "legally cast." Continuing, Scalia wrote, "the counting of votes that are of questionable legality does in my view threaten irreparable harm to [Bush], and to the country, by casting a cloud upon what he claims to be the legitimacy of his election. Count first, and rule upon legality afterwards, is not a recipe for producing election results that have the public acceptance democratic stability requires." Untangled, this rhetoric suggests a remarkably political view of the Court's role. Scalia was concerned less with the ordinary legal procedures than with Bush's "legitimacy" and his "public acceptance"—so much so that he was willing to grant a stay to preserve Bush's narrow victory.

Again, it is not possible to know exactly what motivated the justices to rule as they did, but the stay had an undeniable partisan edge. Scalia was worried that the statewide recount would turn the vote totals in Gore's favor. The question would then become whether the Supreme Court had the intestinal fortitude to undo the Democrat's victory and reinstall Bush as the victor. The stay short-circuited this possibility. Now, thanks to the majority of five, no one would ever know for sure if Gore would have pulled ahead over the weekend.

The clerk's office at the Supreme Court released the stay order at 2:45 P.M. At the time, Gore was on the telephone with Klain, who was simultaneously on another line with Teresa Roseborough, the lawyer who had been handling the appeal in the Eleventh Circuit. The three were celebrating the circuit court's decision earlier in the day to let the recount continue when Jeremy Bash, one of the young lawyers on the Gore team, bounded into Klain's office and told him to pick up another line. Klain waved Bash off, mouthing that he was on with Gore, but Bash insisted that Klain take the call from Andy Pincus, the lawyer who had been designated as the contact person with the Supreme Court. Klain put his two callers on hold and got the news from Pincus.

"Bad news, sir," Klain then told Gore. "The Supreme Court voted five to four to grant a stay."

For the first time in more than a month, the life drained from Al Gore's voice. He was incredulous, outraged—but resigned, too. In Klain's words, Gore had been "ruthlessly optimistic," but even though he didn't say much more than "I see . . . I see," the vice president saw that the election was finally over.

At the Naval Observatory, Gore passed the news to his family and watched the news play out on television. At 3:11 P.M., he sent a BlackBerry message to his chief spokesmen, Mark Fabiani and Chris Lehane: PLEASE MAKE SURE THAT NO ONE TRASHES THE SUPREME COURT.

On a quiet Saturday afternoon at the White House, Bill Clinton had just come off the putting green. His chief of staff, John Podesta, was monitoring the developments on television. After he heard the announcement of the stay, Podesta walked in to tell the president of the decision.

"The Supreme Court," Clinton muttered. "Gore ought to attack those bastards."

At the Leon County public library, a raucous crowd of Bush supporters had gathered to chant and cheer as the judges inside the building conducted their recount in silence. (As usual in Tallahassee, there were practically no pro-Gore demonstrators.) A growing contingent of police officers kept an eye on the scene, and around two o'clock, the cops had surrounded the building with familiar yellow tape on which was printed CRIME SCENE—DO NOT CROSS.

The demonstrators heard the news about the stay before the vote counters did. Then, inside the library, cell phones started to ring, and the judges exchanged shrugs. Should they keep going or not? After a couple of minutes of confusion, Judge Terry Lewis, who had received official confirmation of the order from Washington, called in and told everyone to put the ballots away. There would be no more counting. A Bush lawyer bounded out of the library to tell reporters that the recounted votes were helping his candidate anyway. With almost half of the Miami-Dade undervotes counted, the lawyer said the totals were: Bush 92; Gore 50; 3,236 no-votes; and 137 disputed ballots destined for Judge Lewis.

When a court official told the crowd outside the library that the

Supreme Court had stopped the recount, the Bush demonstrators were jubilant. "We got a stay!" they chanted. "We got a stay!"

A few blocks away, Ron Klain suddenly had another issue to worry about besides the Supreme Court's injunction. He had to figure out a way to stay out of jail.

CHAPTER SIXTEEN

"AL SHARPTON TACTICS"

F IVE WEEKS HAD PASSED. Tallahassee had its recount cus-
toms, and they had to be honored, win or lose. Every major development in the case was followed by dueling press conferences
in the blue-curtained conference room on the senate side of
the Capitol. Since the winner of the latest round usually went
first, Baker made the initial appearance after the United States
Supreme Court granted the stay on Saturday afternoon, December 9. The news was so good that Baker could afford to assume his
statesman role, saying, "We are extremely gratified that the United
States Supreme Court has once again recognized, or seen, what we
think are some very serious deficiencies in the process conducted
down here."

Boies had learned about the stay at the restaurant where he was
eating lunch, and when he returned to the office, he told Klain,
"I'm going home. I'm your Florida lawyer, and that's all over now."
Klain couldn't disagree, but he asked Boies to join him for a final
press conference at the Capitol. The two lawyers knew better than
to try to spin the stay as anything other than a defeat, but Klain
wanted to hold out a measure of hope, too. All morning he had

been in touch with Corrigan and Whouley, who were monitoring the recounts to see how the vote totals were changing. The news from their shop was actually pretty good.

That was how Klain started the news conference. "We're disappointed for several reasons," Klain told the assembled reporters and a national television audience. "First and foremost, we're actually quite pleased with the progress being made at the counts under way here in a number of counties. Our latest information shows that thirteen counties had completely or partially completed their recounts, and in those counties, Vice President Gore and Senator Lieberman had gained a net of 58 votes. Five of those counties were heavily Republican counties, so we believe that . . . we were clearly on a path for Vice President Gore and Senator Lieberman to make up the difference and to pull ahead . . ." (Notably, Klain's numbers did not include the partial results from Miami-Dade.)

After the press conference, Klain returned to his office and started to think about heading north to the Supreme Court argument, which the justices had set for two days later, Monday, December 11. Vaguely, in the background, he heard the usual drone from CNN. A pair of Republican governors, George Pataki and Marc Racicot, were denouncing the Democrats for something new—violating court orders—but Klain didn't pay much attention. Then Mitchell Berger came up to Klain and said, "I don't want to alarm you, but there's a hearing in front of Judge Lewis at six o'clock. He's going to decide whether you should be held in contempt of court."

When Judge Lewis issued his directions for the conduct of the statewide recount, he had said "no partial counts will be done or reported either formally or informally." Klain understood that the judge was instructing county judges and officials—that is, the vote counters themselves—to refrain from giving partial results; Klain did not think there was anything to prevent the lawyers from discussing their own unofficial tallies. The Bush people had already disclosed their counts. At the library, the Republican lawyer had announced his numbers for the Miami-Dade recount, and at Baker's own press conference, he had claimed that the results looked favorable for the Bush side. In light of all of this, Ron Klain was going to be held in contempt of court?

It seemed incredible, but Klain didn't want to take any chances. He decided not to go to Lewis's courtroom himself, so as not to dignify the process. In addition, it would be helpful to not be present if the judge ordered him jailed immediately. Instead, Mitchell Berger and Jeffrey Robinson trooped over to defend their colleague, and Phil Beck came as lead counsel for, as it were, the prosecution. In the meantime, the Klain contempt hearing had become big news. One of Klain's cousins called his mother, who had been in a movie theater in Indianapolis, and she called her son's cell phone. "Are you under arrest, dear?" she asked. Not yet, he said.

Actually not ever. Judge Lewis, who presided over the hearing by telephone, recognized the so-called contempt hearing as the bullying stunt that it was. With his usual common sense, Lewis promptly ruled that Klain had not violated any court order. Later, Beck expressed some embarrassment about the whole undertaking, attributing the idea to some hot-headed younger lawyers in the Bush camp and noting that he never used the precise words "contempt of court." But the vindictive assault on Klain was far from an aberration in the Republican strategy in Florida. The Bush forces always sought victory more than approval. Sometimes, as in the proceeding against Klain, the Democrats fought back; other times, as in the overseas absentee ballots, Gore's side surrendered. But the Republicans never stopped pushing.

By nightfall on Saturday, December 9, in Tallahassee, when the threat against Klain had passed, even the Democrats were making rueful jokes about the lawyer's putative incarceration. Joe Lieber-

man called Klain and vowed that he would have made clerical visits to him in jail, to serve as his spiritual adviser. But when Klain
settled back in his office to think about the upcoming hearing in
the Supreme Court, he heard something that jolted his grateful
reverie about his comrades—and especially about Gore.

Unbeknownst to Klain, the vice president had been working the
phones. Gore was thinking that if the case returned to the United
States Supreme Court, Boies might make a better advocate than
Laurence Tribe. For starters, Gore was not alone in believing that
Tribe had been strangely subdued and only modestly effective in
the first argument. Moreover, as Gore saw it, if the case was seen
as a states'-rights issue and not a matter of federal constitutional
law, he had a better chance to win. Boies was the "symbol" of
Gore's effort in Florida, and he knew the facts of the complicated
litigation there better than Tribe, a constitutional lawyer, who
would need time to learn them. Using Boies would be a signal to
the Supreme Court that the controversy was a state matter that
should be left to the Florida courts to resolve.

Those who knew Gore well were familiar with his history for
conducting phone surveys about the people who worked for him.
The questions he asked tended to become self-fulfilling prophesies
spelling doom for Gore's incumbent of the moment. The vice
president had humiliated any number of staffers and consultants
with this quasi-public process, which invariably leaked to the
press. The campaign operatives Tony Coelho and Craig Smith, the
media adviser Bob Squier, the pollster Mark Penn, and even to
some extent Klain himself had seen Gore toy with their fate in this
way. Now it was Larry Tribe's turn. (By contrast, George W. Bush
had stuck with the same team of people throughout his political
career—and was repaid with their fierce personal loyalty.)

Klain decided to fight the shift to Boies. He felt a sense of personal obligation to Tribe, and he believed that the Harvard professor was the better lawyer for the job. Klain admired Boies, but
arguing before the Supreme Court was a specialized skill. Boies
had done it only once, in the famous Pennzoil-Texaco case of

1987, and he had lost nine to nothing—with Tribe as opposing counsel. As for Gore's idea of Boies as a signal to the justices that the case was really about Florida law, Klain saw it as a typical Washington overanalysis. Why not just hire the best Supreme Court advocate available?

Gore was unmoved by Klain, but the vice president agreed to convene a final conference call on Saturday to weigh the Boies-versus-Tribe question. By then, the deck was stacked. Warren Christopher, Frank Hunger, Walter Dellinger, and Mark Fabiani had all spoken up for Boies. Besides Klain, the only other person on Gore's staff in favor of Tribe was Bill Daley, who added, characteristically, "It doesn't matter, because we're going to lose anyway."

Christopher volunteered to make the trip to the Watergate hotel, where Tribe was finishing the brief, to tell him that he was out. "I always find that it's best to deliver unpleasant news in person," Christopher said when he arrived. Though shocked and devastated by the news, Tribe agreed to complete the brief and assist Boies in any way he could. In the meantime, Boies had returned home to Westchester without knowing he was being considered for the Supreme Court argument. When Gore told him of the new assignment, the lawyer said he would go to Washington the following morning. Boies had a little less than one full day—Sunday, December 10—to prepare.

It had only been ten days since the first argument before the justices, but the grand chamber of the United States Supreme Court seemed like a different place on Monday morning, December 11. The cheerful buzz that had preceded the last argument was replaced by a sullen hum. It had once seemed possible that the Supreme Court would rise above the partisan rancor of the post-election battle, but after issuing the stay on Saturday, the Court was no longer a place apart from the political struggle; it was simply another venue. The justices had apparently taken to voting in court just as they had in their voting booths on Election Day.

Ted Olson had to do only one thing in his argument: stay out of trouble. He had already won five votes for the stay, so all he had to do was keep his winning coalition together. He began by playing it safe, attacking the Florida Supreme Court for its failure to make "a single reference" to the U.S. Supreme Court's opinion of just days earlier. Olson also tried to take a narrow approach to the legal issues, starting with his argument that Article II of the Constitution said that state legislatures alone, not state courts, could make the rules for presidential elections. A decision based on this rarely invoked provision of Article II would allow the Court to rule for Bush without disturbing any settled precedents. But then Justice Anthony Kennedy, one of the swing votes, ripped that idea from its moorings, correctly noting that courts interpret the words of legislators all the time. Olson was quickly forced to concede, "It may not be the most powerful argument we bring to this Court."

"I think that's right," Kennedy replied.

Olson then turned to his argument that federal law prohibited Florida from changing the rules of the vote counting after the ballots had been cast. This law, too, was a sufficiently obscure provision that it would allow the Court to rule in a narrow way. Again, Justice Kennedy turned Olson away, saying, "I thought your point was that the process is being conducted in violation of the equal-protection clause, because it's standardless."

It was easy to see why Olson had buried this particular claim, giving it less than five pages in his fifty-page brief. In the first election case, earlier in the month, the Supreme Court had explicitly rejected Bush's lawyers' attempt to raise a claim based on the equal-protection clause of the Fourteenth Amendment. This wasn't especially surprising. The doctrine of equal protection had fallen into relative disuse in the Rehnquist Court. In recent years, the Court had used equal protection only to strike down laws that explicitly discriminated against groups the Constitution protected, most notably racial minorities. Unless a government action intentionally targeted such a group, the conservatives on the Court were reluctant to invoke the equal-protection clause.

In this case, of course, Olson could not identify the kind of in-vidious discrimination that the Supreme Court usually required. In the cursory, almost throwaway argument about equal protec-tion, Olson's brief suggested that the Florida recount order vio-lated the principle of "one person, one vote," because some ballots were reviewed more than others. (Tribe's brief, in reply, suggested that it could not be a violation of equal protection to make accu-rate counts of valid ballots that were initially designated under-votes. Indeed, he noted, "it is the exclusion of these ballots, not their inclusion, that would raise questions of unequal treatment.")

Not surprisingly, then, Olson ducked Justice Kennedy's invita-tion to explain his equal-protection argument at length, and in any event, the lawyer was soon distracted by a series of questions from Justice Stephen Breyer. A former colleague of Tribe's at Harvard Law School, Breyer prided himself on his ability to find common ground with his more conservative colleagues on the Court. Breyer was looking for a compromise—a remand of the case back to the Florida Supreme Court, with instructions to designate a single standard for counting all the undervote ballots. So, Breyer asked Olson, "what would the standard be?"

As the Bush lawyers had done from the beginning of the re-count, Olson dodged this question; he wanted an accurate recount to be an impossibility. But Olson's answers mattered less than Breyer's questions. In a familiar tactic for Supreme Court justices, Breyer was floating a proposal to his colleagues. He drew immedi-ate interest from his fellow dissenters David Souter and Ruth Bader Ginsburg, but not from any of the five who might change the outcome. Like so many Democrats who reached out in this re-count, Stephen Breyer discovered that the other side cared more about winning than dealing.

Joe Klock only had ten minutes to argue, but it was long enough to win a measure of immortality. As Katherine Harris's lawyer, Klock had been critical in preserving Bush's victory. Like Mac Stipanovich, he had pushed hard for Harris to reject the recounts, and had also established a fast kinship with Judge Sanders Sauls during the contest.

Souter and Breyer began by pursuing Klock on an issue they had raised with Olson. What would be a fair standard for counting the votes? Klock also refused to give a straight answer, and Justice Stevens followed up with a tricky hypothetical. Suppose a machine damaged some ballots. Wouldn't it be permissible to set a standard to evaluate whether any of those votes should be counted? "What standard would you use in the situation I proposed then?"

Klock replied, "Well, Justice Brennan, the difficulty is that under . . ." Suddenly, the courtroom was rocking with laughter. Justice William Brennan had retired in 1990 and died in 1997. Brennan used to go down to Miami on holidays, and Klock had once had dinner with him. During a moot-court rehearsal, Klock had confused Stevens and Brennan in just this way.

After Klock struggled for a moment to regain his footing, Justice Souter followed up on the subject of the standard. "They have to throw their hands up?" he asked.

"No. Justice Breyer, what I'm saying is that—"

"I'm Justice Souter. You've got to cut that out."

The laughter broke like a thunderclap in response to Klock's second such mistake in less than a minute. The error focused so much attention on the hapless lawyer that it obscured something more important: Souter wasn't laughing. Indeed, the taciturn New Hampshire bachelor was suffering. More than any other justice, Souter believed that the majority was engaged in a deeply illegitimate exercise. No justice had greater reverence for the Supreme Court as an institution than David Souter, and no one was more disappointed by the performance of his colleagues.

Justice O'Connor had been relatively quiet through the first two arguments but jumped into the fray when Boies stood up to speak. (Among the justices, only Clarence Thomas remained silent for both oral arguments.) "I did not find, really, a response by the Florida Supreme Court to this Court's remand in the case a week ago. It just seemed to kind of bypass it and assume that all those changes in deadlines were just fine and they'd go ahead and adhere to them," she said. "And I found that troublesome." Far from a defender of states' rights in this case, O'Connor was furious at the perceived insolence of the Florida justices.

The heart of Boies's argument should have come when Justices Kennedy and Souter asked him about variation in counting standards between different counties. What if dimpled ballots were recognized as votes in one county but not in another? "There may be such variation, and I think we would have a responsibility to tell the Florida courts what to do about it," Souter said. "On that assumption, what would you tell them to do about it?"

Boies had a temporary mind freeze. It was perhaps the most important question of the argument, and he simply didn't have an answer. Weeks of little sleep, not to mention inadequate time to prepare, had taken their toll.

"Well, I think that's a very hard question," Boies said simply.

Justice Stevens tried to come to Boies's rescue. "Does not the procedure that is in place there contemplate that the uniformity will be achieved by having the final results all reviewed by the same judge?"

Boies grasped the life preserver. "Yes," he said. "That's what I was going to say, Your Honor."

It took Justice Ginsburg to give an even better reply to the equal-protection argument. True, as Stevens and Souter both suggested, Judge Lewis served as a fairness check for the process, but in a larger sense, no court had ever required a state to give all its voters the same technology or to evaluate all its ballots by a single standard. When Olson rose to give his rebuttal, Ginsburg said, "Well, there are different ballots from county to county, too, Mr. Olson. And that's part of the argument that I don't understand. There are machines, there's the optical scanning, and then there are a whole variety of ballots. There's the butterfly ballot that we've heard about and other kinds of punch-card ballots. How can you have one standard when there are so many varieties of ballots?"

Time was up before Olson could give a complete answer. Both sides had made competent, if uninspired, arguments, but Bill Daley probably had it right. The vote on the stay had been five to four in Bush's favor, and nothing in the oral argument suggested that any of the justices had changed their minds.

When no decision came immediately from the Court, Al Gore did what came naturally to him. He sat down and wrote an op-ed piece for *The New York Times*. He wrote it on the assumption that the Supreme Court would rule in his favor—and that the renewed vote counting would cause a moan of impatience around the country. Gore was probably wrong. The nation at large never had any problem with the actual counting of votes, only with the legal wrangling about the ballots. But the pundits and pros had declared their impatience with the process. Now the vice president sat down once more to try to win their favor in their forum of choice.

Gore again called the editor of the *Times* editorial page. "Howell Raines is holding space open for me," the vice president told his adviser Walter Dellinger. "The identity of the person who has been chosen by the people is locked in boxes in Tallahassee," Gore wrote. "And we cannot forgive ourselves if we do not open those boxes."

"But what if they rule against you?" Dellinger asked.

"They are not going to rule against me," Gore said. "They are going to rule in my favor."

In a real sense, the case—and thus the election—was over within minutes of the completion of the oral argument on Monday, when the justices retreated to the secrecy of their conference room. The majority for Saturday's stay remained intact forty-eight hours later, in favor of reversing the Florida Supreme Court.

Rehnquist often said he cared more about the Court's results than its written opinions. So once the chief justice had secured the five votes, he split up the drafting among his clerks and waited for his colleagues to fall into place. Scalia and Thomas joined Rehnquist in the view that the Florida court, by ordering the statewide recount of the undervotes, had usurped the role that Article II of the Constitution assigned to the state legislature. Kennedy and O'Connor said that they too wanted to reverse the Florida judgment, but they weren't yet sure of the grounds.

On the other side, Breyer and Souter weren't ready to surrender. The other dissenters, Stevens and Ginsburg, felt that the ruling of the Florida Supreme Court should be upheld in all respects; they saw no conceivable common ground that might bring one of the majority with them. But Breyer in particular thought he could craft a compromise that might nudge Kennedy, or, less likely, O'Connor, over to his side. After the customary brief-conference meeting—Rehnquist didn't care for what he called a "debating society"—the justices went to their chambers to begin drafting. O'Connor and Kennedy, who had nothing to write at first, awaited the courtship of Breyer and Souter on the one hand and Rehnquist, Scalia, and Thomas on the other.

In his opinion, Breyer wrote that the Supreme Court should have sent the case back to the Florida court with a simple instruction: Establish one statewide standard (that is, include or exclude all dimpled- and hanging-chad ballots) and recount all the undervotes in the state—"whether or not previously recounted prior to the end of the protest period." Breyer and Souter said that it should be up to the Florida courts to determine whether there was time to complete such a recount by December 18, the date of the Electoral College meeting. Souter observed acidly that Florida probably would have been able to complete its recount "if the state proceedings had not been interrupted" by the Supreme Court's unwise stay.

In light of these polarized positions, O'Connor and Kennedy set out, with time exceptionally tight, to write their own opinion. Like the first opinion, the author would be per curiam rather than by any individual justice. The work took place mostly on the morning of Tuesday, December 12. Though the wording was mostly Kennedy's, the sense of pique—and the desire simply to get the matter over with—was more O'Connor's. Their opinion amounted to only twelve pages, most of which were devoted to reciting the facts. Even defenders of the Court's result have found little to admire in the shallow reasoning and meager explanation in what became the majority opinion.

The justices simply announced that the "absence of uniform rules to determine" the intent of the voters violated the Constitution— even though the Court had never before suggested that different voting systems offended the equal-protection clause of the Fourteenth Amendment. Under contemporary equal-protection doctrine, the majority should have identified the purported targets of this constitutional violation—blacks? women? the poor? Of course, the Court could point to no such class of victims, because there weren't any.

But if it was difficult to identify the victims, it was simple to find the single beneficiary of this new rule of constitutional law: George W. Bush. Late in the process on Tuesday, O'Connor and Kennedy made this point explicit in a sentence that quickly became the most notorious in their opinion: "Our consideration is limited to the present circumstances, for the problem of equal protection in election processes generally presents many complexities."

The basic obligation of a court devoted to precedent is to create rules of general application. Here, however, the Supreme Court was announcing in advance that the case of *Bush v. Gore* existed to serve only the Republican candidate for president in 2000. For those who would see cynical motives in the work of the majority— who thought they were acting more from political than principled motives—this sentence looked like a confession. O'Connor, Kennedy, and the others, it appeared, limited themselves to "the present circumstances" because that was what was necessary to assure their candidate's victory.

If anything, the majority's treatment of the election deadline was even more shoddy. Florida law was silent on whether the electors should be chosen by December 12 or December 18. So O'Connor and Kennedy simply inferred that Florida really wanted the deadline to be December 12—even though the legislature never said any such thing. "Because it is evident that any recount seeking to meet the December 12 date will be unconstitutional for the reasons we have discussed," the per curiam decision stated, "we reverse the judgment of the Supreme Court of Florida ordering a recount to proceed." In the tortured language of the opinion, this was as close as the justices came to stating their bottom line. The December 12 deadline had passed—even though it was a deadline of the Court's own invention.

In their conclusion, Kennedy and O'Connor tried to bulk up their support for their holding by stating, "Seven justices of the Court agree that there are constitutional problems with the recount ordered by the Florida Supreme Court that demand a remedy." Thus, the five-to-four majority tried to suggest that the vote was really seven to two. But Breyer joined Stevens's all-out dissenting opinion, and Souter said clearly that he thought the recount should have proceeded. Notwithstanding the majority's attempt at marketing, the opinion was nothing more, and nothing less, than a decision to award the presidency to George W. Bush by a vote of five to four.

Ruth Bader Ginsburg had watched the last round of jockeying with some disgust. Before becoming a judge, she had devoted her life as a lawyer to the equal-protection clause of the Fourteenth Amendment, specifically to the task of making women beneficiaries of its protections. She was appalled to see the majority distort the meaning of the clause. In a late draft of her dissenting opinion, she drew on the early press reports about the black vote in Florida to observe that if there was any equal-protection violation by the state, it was more likely by the local and state authorities than by the Florida Supreme Court. When Antonin Scalia saw Ginsburg's draft, however, he wrote a memorandum accusing her of using the Supreme Court to engage in "Al Sharpton tactics" about the election.

Scalia's memo, like so many Republican thrusts over the previous thirty-five days, posed a dilemma for Ginsburg. Should she fire back with equal fury and engage her adversary at the same rhetorical temperature, or should she take the high road and tone down the confrontation? Like so many Democrats—and like Al Gore himself—Ginsburg chose not to fight. She removed the reference to race from her opinion.

At precisely 10 P.M. on Tuesday, December 12, the hastily printed opinions were handed to the reporters in the Supreme Court press room, who sprinted to their camera positions and attempted to untangle what the justices had wrought.

After the Supreme Court granted the stay on Saturday, Karl Rove went north to the Bush transition office in the Virginia suburbs to witness the denouement. On Tuesday night, Rove was watching the television journalists struggle to make sense of the ruling, and he called his boss to celebrate the good news. Though it was just after 9 P.M. in Austin, George W. Bush was already in his pajamas at the governor's mansion. "Congratulations, Mr. President," Rove said. "This is great news."

"What are you talking about?" Bush replied. "This is terrible."

"What channel are you watching?" Rove asked.

Bush was watching CNN, and Rove was watching NBC, which was faster to recognize the implications of the decision.

"You know what," Bush said at last. "I'm going to call a lawyer."

On the night of December 12, James Baker was still at his post in Tallahassee, and he convened a quick conference call with Olson, Ben Ginsberg, and the other lawyers to get their reading on the Supreme Court's opinion. Moments after Bush's phone conversation with Rove, Baker called the Texas governor. As he had so many times over the previous thirty-five days, Baker settled the issue. When Bush came to the phone, Baker said, "Congratulations, Mr. President-elect."

.   .   .

In an act of reckless optimism, Ron Klain returned to Tallahassee after the argument on Monday morning. In theory, he was going to continue to lead the recount effort after the justices in Washington affirmed the Florida Supreme Court. With his small corps of loyalists—including Mitchell Berger, Jeremy Bash, Jack Corrigan, and a handful of others—Klain watched the instant analysis of the Supreme Court's opinion on Tuesday night. After an agonizing wait for the fax to arrive, Klain did a page-by-page explanation on the telephone for Gore. When page twelve finally came through, Klain said, "I think we're kind of hosed here." Still, Klain told Gore, he thought there might be a sliver of hope in the opinion. The vice president agreed to let Klain's team work through the night one more time. (He withdrew his op-ed piece.)

Mostly recognizing the futility of their mission, they nevertheless produced a twenty-seven-page brief that asked the Florida Supreme Court to restart the recount with the single standard. "This Court should direct the counting of all ballots which contained a discernible indentation or other mark," the lawyers wrote, making a last stand in favor of dimples. But the justices' adherence to the December 12 deadline, unjustified as it may have been, doomed Klain's final mission. Gore and Klain spoke early on the morning of Wednesday, December 13, and they agreed that the brief would not be filed. At about 9:30 A.M., Daley called his counterpart, Don Evans—just as he had thirty-six days earlier—to arrange for Gore's concession phone call to Bush.

At 11:50 A.M., Klain put Gore on the speakerphone so that everyone in the Tallahassee office could hear him. "Hey, Ron, that was some election night!" the vice president began. "There are no words to express my gratitude. You guys are just unbelievable. The decision last night is a testament to what you made it impossible for them to say. You left them no alternative to saying what they said in the way that they said it." This was as close as Gore could bring himself to criticizing the Supreme Court's opinion, even among his own staff. Gore was hosting a long-scheduled Christmas party that night in Washington. "I want you all to come to my house," Gore said. "You'll know it when you hear a bunch of people yelling, 'Get out of Cheney's house!'"

In his meticulous way, Gore wanted to make sure to do certain things in his concession speech. Sitting in his family room at the Naval Observatory on Wednesday afternoon, dictating to his speechwriter Eli Attie, Gore said he wanted to make sure that he used specific words that evening. In the rancor generated by the Supreme Court's opinion, some Democrats were suggesting that Gore register some sort of protest with his departure speech. He might say *withdraw* rather than *concede,* or refuse to refer to Bush as the president-elect. As ever, Gore wanted no part of these hardball tactics. To Attie, and later to Daley, Shrum, and Eskew, who joined in the drafting, Gore said he wanted to make sure that his concession was both gracious and complete.

Gore arrived at the Old Executive Office Building, just across a small alleyway from the White House, shortly before nine. He went to the office of his official press secretary, Jim Kennedy, and picked up the phone to call George W. Bush in Austin. Their exchange was polite but perfunctory, and the vice president immediately stepped to a podium in the room next door to speak to the nation. His wife and four children—the only intimates Gore had ever had or needed—stood at his side.

"Just moments ago, I spoke with George W. Bush and congratulated him on becoming the forty-third president of the United States—and I promised him that I wouldn't call him back this time."

It was the first of five references, in a seven-minute speech, to Bush as president or president-elect. "Neither he nor I anticipated this long and difficult road. Certainly neither of us wanted it to happen. Yet it came, and now it has ended, resolved, as it must be resolved, through the honored institutions of our democracy." The words in this passage were a conscious evocation of Lincoln's second inaugural address ("the war came"), a subtle reminder of the magnitude of the events the country had just endured.

"I know that many of my supporters are disappointed. I am, too. But our disappointment must be overcome by our love of country." Gore praised the Liebermans, and quoted his father—"No matter how hard the loss, defeat might serve as well as victory to shape the soul and let the glory out." He thanked his "truly tireless campaign staff and volunteers, including all those who worked so hard in Florida for the last thirty-six days."

"And now, my friends, in a phrase I once addressed to others"— at the 1992 Democratic National Convention—"it's time for me to go."

A wicked sleet bounced off the granite steps as Gore raced to his car. Several hundred drenched staffers had waited in the cold to cheer him on his way. The bursts of the photographers' flashes made a strobe pulse against the tiny icicles and the former candidate, so the journey of just a few steps seemed as if it took a very long time.

MOVING ON

Within an hour of Gore's concession, George W. Bush was standing before a cheering crowd at the Texas House of Representatives in Austin. The president-elect's advisers chose the Democrat-controlled House as a symbol of Bush's commitment to bipartisanship. "Our nation must rise above a house divided," he said. "Americans share hopes and goals and values far more important than any political disagreements. Republicans want the best for our nation, and so do Democrats. Our votes may differ, but not our hopes."

Bush thanked Gore for his concession, then promptly outlined his agenda for the nation—reforming education, strengthening Medicare, and delivering "broad, fair, and fiscally responsible tax relief." Bush could have delivered essentially the same speech thirty-six days earlier had Gore not called to withdraw his concession. The moment may have been delayed, but Bush had won, Gore had lost, and that was all that mattered.

Far from ending with the inauguration, the politics of the recount became a touchstone of the new administration. To be sure, the recount reflected the personalities of the two candidates, but the early days of the Bush presidency also suggested that those thirty-six days displayed the DNA of the contemporary Democratic and Republican parties: the party of process versus the party of results, reliance on elite opinion versus trust in public opinion, the agony of deliberation versus the exercise of power. It took a little while for quasi-official Washington to understand this. For example, on the day after Bush declared victory, R. W. Apple, Jr., wrote in *The New York Times:* "Mr. Bush will need to foster the kind of bipartisan cooperation he promised during his campaign. To accomplish that, the Texas governor will have to choose his issues carefully and weigh with caution how hard to push his viewpoint on contentious questions like abortion and the sweeping tax cut he has pledged." If he had won, Al Gore might actually have taken this kind of advice.

George W. Bush, by contrast, ran his new administration with the same air of jaunty confidence he had exhibited during the recount. The symbols and words of bipartisanship turned out to be just that. On his first day in office, Bush signed an executive order banning U.S. funding for international family-planning organizations that provide or counsel for abortions. As his first major legislative initiative, he advocated and won passage of the largest income-tax cut in a generation, just as he had pledged to do during the campaign. Bush didn't modulate his views or his agenda just because the conventional wisdom suggested that he should. He had run as a committed political conservative, and that was the kind of president he would be.

Bush's straight-ahead approach did exact costs in the closely divided capital. In May 2001, Republican senator Jim Jeffords, of Vermont, citing the rightward tilt of the Bush administration, switched to an independent affiliation, putting the Senate in Democratic hands for the first time in more than six years. But Jeffords's defection had no discernible impact on the way Bush conducted his presidency. George W. Bush was a man of strong and steady convictions. And nothing—not the loss of the Senate, the advice of the Washington establishment, or the extraordinary circumstances of his victory—would change what he believed or how he behaved.

True to his loyal nature, Bush rewarded the people who had worked so hard for him in Florida. One of James Baker's deputies in Tallahassee, Robert Zoellick, became United States trade representative and another, Margaret Tutwiler, was named ambassador to Morocco. The new president appointed his campaign chairman Don Evans secretary of commerce, and campaign manager Joe Allbaugh director of the Federal Emergency Management Agency. (Ben Ginsberg did not seek a government job and returned to his law firm.) Many of the middle- and lower-level operatives for Bush in Florida found important positions throughout the federal bureaucracy. For example, David Aufhauser, the architect of the Republicans' legal strategy on the overseas absentee votes, became general counsel to the Treasury Department. Indeed, it quickly became apparent that service during the Florida recount was the indispensable credential in George W. Bush's Washington. The president's first two appointments to the United States Court of Appeals for the District of Columbia circuit—generally regarded as the stepping-stone to the Supreme Court—went to Miguel Estrada and John G. Roberts, Jr., who had played important behind-the-scenes roles in the Florida litigation.

James Baker sought no favors from the new president, but he did bask in the victory he had done so much to secure. Shortly after the inauguration, Baker attended the annual Alfalfa Dinner in Washington, a white-tie affair for the city's power brokers. There, he encountered former senator John Danforth, who had spurned Baker's overtures to represent Bush in the federal lawsuit challenging the manual recounts. "I guess that equal-protection theory wasn't so bad after all!" Baker needled his old acquaintance. Baker could have mentioned, but didn't, another one of Danforth's predictions—that the lawsuit "would destroy the reputation of everyone involved on the Bush side." Theodore B. Olson, the lawyer who took on the role Danforth would have played, far from being destroyed, was rewarded by the president with perhaps the greatest prize any litigator can receive: Bush named Olson solicitor general of the United States, the government's chief advocate before the Supreme Court.

As it happened, the vote on Olson's nomination took place just as the Senate was switching from Republican to Democratic hands, and the Democrats could easily have prevented it from coming to a vote. Because of Olson's role in the election controversy—as well as his questionable activity in support of extreme anti-Clinton organizations—some in the Democratic Party wanted to deny him this plum appointment. But in a not-so-distant echo of the Democrats' approach and behavior during the recount, the new Senate leadership decided to be gracious and allow Olson to assume his post. During the Clinton years, the Republican-controlled Senate had refused to confirm any number of Democratic appointees who were far less controversial than Olson. Indeed, Senator Jesse Helms and others had stopped Gore's adviser Walter Dellinger from *ever* getting a vote on his nomination to be solicitor general. But Senate Democrats, showing off their gene for unrequited conciliation, handed Olson a pass for the same job. (Olson's confirmation gave rise to some rueful speculation by some of Gore's Florida operatives. If Gore had won, they figured, the Senate Republicans would have refused to confirm them for anything—and President Gore would have sacrificed them rather than force the issue.)

There was one more postscript to Baker's service on the recount. In light of the Republican victory, Vice President–elect Cheney had to step down from all of his board memberships, including one with EDS, the Texas-based computer-services firm on whose board Baker also served. Baker came up with the idea for Cheney's replacement. Indeed, months later, Baker would still laugh mischievously about what a good idea it was to ask Gore's campaign chairman Bill Daley to take Cheney's place. After the election, Daley moved to New York to pursue business interests at EDS and elsewhere.

When the position of Florida secretary of state ceases to exist in 2002, Katherine Harris will most likely run for Congress. In the heavily Republican district where she lives, Harris will be a strong favorite to win.

Notwithstanding the rancor surrounding *Bush v. Gore,* the United States Supreme Court continued its work without notable change or interruption. Nineteen days after the decision, Justices Ginsburg and Scalia celebrated New Year's Eve together with their families, as they had done for many years. In the next few months, several justices on both sides of the decision gave speeches saying that they continued to respect their colleagues and believed that the Court remained essentially an apolitical institution. (Notably, Justice Souter gave no such testimonial.) Polls showed that public esteem for the Court was essentially unchanged, though critical reaction to the opinion in *Bush v. Gore* remained harsh. Even defenders of the result had few kind words for the Court's reasoning, arguing instead that the justices simply acted to save the country from further uncertainty. In all, the Supreme Court's performance in the election cases vindicated once more the famous observation offered by Justice Robert Jackson in 1953: "We are not final because we are infallible, but we are infallible only because we are final."

Al Gore received 50,996,582 votes for president, the second-highest total in history, behind only Ronald Reagan's landslide in 1984. In the nationwide total, Gore defeated Bush by 540,520 votes, or .51 percent, which was more than four times greater than John F. Kennedy's margin over Richard Nixon in 1960. In Florida, Ralph Nader received 97,488 votes, meaning that if one out of a hundred Nader supporters in the state had switched to Gore, he would have won the state, and the presidency, with relative ease.

If the former vice president agonized about the excruciatingly close defeat, he gave no sign of it, not even to close friends. In his own way, Al Gore was as transparent as George W. Bush. Cautious, analytical, distant, Gore made a conscious effort to avoid dwelling on the election. He took short-term teaching jobs near where his mother and children lived, and he planned to write a book with his wife about family issues—an outgrowth of the annual Vanderbilt conferences he enjoyed so much. In his teaching assignments, Gore relied mostly on guest speakers, which saved him from any kind of forced introspection.

It is possible, of course, that nothing Gore and his campaign might have done would have made any difference in the final result. (This was the post-recount view of Bill Daley, who described himself as a "realist" rather than a "pessimist" or "defeatist.") If the election had been thrown into the Congress or if the Florida legislature had chosen to assign the state's electoral votes, Gore might have lost as well. If the recounts had proceeded, they might not have gone Gore's way. But the fact remains that Gore did not do nearly everything he could to secure his victory, so the nation can never know whether a more determined effort might have succeeded.

Al Gore's performance during the recount raises a question that is simple to pose but difficult to answer: Was the vice president a statesman or a sap? Gore decided to forgo appeals that would have left him open to charges of hypocrisy (the Seminole and Martin claims), demagoguery (the street protests and the racial issues), or putting his own interests ahead of those of the military (the overseas-absentee-ballots issue). Running away from these fights would be admirable only if the accusations against him had merit, but not simply because they were raised. Gore's analytical powers were such that he even convinced himself not to make the very claims that might have won him the election in an honorable way. If Bill Clinton was a prisoner of his id, Gore was bedeviled by his superego—an internal censor so strong that it wiped out not only the killer instinct but also the fighting spirit. It is perhaps not surprising that Gore failed to attract passionate followers.

With the election finally over, Gore's supporters resumed their lives. The consultants (Shrum, Eskew, Devine) went off to find other candidates, and the lawyers (Boies and the others) returned to their firms. When Ron Klain returned to O'Melveney & Myers, he decided to use his newfound expertise in election law to build a sideline in redistricting controversies. Among his first clients were the Democrats in the Florida legislature.

By and large, Gore's advisers took their cue from the candidate and beat a respectful retreat into private life. There was one stealthy exception. Few people aroused the ire of Gore partisans more than their ostensible ally Alex Penelas, the mayor of Miami-Dade County, who had done so little to support the manual recount. After Gore's concession, the South Florida locals on Gore's team—including Mitchell Berger, Kendall Coffey, and Ben Kuehne—decided to seek a little revenge. They set out to sabotage Penelas's pet project, the conversion of the former Homestead Air Force Base into a commercial airport. The lawyers, who opposed the idea on environmental as well as personal grounds, reached out to every connection they could think of in the final days of the Clinton administration. On January 16, four days before George W. Bush's inauguration, the air force announced it had killed Penelas's plan.

Al Gore has remained silent about his political future, but he has taken the first steps toward restarting a campaign operation. He planned to begin giving speeches in late 2001, to hire a few political aides, and to make appearances for Democratic candidates in the 2002 elections. Of the two dozen or so top officials of the Gore campaign and recount operation, only one, Mitchell Berger, who had said that he would take a bullet for his friend, endorsed another Gore bid for president. Though no losing candidate in history had come closer to winning the presidency than Al Gore, almost no one who helped him get there wanted to see him try again.

Because Florida law guarantees public access to ballots even after an election, several news-media groups conducted analyses to explore the question of "who really won." Alas, what was intended to bring some clarity to this benighted election was quickly muddied by familiar problems—rules disputes, partisan acrimony, and general confusion.

In a modest way, the media recounts help answer some lingering, important questions about the vote in Florida. First, if the Supreme Court had not granted a stay on Saturday, December 9, and the recounts of the undervotes had continued, which candidate would have come out ahead? Second, if the votes in all the counties had been recounted—overvotes as well as undervotes—what would the result have been? And finally, what do the media recounts reveal about the strategies of both sides?

A joint study of some 64,000 ballots by *USA Today, The Miami Herald,* and the Knight Ridder newspapers sought, initially, to answer the first question: What if there had been no stay? This study examined only undervotes; it did not include the ballots in the seven counties that had completed their manual recounts by the time the Supreme Court entered its stay or those precincts in Miami that were recounted before the local canvassing board decided to stop all counts. Under three of four scenarios, Bush won this recount. If the standard for counting ballots was lenient—that is, dimples allowed—Bush won by 1,665. If the standard was similar to that applied in Palm Beach, Bush won by 884. If two corners had to be detached, Bush won by 363. Only by a strict standard—fully detached chads required—did Gore win, and by a total of only 3 votes.

At first glance, these results are curious: The Gore forces were always fighting for a lenient standard, and it now seems that Bush would have prevailed under such a rule. But this apparent anomaly can be explained by examining the counties that were not included in the study, which were the most Democratic areas in the state—all of Broward and Palm Beach as well as the northern part of Miami-Dade. If these areas were included—that is, if the undervotes in all sixty-seven counties were examined—then the race shifted in Gore's direction.

A later *USA Today, Miami Herald,* and Knight Ridder review of 176,000 ballots, including 111,000 overvotes (mostly from optical-scan machines) helps to answer the second question: What if there had been a true statewide recount? Here, Gore did better. Under the lenient standard for a statewide recount, Gore won by 393 votes; under a Palm Beach approach, Gore won by 299; under a two-corner rule, Bush was the winner by 352; under the strict test, Bush won by 97. In other words, when the recount included the seven-plus mostly Democratic counties, Gore won under two of the four standards.

What conclusions can be drawn from this blizzard of numbers? Rather few. First, as *The New York Times* reported shortly after the *USA Today* study appeared, hundreds of ballots simply disappeared between election night and the time of the media recounts. For example, only eight counties were able to produce the exact number of undervotes they reported on election night. This kind of seepage is not especially surprising in light of the chaotic post-election environment in Florida, but with margins so close, these missing ballots would surely have made an important difference. At some level, too, the media recounts misconceived how the official recounts were conducted in Florida. The canvassing boards evaluated the ballots in rooms thick with political intrigue and in environments full of overbearing lawyers (of both parties), hot-blooded protesters (invariably Republican), and impatient journalists. It is interesting to compare these raucous exercises with the contemplative after-the-fact analysis of neutral inspectors, but it is folly to pretend that they are the same thing. Many factors affected the vote totals in Florida, and the actual appearance of the ballots was just one of them.

Still, the media recounts do suggest at least some tentative conclusions about the candidates' strategies. They lend credence to the argument that Gore's campaign should have sought a full statewide recount at the outset of the controversy. The numbers suggest that Jack Young was right after all: The broader the recount—one that included overvotes and undervotes, punch-card and optical-scan ballots—the better Gore's chance of winning. More important, a broader recount (if Gore had been able to obtain one) would have been perceived to be more fair than the selective approach he took. Ironically but fittingly, Gore chose the limited recount in an attempt to ingratiate himself with Washington—and crippled himself in the course of that futile attempt. As for the Republicans, the media recounts suggest that James Baker had it right all along. From election night forward, Bush was always ahead; any recounts jeopardized his lead. Baker's cynical war on the recounts—which he fought in courtrooms, in television studios, and in the streets—was the best way to make sure that George W. Bush became president.

For an event of such seismic importance, the Bush-Gore recount left modest footprints on the American landscape. If there was one point of universal consensus in the aftermath of the Florida fiasco, it was that voting procedures around the country needed a massive overhaul. By the middle of 2001, however, the momentum for such changes had slowed. To its credit, Florida passed comprehensive reform legislation that will, among other things, outlaw the punch-card ballot in future elections. However, not one other state followed suit, although Georgia passed some modest reforms. No federal legislation appears imminent or even likely.

George W. Bush has become a president like any other, with his popularity based on his performance in office rather than the circumstances of his arrival. By 2004, when he runs for re-election, the recount will probably have faded to a politically irrelevant memory. As new disclosures raise ever more troubling questions about the vote in Florida, Ari Fleischer, the White House press secretary, has a stock response: "The nation, the president, and all but the most partisan Americans have moved on." So, undoubtedly, they have.

But still, the election of 2000 will not go away, because in any real, moral, and democratic sense, Al Gore should have been declared the victor over George W. Bush—in the popular vote, in Florida, and in the Electoral College. No one seriously suggests that 3,407 people intended to vote for Patrick Buchanan in Palm Beach County; no one believes that thousands of black voters in Duval County had no preference in the race for president. The 680 questionable overseas absentee ballots identified in July 2001 by *The New York Times* assuredly, and improperly, went to Bush by a wide margin. If the simple preference of the voters behind their curtains was the rule—and it *is* supposed to be the rule in a democracy—then Gore probably won the state by several thousand votes, approximately the margin of the original network exit polls. Should Gore have won in a legal sense as well? He probably should have, and a Supreme Court opinion that is doomed to infamy denied him this opportunity, too.

In the cynical calculus of contemporary politics, it is easy to dismiss Gore's putative victory. But if more people intended to vote for Gore than for Bush in Florida—as they surely did—then it is a crime against democracy that he did not win the state and thus the presidency. It isn't that the Republicans "stole" the election or that Bush is an "illegitimate" president. But the fact remains: The wrong man was inaugurated on January 20, 2001, and this is no small thing in our nation's history. The bell of this election can never be unrung, and the sound will haunt us for some time.

SOURCE NOTES AND ACKNOWLEDGMENTS

I spent almost every day of the post-election period in Florida (mostly in Tallahassee), and also attended the two arguments before the United States Supreme Court. This book is based primarily on my observations there and on my subsequent interviews with more than a hundred participants in the story. All quotations from private conversations come either from the person who made the comment or a person who heard it. All quotations from court proceedings come from official transcripts. I am thankful for the broad degree of cooperation that I received from participants on both sides. I should add, however, that President Bush, former Vice President Gore, and the justices of the United States Supreme Court declined to be interviewed.

I have steeped myself in the voluminous press coverage of the recount controversy, and I am grateful, as ever, for the work of my fellow reporters. In particular, I read the following books with care:

Bugliosi, Vincent. *The Betrayal of America: How the Supreme Court Undermined the Constitution and Chose Our President.* New York: Thunder's Mouth Press, 2001.

Correspondents of *The New York Times*. *36 Days: The Complete Chronicle of the 2000 Presidential Election Crisis*. New York: Times Books, 2001.

Dershowitz, Alan M. *Supreme Injustice: How the High Court Hijacked Election 2000*. New York: Oxford University Press, 2001.

Dionne, E. J., Jr., and William Kristol, eds. *Bush v. Gore: The Court Cases and Commentary*. Washington: Brookings Institution Press, 2001.

Greenfield, Jeff. *"Oh, Waiter! One Order of Crow!": Inside the Strangest Presidential Election Finish in American History*. New York: G. P. Putnam's Sons, 2001.

Issacharoff, Samuel, Pamela S. Karlan, and Richard H. Pildes, eds. *When Elections Go Bad: The Law of Democracy and the Presidential Election of 2000*. New York: Foundation Press, 2001.

Lewis, Terry. *Conflict of Interest*. New York: Pinnacle Books, 1997.

Merzer, Martin, ed. *The* Miami Herald *Report: Democracy Held Hostage*. New York: St. Martin's Press, 2001.

Posner, Richard A. *Breaking the Deadlock: The 2000 Election— The Constitution and the Courts*. Princeton, New Jersey: Princeton University Press, 2001.

Sammon, Bill. *At Any Cost: How Al Gore Tried to Steal the Election*. Washington: Regnery Publishing, Inc., 2001.

Staff of *The Washington Post*. *Deadlock: The Inside Story of America's Closest Election*. New York: Public Affairs, 2001.

Tapper, Jake. *Down and Dirty: The Plot to Steal the Presidency*. Boston: Little, Brown and Company, 2001.

I also studied the day-to-day coverage of the recount in *The New York Times*, *The Washington Post*, the *Tallahassee Democrat*, the *Orlando Sentinel*, *The Palm Beach Post*, and *The Miami Herald*. I would like to acknowledge Frank Cerabino's thirteen-part series on the election, which was published in *The Palm Beach Post* in early 2001; John Mintz and Peter Slevin's June 1, 2001, report in *The Washington Post*, which first disclosed the shortcomings of the automatic recount; Marjorie Williams's analysis of the Gore-Clinton relationship in the July 2001 *Vanity Fair;* and David Barstow and Don Van Natta, Jr.'s, dissection of the Bush strategy on overseas absentee ballots in *The New York Times* of July 15, 2001. As a public service, a news researcher named Liz Donovan built an extraordinary archive of on-line resources regarding the 2000 election. That collection, at http://home.infi.net/~edonovan/behind/collect1.html, was of enormous help to me.

I have pre-existing relationships with several participants in this story, which readers may wish to consider in evaluating my judgments. In the mid-1980s, I became friends with Jack Corrigan and Ron Klain at Harvard Law School, where they were fellow students. For two years, Corrigan and I were roommates. Also during that time, I worked as a research assistant to Professor Laurence Tribe. In 1990, I became involved in a dispute with the federal government over my right to publish a book about my experiences as a prosecutor in the Iran-contra case. David Boies, then of Cravath, Swaine & Moore, agreed to have his firm represent me pro bono in the controversy.

Over nearly a decade, I have been fortunate to work with a superb, and blessedly stable, cast of journalists and publishers, who happen to be terrific people as well. At *The New Yorker,* David Remnick has always been an inspiration—first as friend, then as boss and friend. Dorothy Wickenden and Jeffrey Frank have long edited my work with skill and grace. My colleague Julie Tate provided extraordinary research assistance on this book. I offer thanks, too, to my friends at ABC News, with whom I shared so much of this story.

I am privileged, once again, to be published by Random House, where I bask in the support and protection offered by my editor, Ann Godoff. Sunshine Lucas gave the manuscript the kind of attention that's not supposed to exist in publishing anymore, and Veronica Windholz copyedited fast and well. I am also grateful to Beth Pearson and Carole Lowenstein, as well as to Liz Fogarty, Tom Perry, and Carol Schneider. But could it be that we all work so hard because we are afraid of getting in trouble with my agent, the great Esther Newberg?

This recount, of course, had a tangled legacy, but at least one good thing came out of it—a smashing if tardy eighth birthday celebration for Adam Toobin with his dad in Cooperstown. As for his ten-year-old sister, Ellen, may the dedication of this book inspire her to use her vote and her life to help build a better world. For guidance about this and everything else, Ellen could not do better than to look to her mom, Amy McIntosh, my partner, pal, and true love.

New York City
August 2001

INDEX

Aaronson, Burt, 13
ABC, 18, 19, 20, 21, 22
abortion, 60, 113, 183, 272
Abrams, Dan, 129
Ahmann, John, 221–22, 223
Allbaugh, Joe, 42, 47, 52, 94, 238–39, 273
Alper, Jill, 29, 31, 32
Altman, Jennifer, 221–22
Anstead, Harry, 232, 235
Apple, R. W., Jr., 38, 82, 272
"Arrive with Five" initiative, 169–70
Askew, Reubin, 112
Attie, Eli, 20, 270
Atwater, Lee, 96
Aufhauser, David, 96, 131, 273
Avram, Eric, 129
Azar, Alex, 184

Baker, James A., III:
    Bush's relationship with, 7–8, 53, 94, 238, 267, 273, 274
    Christopher compared with, 45–46, 52, 57, 133
    Christopher's meeting with, 39, 45–46, 52
    election-day activities of, 40–42
    at Florida Supreme Court hearings, 133, 134, 137, 230
    foresight of, 42, 47, 94, 132, 176
    Harris's meetings with, 70
    legal team of, 8, 33, 46, 48–49, 74, 76, 83, 85, 95–96, 99–100, 110, 111,
    127–28, 133, 153, 207, 208–10, 240–41, 246, 247, 256
    media operations of, 46, 110, 111, 126, 137, 207, 225, 256
    political background of, 40–41
    Republican effort led by, 42, 45–51, 52, 63, 94–97, 206–7, 208
    Republican support for, 8, 45, 48–49, 74, 76, 110, 120
    strategy of, 47–52, 53, 57, 85, 119, 127–28, 132, 137–38, 161–63, 181, 184–85, 193, 206–7, 256, 280
    Tallahassee headquarters of, 46–47, 53
    at U.S Supreme Court hearing, 254
Baker, Susan, 42
Baker Botts, 40, 207, 210
Baldick, Jackie, 22, 32
Baldick, Nick, 16, 18–19, 21–22, 32
ballots:
    absentee, 4, 78, 93, 96, 105, 113–14, 117, 124, 129–32, 170–71, 174–75, 176, 185, 196, 197–202, 207, 208–10, 224, 226, 229, 233–34, 240, 256, 273, 281
    "bulging" chads of, 86, 87, 161–62
    butterfly, 14–16, 28, 31, 33, 35, 39, 42, 54, 77, 81, 88, 168, 172, 173, 200, 234, 262
    "caterpillar," 172–73
    chads of, 28, 34, 85–86, 87, 135, 161–68, 217–18, 221–22, 236, 241, 278, 279
    design of, 13–14

ballots (*cont.*)
  dimpled (indented) chads of, 135, 166,
    167–68, 217–18, 236, 278
  disqualified, 33, 39, 169
  "hanging" chads of, 87, 88, 161–62,
    164–65, 241, 278, 279
  missing, 279
  name placement on, 13–15
  non-governmental scrutiny of, 6–7, 66,
    277–80
  provisional, 15
  recounts of, *see* recounts, ballot
  secrecy of, 199
  special instructions for, 15–16
Barnett, Martha, 32, 33
Bartlit, Fred, 210, 220
Bash, Jeremy, 98, 202, 203, 251, 268
Bauer, Bob, 98, 99
Baur, Katie, 190
Baxter, Ethel, 64–65
Beck, Phil, 210, 218–20, 221, 240–42,
    256
Beckstrom, Gus, 113–14
Berger, Mitchell, 34, 39, 97, 99, 120,
    195, 199, 202, 203, 210, 255, 256,
    268, 277
Berger Davis & Singerman, 97, 109, 127,
    138, 157, 162
Berra, Yogi, 189
Bible, 68, 129
Biden, Joe, 201
Bill of Rights, 183, 185
BlackBerry, 179, 227, 238, 252
Boczar, Jim, 59–60
Boies, David, 195–97, 200, 201, 242,
    245–46, 254–55
  Cult of (COB), 110
  Democratic "contest" pleaded by,
    180–81, 204–5, 210, 211–12, 213,
    216–17, 220, 221, 242
  Florida Supreme Court appearances
    of, 112, 113–14, 120, 124, 125,
    133, 134, 180, 195, 211, 230–31,
    232, 254, 257
  Gore's relationship with, 110, 111, 180
  law practice of, 106–7, 110–12, 276
  Tribe and, 257–58
  U.S. Supreme Court appearance of,
    257–58, 262
Boies, Jonathan, 112
Boies, Mary, 180–81
Boyd, Joseph, 112
Brace, Kimball, 217–18, 219
Bradley, Bill, 99
Brazile, Donna, 27, 82, 225–26, 227
Brennan, William, 261
Breyer, Stephen, 249, 250, 260, 261,
    264, 266
Bristow, Daryl, 207, 209
Brockovich, Erin, 54

"Brooks Brothers riot," 156, 179, 245
Broward County, Fla.:
  Buchanan's total in, 33
  canvassing board of, 147, 160–63,
    165, 188
  electoral process in, 6, 116–17
  Emergency Operations Center of, 161
  Harris's advisory opinion and, 92
  recount for, 39, 71–72, 83, 84, 92,
    101, 115, 116–17, 118, 137, 138,
    151, 160–63, 167, 168, 188, 236,
    278
  undervotes in, 39, 219, 236
  vote margin in, 19, 149, 162, 163,
    165–66, 176
Brown, Lisa, 211
Brown, Reg, 171, 190, 191
Brown v. Board of Education, 216
Buchanan, Pat:
  ballot placement of, 14
  Jewish antipathy to, 4, 15, 81
  Palm Beach County returns of, 4, 15,
    33, 35, 81, 88, 280–81
Burger, Warren, 182
Burton, Charles:
  Carpenter's influence on, 85–87, 90
  legal ruling solicited by, 73, 74–76,
    101, 102
  legal testimony of, 220–21
  on Palm Beach County canvassing
    board, 74–76, 77, 81, 82, 85–92,
    117, 164–67, 186–88, 228
  political background of, 77–78
Bush, George H., 41
Bush, George W.:
  acceptance speech of, 271
  administration of, 271–73, 280
  Baker's relationship with, 7–8, 53, 94,
    238, 267, 273, 274
  ballot placement of, 14
  bipartisanship of, 271–72
  conservatism of, 271–73
  Crawford, Tex. ranch of, 53, 119, 213
  Gore's phone calls to, 24–25, 268, 269
  media coverage of, 51, 213
  personal loyalty to, 10, 99, 257,
    273–75
  political campaign of (2000), 61, 96
  political legitimacy of, 49, 250–51,
    265, 271–73, 280–81
  transition team of, 51, 213, 238
  victory important to, 7–8, 53, 94,
    271–73
Bush, Jeb:
  Clinton's views on, 194
  Cuban-American support for, 146
  as governor, 6, 14, 32, 77, 113, 128,
    138, 189, 208–9
  gubernatorial campaign of (1994), 68,
    74

gubernatorial campaign of (1998), 60, 61, 74
judicial appointments of, 77, 113, 208–9
legal staff of, 62, 74, 75–76, 170–71, 176, 189–90, 198
"One Florida" initiative of, 169
political influence of, 6, 33, 76, 87, 95, 97, 115
school-choice initiative of, 171
Bush campaign:
headquarters of, 46–47, 53
management of, 10, 24, 42, 49, 50
media operations of, 46, 110, 111, 126, 137, 207, 225, 256
mobilization of, 8, 45, 48–49, 74, 76, 110, 120
post-election strategy of, 7–8, 44–45, 48, 74, 201, 271–72, 274
Bush v. Gore, 248, 265, 275
see also Supreme Court, U.S.
Butterworth, Bob, 92, 128, 161

Cardenas, Al, 62, 75, 76, 101, 146, 209
Carollo, Joe, 140, 148
Carpenter, Kerey, 72, 73–74, 84, 85–87, 90
Carroll, Jane, 160, 161, 162
Carvin, Michael, 96, 133, 134, 135, 231–32
Cass, Terre, 108, 123
Castro, Edward, 234, 235, 237
Castro, Fidel, 141–42
CBS, 18, 19, 20, 21, 22, 111, 225
Cepero, Evilio, 153
certificate of ascertainment, 190–91, 199
chads, *see* ballots
Cheney, Dick, 41, 44, 45, 53, 157, 269, 274
Cheney, Lynn, 41
Chiles, Lawton, 46–47, 59, 60, 98, 112, 113, 125, 208
Christopher, Warren:
Baker compared with, 45–46, 52, 57, 133
Baker's meeting with, 39, 45–46, 52
Gore's relationship with, 54, 55–57, 257
Harris's meetings with, 70–71
law firm of, 10, 11, 45–46, 106
political background of, 30, 34
at U.S. Supreme Court hearing, 213–14
Churchill, Winston S., 26
Clark, Nikki Ann, 202, 208–10, 229, 233–34, 240
Clinton, Bill:
Elián González case and, 143–44, 148–49

Florida recount as viewed by, 192–94, 197, 252
Gore's relationship with, 10, 192, 193–94
impeachment of, 8, 106, 192, 193, 194
legal team of, 96, 106
media coverage of, 194
pardons issued by, 192–93
political appointees of, 5, 274
political legacy of, 10
presidential campaign of (1992), 10, 37, 41, 140
presidential campaign of (1996), 19, 149, 173
Republican opposition to, 8, 45, 95, 99, 193
CNN, 73, 124, 225, 255, 267
Coelho, Tony, 10–11, 37, 44, 257
Coffey, Kendall, 34, 36, 39, 139–44, 150, 151, 154, 157, 210, 222, 277
Conflict of Interest (Lewis), 104
Congress, U.S., 44–45, 153, 206, 226, 276
Constitution, U.S., 35, 50–51, 100–101, 137, 181, 182, 183, 222, 227, 230–31, 246, 259–60, 264, 265, 266
Corrigan, Jack, 83–84, 89, 165, 244, 245, 254–55, 268
Cote, Denise, 166–67
Cravath, Swaine & Moore, 111–12
Crawford, Bob, 189
Cruz, Ted, 184

D'Alemberte, Sandy, 115, 128
Daley, Eleanor "Sis," 37
Daley, Richard J., 36–37, 54, 98
Daley, Richie, 37
Daley, William, 274
Clinton's relationship with, 192, 193, 194
in Democratic recount effort, 29, 30, 34, 37–38, 43, 51–52, 54–56, 57, 97–98, 103, 121, 139, 199, 227, 230, 239, 258
Gore's campaign managed by, 11, 17, 20, 22, 37–38, 268, 276
Gore's first concession speech and, 20, 23, 24, 26–27
Harris's meeting with, 71
political background of, 37–38, 97–98
at Tallahassee headquarters, 34
at U.S. Supreme Court hearings, 213–14, 258, 262
Danforth, John, 49–50, 95, 273
Daschle, Tom, 10
Database Technologies (DBT), 169
Data-Punch machines, 14
Daytona Beach, Fla., 113–14

death penalty, 113, 234, 235
DeGrandy, Miguel, 151, 154
DeLay, Tom, 179
Dellinger, Walter, 106, 257, 263, 274
Delray Beach, Fla., 3–4, 80–81
Democratic National Committee (DNC),
     31, 178, 226
Democratic National Convention (1992),
     270
Democratic National Convention (1996),
     111
Democratic Party:
   ballot placement of, 14
   corruption in, 44–45
   get-out-the-vote operations of, 3–4, 12,
     17
   as incumbent party, 8
   poll workers of, 3–4, 15–16
   Republican Party compared with, 201,
     271–72, 274
Devine, Tad, 27, 148, 150, 151, 226, 276
Dewey Square Group, 12, 16, 22
Diaz, Manny, 143, 144
Diaz-Balart, Lincoln, 143, 149, 153
Dion, Ed, 162
Division of Elections, Florida, 62–65,
     73–76, 85, 101
Dixon, Monica, 22, 30, 234
Dole, Robert, 145
Douglas, William O., 214
Douglass, Dexter, 47, 98, 105, 120, 121,
     133, 202–5, 210, 213, 247
Downs, Timothy, 28, 34, 44
Dugger, Ronnie, 178
Dukakis, Michael, 84
Duval County, Fla.:
   absentee ballots in, 170–71, 174–75
   African-American population of, 39,
     171–72, 173, 175, 201, 281
   canvassing board of, 172–75
   illegal votes in, 169
   overvotes in, 173
   recount of, 173–75
   undervotes in, 39, 171–72, 281
   vote margin in, 173, 174–75

Ebbeson, Anders, 59, 129, 185–86
Election Data Services, 217–18
elections:
   of 1876, 6, 195
   of 1960, 36–37, 275
   of 1968, 9
   of 1976, 112
   of 1981, 144–45
   of 1984, 27, 43–45, 275
   of 1988, 84
   of 1989, 27, 29
   of 1990, 86
   of 1992, 10, 37, 41, 140, 270
   of 1994, 27, 28, 60, 68, 74, 153

   of 1996, 19, 111, 113–14, 145, 148,
     149, 173
   of 1997, 141, 169
   of 1998, 27, 60–61, 74, 219–20
   of 2000, see presidential election of
     2000
   of 2002, 277
Electoral College:
   certificate of ascertainment sent to,
     190–91, 199
   electors designated for, 195–96
   Florida's votes in, 5, 18, 134, 137–38,
     190–91, 195, 206, 230–31, 265–66,
     276
   meeting of, 195, 204, 264, 265–66
   vote margin in, 5, 280
Ellis, John, 17
Enos, Tony, 14
Eskew, Carter, 17, 18, 27, 30, 54, 205,
     227, 239, 269, 276
Estrada, Miguel, 184, 273
Evans, Don, 24, 42, 49, 50, 239, 268,
     273
exit polls, 17, 18, 19, 20, 21, 39, 281

Fabiani, Mark, 16–17, 26, 33, 81, 98,
     119, 179, 226, 227, 252, 258
Fagan, Shawn, 184
Falcon, Willie, 140
Fanjul, Pepe and Alfy, 115
federalism, 48, 183, 185, 249, 257
Federalist Society, 74, 184
Feldman, Michael, 22–23
Fifth Amendment, 222
Flagler, Henry, 79
Flanigan, Tim, 184
Fleischer, Ari, 280
Florida:
   African-American population of, 17,
     39, 80, 168–72, 173, 175, 194, 201,
     226, 281
   ballot recounts in, see recounts, ballot
   canvassing boards of, 38, 46, 47, 63,
     72, 95, 103, 136, 147, 170, 278,
     279
   constitution of, 105
   county supervisors in, 65
   county vs. state electoral process in, 6,
     65
   electoral votes of, 5, 18, 134, 137–38,
     190–91, 195, 206, 230–31, 265–66,
     276
   legislature of, 60–61, 63, 137–38, 181,
     206, 215–16, 230–31, 259, 264,
     276, 277
   popular-vote margin in, 16–25, 29,
     52–53, 55–56, 63, 67, 72, 78, 79,
     88–89, 103, 114, 117, 128, 138,
     151, 176, 185, 187, 189, 196–97,
     198, 207, 232, 236, 255, 278–81

pro-Bush demonstrations in, 51,
    145–47, 152, 153–59, 179, 207,
    245, 252–53
pro-Gore demonstrations in, 79, 80,
    82, 193, 226, 252, 276
referendum in (1976), 112
Supreme Court of, *see* Supreme Court,
    Florida
see also specific counties
Florida Canvassing Election
    Commission, 188–89
Florio, Jim, 145
Folger, Lee and Julie, 248–49
Fourteenth Amendment, 50–51, 259–60,
    265, 266
Francisco, Noel, 184

Gallagher, Sean, 184
Garnett, Rick, 184
Gejdenson, Sam, 27
Geller, Joe, 150, 155–56
*George W. Bush v. the Palm Beach County
    Canvassing Board*, 215
Gingrich, Newt, 44–45
Ginsberg, Ben, 128, 208, 227, 267, 273
    at Florida Supreme Court hearing,
        133–34, 135, 137
    legal teams approved by, 95–96
    as recount specialist, 42–45, 46,
        48–49, 74, 94, 97, 109
Ginsberg, David, 178, 179
Ginsburg, Ruth Bader, 5, 249, 250, 260,
    262, 264, 266–67, 275
Glendening, Parris, 28
Glock, Robert, 234, 235, 237
Glover, Nat, 172
Goller, Leslie, 174
González, Delphin, 144
González, Elián, 141–44, 146, 148–49,
    153, 157
González, Juan Miguel, 142, 143
González, Lázaro, 142, 144
Goodman, Adam, 67
Gore, Al:
    advisers of, 53–57, 179–80, 199–202,
        257–58, 268–69, 276–77
    ballot placement of, 14
    Bush called by, 24–25, 268, 269
    Bush compared with, 7–8, 10, 54, 94,
        99, 257, 271–72, 275
    charisma lacked by, 10, 11, 98–99,
        224–26
    Christopher's relationship with, 54,
        55–57, 257
    Clinton compared with, 276
    Clinton's political legacy as burden to,
        10
    Clinton's relationship with, 192,
        193–94
    credibility of, 30, 31, 103, 224–25

    defeatism of, 229–30, 251–52
    Democratic support for, 110, 225–26,
        229–30
    establishment opinion as important to,
        7, 21, 30, 38, 82, 103, 120, 178,
        180, 201, 224–25, 230, 280
    family of, 16, 54, 178, 214, 269,
        275–76
    first concession speech of, 20–27, 41,
        193, 271
    intellectual approach of, 111, 177–78,
        197, 275, 276
    media coverage of, 118–20, 224–25
    op-ed piece of, 262, 268
    personal morality of, 201, 276
    post-election activities of, 275–76, 277
    recount strategy approved by, 53–57,
        177–81, 224–27
    Republican opposition to, 178–79
    second concession speech of, 5, 268,
        269–70, 271
    as "sore loser," 28–29, 31, 56–57, 103,
        226
    speeches of, 20–27, 41, 118–20, 205
    U.S. Supreme Court decisions as
        viewed by, 251–52, 257–58, 263,
        268, 269
    vice-presidential campaign of (1996),
        111
Gore, Tipper, 16, 54, 178
Gore campaign:
    African-American support for, 17, 226
    communications center of, 11, 19, 21
    defeatism of, 229–30, 233–34
    factions in, 17
    headquarters of, 21, 26–27
    legal team of, 32, 33–37, 48, 83, 95,
        97, 99–100, 110–11, 120–21, 122,
        127, 133, 152–53, 184, 210,
        226–27
    management of, 10–11, 17, 20, 22,
        37–38, 268, 276
    media operations of, 16–17, 30, 31, 33
    phone-bank operations of, 12, 16
    post-election strategy of, 7–8
    recount effort of, 30, 42, 51–52,
        55–57, 97, 139, 199, 201
Gore v. Harris, 248
"Government in the Sunshine" law, 104,
    242
Graham, Bob, 112
Gray, Hannah, 40
Greenberg Traurig, 33, 95
Griffin, Ben Hill, Jr., 58–59
Gunzburger, Suzanne, 160, 161
Gutierrez, Armando, 141, 142, 143–44,
    150

Hancock, Paul, 134
Harding, Major, 128, 231, 232, 235

Harris, George W., Jr., 59
Harris, Katherine, 58–76
  advisory opinions issued by, 72–76,
    89–93, 101, 136, 160–61, 164, 228
  "bring the election in for a landing"
    strategy of, 69–70, 71, 82, 102, 103,
    118, 187
  election certified by, 67, 69, 83, 93,
    101–9, 110, 114–18, 120–29,
    132–38, 147, 151, 152, 160, 171,
    175, 176, 180, 184, 185–91, 195,
    196, 202, 224, 228, 229, 234, 247,
    249–50
  as Florida secretary of state, 19, 29,
    58, 62–76, 128–29, 266,
    274–75
  Florida Supreme Court's ruling
    against, 124, 126–29, 130, 132–38,
    151, 185–86
  legal staff of, 33, 62–72, 129, 137
  Lewis's rulings and, 103–9, 110,
    114–18, 120–25, 202
  media coverage of, 63, 67, 70, 116–17,
    118, 188–89
  political background of, 58–62, 70
  recount as viewed by, 34, 57, 63–67,
    72–76
  Republican affiliation of, 58, 61–62,
    67, 69, 75–76, 84, 85, 86, 120–21,
    129, 187
  requests for extension rejected by,
    116–18
  staff of, 62–63
  as state senator, 60–61
  Stipanovich's influence on, 69–70, 73,
    76, 82, 102, 114, 118, 185–86, 187,
    188, 189, 260–61
  website of, 19, 29
Harry N. Jacobs v. the Seminole County
  Canvassing Board, 207
Harvest of Shame, 80
Hatch, Orrin, 201, 214
Hattaway, Doug, 98
Hayes, Rutherford B., 6, 195
Hengartner, Nicolas, 218–20, 221, 222,
  241
Henry V (Shakespeare), 12
Herron, Mark, 131–32, 170, 174
Hiaasen, Carl, 140
Hill, Anita, 201
Hill, Tony, 169–70
Hogan, Wayne, 175
Holland & Knight, 32, 33, 97
Homestead Air Force Base, 148, 277
House of Representatives, U.S., 44–45,
  153
Howard Hughes Medical Institute, 40
Hughes, Karen, 51, 130, 239
Hungar, Tom, 184
Hunger, Frank, 54, 199, 257

Hutton, Barbara, 79–80
Hyman, Lester, 3–4, 11
Hyman, Liz, 4, 11, 80
Illinois, 36–37, 168
Indiana, Eighth Congressional District
  race in (1984), 27, 43–45

Jackson, Jesse, 18, 79, 80, 82, 194, 208
Jackson, Robert, 275
Jacksonville, Fla., 170, 171–72
Jeffords, Jim, 272
Jimenez, Frank, 62, 73–75, 91, 95,
  170–71, 190, 191
Johnson, Jim, 239
Jones, Paula, 193

Kamen, Al, 178
Kantor, Mickey, 239
Kast, Ed, 62
Kean, Tom, 144–45
Kearney, Deborah, 67, 104–5
Kelley, Bill, 184
Kennedy, Anthony, 215, 249, 259, 260,
  262, 264–65
Kennedy, Edward M., 78
Kennedy, Jim, 269
Kennedy, John F., 36–37, 275
Kennedy, Robert F., 9
King, James Lawrence, 150
King, Lawrence D., 149–50, 154,
  156–57, 158
King, Martin Luther, Jr., 172
Kitchen, E. C. Deeno, 210–11, 217
Klain, Ron:
  contempt-of-court charge against, 253,
    254–57
  Democratic recount initiative
    organized by, 28, 29–34, 54, 55, 93,
    98, 100, 102, 103, 106, 110,
    119–20, 122, 138, 152–53, 157,
    165, 195–202, 229, 245–47, 251,
    253, 268
  Gore's campaign managed by, 10–11,
    99
  as Gore's communications director, 11,
    21, 27
  Gore's relationship with, 10–11, 177,
    179–80, 233, 257–58, 268
  Hyman's call to, 5, 9
  law practice of, 9–10, 276–77
  recount deadline determined by,
    195–97
Klein, Joel, 106
Klein, Ron, 15
Klock, Joe, 114–17, 122, 204, 217, 228,
  260–61
Knight Ridder newspapers, 173, 278–79
Korge, Chris, 150
Kristol, Bill, 130
Kuehne, Benedict, 83, 277

LaBarga, Jorge, 92, 93, 162, 164, 166
Lake County, Fla., 66
Lake Ida Shopping Plaza, 3–5, 8
Lang, David, 202–3
Langton, Mark, 173
lawsuits:
    on absentee ballots, 170–71, 175, 200,
        202, 208–10, 226, 229, 233–34,
        240
    on disqualified ballots, 33, 39
    federal vs. state, 47–48, 49, 95, 99
    media coverage of, 104
    political dangers of, 28–29, 193–94,
        226
    on recounts, 28–29, 34–37, 39,
        47–49, 53, 54, 67, 83, 92–93,
        99–101, 119, 206
Leahy, David, 148, 149, 150, 151, 152,
    153–57, 158, 244
Leahy, Patrick, 214
Lee, Robert W., 160, 161, 163, 174
Lehane, Chris, 18, 27, 30, 80–81, 98,
    119, 179, 252
Lehr, Myriam, 149–52, 158
Leon County Circuit Court, 202–3, 208
LePore, Theresa:
    as Palm Beach County supervisor of
        elections, 12–16, 77, 78–79, 82, 84,
        90, 91, 165, 166, 167, 172, 200
    political background of, 13–14
    recounts supervised by, 78–79, 90, 91,
        92, 93, 122, 188, 197
Lewinsky, Monica, 45, 115, 192
Lewis, R. Fred, 231, 232, 234, 235
Lewis, Terry:
    first ruling of (Lewis I), 103–9, 110,
        123
    Klain's contempt-of-court charge
        before, 253, 254–57
    legal background of, 203
    Martin County challenges heard by,
        229, 233–34
    novel written by, 104, 208
    recount supervised by, 240–57
    second ruling of (Lewis II), 120–25,
        126, 128, 136–37, 151, 202
Lieberman, Joe:
    absentee ballots as viewed by, 131–32,
        170, 175, 176, 199, 226
    campaign plane of, 29, 31–32
    defeatism of, 229–30
    Klain's contempt-of-court charge and,
        256–57
    private vs. public statements of, 56,
        131–32, 226
Lincoln, Abraham, 269
Lucas, Richard, 98

McBride, Andrew, 184
McCain, David, 112

McCain, John, 96
McCloskey, Frank, 44
McIntyre, Richard, 44
McKay, Ben, 67, 69, 188–89
McPherson v. Blacker, 230
Magluta, Sal, 140
Manatee County, Fla., 64
Manning, John, 50, 184
Marais, Laurentius, 221
Markey, Ed, 10
Marshall, Goody, 214
Marshall, Thurgood, 214
Martin County, Fla., 197–202, 207, 229,
    234–35, 276
Martinez, Bob, 203
Meek, Kendrick, 169–70
Meet the Press, 131–32, 226
"Memorandum to All Supervisors of
    Elections" (Roberts), 65–66
Meros, George, 171
Meyers, Andrew, 162
Miami, Fla.:
    Cuban-American community in,
        141–49, 153–59
    mayoral race of (1997), 141, 169
    political situation in, 139–40
Miami-Dade County, Fla.:
    Buchanan's votes in, 33
    canvassing board for, 147–59, 188,
        212, 217, 232, 245
    Clark Center meeting in, 152, 153–59,
        179, 245
    disputed ballots requested from,
        211–13, 217, 232, 243
    electoral process in, 6, 116–17
    recount for, 39, 71–72, 83, 102, 115,
        116–17, 118, 137, 138, 147–59,
        160, 180, 188, 199–200, 222, 231,
        235–36, 243, 244–45, 252–57, 278
    undervotes in, 39, 152, 154, 157, 219,
        231, 232, 243, 244–45, 252
    vote margin in, 19, 149, 176, 196,
        197, 199–200
Miami Herald, 278–79
Middlebrooks, Donald M., 100–101,
    122, 183, 206, 246
Montgomery, Bob, 83, 84, 90
Morehouse, David, 23–24
Morgan, Lucy, 68
Mortham, Sandra, 60–61, 70
Moya, Miguel, 140
Muchachos, Los, 140, 147
Mullaney, Rick, 175
Murrow, Edward R., 80

Nader, Ralph, 275
Nashville *Tennessean,* 177–78
Nassau County, Fla., 196, 197, 199, 207,
    228, 236
National Enquirer, 145

NBC, 18, 19, 20, 21, 22, 267
Newman, Dennis, 165, 166
Newton, John, 98, 120, 202, 209
Newton, Wayne, 159
New Yorker, 178
New York Times, 33, 38, 39, 54, 82, 86,
    120, 133, 153, 158, 176, 178, 224,
    262, 272, 279, 281
Nides, Tom, 199
Nixon, Richard M., 216, 275
Nixon, United States v., 216
North, Oliver, 96, 207

O'Connor, Sandra Day, 184, 215,
    248–49, 261–62, 264–65
Olson, Barbara, 214
Olson, Theodore, 49, 50, 95, 97, 100,
    181–82, 184, 206, 214, 215, 248,
    259–60, 261, 262–63, 267, 273–74
O'Melveney & Myers, 9, 11, 45–46, 106,
    276–77
Operation Pedro Pan, 141–42
Opperman, Vanessa, 24
Orlando Sentinel, 66
Osborne, Kathy, 45–46

Palm Beach, Fla., 79–80
Palm Beach County, Fla., 77–93
    African-American population of, 80
    ballot used in, 14–16, 28, 31, 33, 35,
        39, 42, 54, 77, 81, 88, 168, 172,
        173, 200, 234, 262
    canvassing board of, 33, 73–92, 102,
        117, 147, 164–68, 185, 186–88,
        212, 217, 228, 232
    Democratic Party of, 3–5, 80–81, 84
    disputed ballots requested from,
        211–13, 217, 232
    electoral process in, 6, 8, 116–17
    Emergency Operations Center of,
        91–92, 93, 161, 186–88
    Harris's advisory opinion and, 72–76,
        89–93, 164
    Jewish population of, 4, 15, 80, 81
    lawsuits against, 28–29, 34–37, 39,
        54, 67
    media coverage of, 15
    overvotes in, 33, 35, 75, 81, 88
    popular-vote margin in, 36, 79, 85, 86,
        88–89, 199–200, 207
    recount for, 39, 71–76, 81–93, 101,
        102, 115, 118, 121, 122, 126, 137,
        138, 151, 160, 163, 164–68,
        185–88, 199–200, 218–20, 231,
        235–36, 278, 279
    undervotes in, 33, 35, 39, 75, 81, 86,
        167, 218–20, 221, 231, 232, 236
    vote margin in, 149, 166, 176, 196–97
    voter complaints in, 3–5, 9, 12–13, 15,
        31, 80–81

Palm Beach Post, 86, 167
Pariente, Barbara, 135, 137, 231, 232,
    234, 235
Pataki, George, 255
Patton Boggs, 45
Penelas, Alex, 148–51, 277
Penn, Bob, 257
Perez-Roura, Armando, Jr., 146–47
Perez-Roura, Armando, Sr., 146–47, 153
Perot, Ross, 41
Pincus, Andy, 251
Podesta, John, 192, 194, 252
Portman, Rob, 153
Post, Jim, 174–75
postmarks, on absentee ballots, 96,
    131–32
presidential election of 2000:
    cast of characters in, xiii–xvi
    certification of, 67, 69, 83, 93, 101–9,
        110, 114–18, 120–29, 132–38, 147,
        151, 152, 160, 171, 175, 176, 180,
        184, 185–91, 195, 196, 202, 224,
        228, 229, 234, 247, 249–50
    chronology of, xvii–xxi
    closing of polls for, 5
    constitutional crisis in, 182, 246
    democratic principles in, 194, 214,
        250–51, 269, 280–81
    election of 1876 compared with, 6
    electoral-vote margin in, 5, 280
    final result in, 6–7
    Florida recount in, *see* recounts, ballot
    fraud as issue in, 114, 119
    legal basis of, 5–6, 30, 152–53, 193,
        197, 214, 281
    as political process, 5–6, 51–52, 101,
        152–53, 193–94, 197, 249, 280–81
    popular-vote margin in, 12, 16–25, 30,
        39, 194, 275, 280–81
    post-election period of, 5–6
    U.S. Supreme Court's decisions on, 6,
        42, 48, 92, 176, 181–85, 206, 249,
        258, 263, 265, 266, 275, 281

Quince, Peggy, 113, 135, 232, 234, 235

Racicot, Marc, 153, 225, 255
Radio Mambi, 146–47, 153
Raines, Howell, 263
Rawls, Wendell, 178
Reagan, Ronald, 41, 46, 144, 275
Recount Primer, The (Young, Downs and
    Sautter), 28, 34, 44
recounts, ballot:
    automatic, 72–73, 78–79, 119, 196
    broad vs. restrictive, 72–73, 90,
        161–62, 167–68, 278, 279–80
    "contests" in, 102–3, 124–25, 180–81,
        201–2, 204–5, 207, 208, 210–13,
        216–23, 228–29, 231, 235, 242

"counting claims" in, 199–200
counting teams for, 163, 166–67
deadlines for, 101–9, 114–18, 120–25,
    132–38, 147, 154, 171, 175, 184,
    185–88, 195–97, 204, 243, 265–66,
    268
Democratic support for, 27–34, 48,
    97–98, 187–88, 245–46
"equal protection" issue in, ix, 50–51,
    100–101, 185, 259–60, 262, 265,
    266, 273
extensions for, 116–18, 186–88
Florida law on, 22, 23, 29, 35–36, 50,
    63, 64, 65–67, 70, 71, 72–73, 101,
    126–27, 135–37, 160, 171,
    230–31
Florida Supreme Court's approval of,
    152, 154, 164, 166, 176, 182, 186,
    188, 211, 212, 230–57, 264
Herron memo on, 131–32, 170, 174
intentional delays in, 204–5, 220,
    228–29
judicial supervision of, 240–53
late returns in, 108–9, 114–18
lawsuits on, 28–29, 34–37, 39, 47–49,
    53, 54, 67, 83, 92–93, 99–101, 119,
    206
machine, 34, 36, 50, 52–53, 55–57,
    63–67, 78–79, 119, 135, 245, 261
mandatory, 22, 29, 34
manual, 35–36, 37, 50, 56, 70, 84–93,
    100–103, 113–20, 121, 126, 135,
    137, 149–52, 158, 160, 161, 173,
    216–17, 221–22, 223, 236–53, 273,
    278
media coverage of, 38, 55, 66, 73, 84,
    103, 130, 131–32, 180, 237,
    277–80
observers of, 84–85, 154, 165–66,
    186, 239–40
of overvotes, 33, 35, 75, 81, 88, 173,
    278–79
partial results in, 253, 254–57
"principled," 165, 166
"protests" in, 29, 35–36, 71–72, 102,
    103
public opinion on, 103, 124–25,
    224–25
recanvasses vs., 28
Republican opposition to, 47–49, 50,
    73–76, 83, 85, 90–92, 94, 187–88,
    204, 246, 280
Roberts memo on, 65–66
safe-harbor provision and, 195–96,
    243
"selective," 50–52
standards for, 27–28, 84–92, 161–68,
    175, 176, 219, 241–42, 243, 246,
    259, 260, 262, 278
statewide, 38, 45, 46, 50–52, 56, 94,

    118–20, 194, 197, 198, 201, 223,
    225, 232, 236–57, 264, 278–79
statistical analysis of, 160, 218–21
"sunshine standard" for, 85–86
tally sheets in, 29
time as factor in, 36, 70, 82, 93,
    101–3, 195, 204–5, 213, 220,
    228–29, 235, 236–37, 243
of undervotes, 33, 35, 39, 75, 81, 86,
    152, 154, 157, 167, 171–72,
    218–20, 221, 231, 232, 236–37,
    243, 244–45, 252, 260, 264, 278,
    281
U.S. Supreme Court's stay of, 246,
    247, 248–55, 258–69, 278, 281
recusal motions, 208–10, 234, 240
Rehnquist, William H.:
    as chief justice, 183, 214–15, 228,
        248, 259, 263–64
    Clinton's views on, 194
    legal background of, 182–83
Reno, Janet, 10, 140
Republican National Committee (RNC),
    45
Republican National Convention (2000),
    61
Republican Party:
    ballot placement of, 14
    Clinton's policies opposed by, 8, 45,
        95, 99, 193
    conservative wing of, 44–45, 48, 74,
        201
    Democratic Party compared with, 201,
        271–72, 274
    political influence of, 44–45, 61–62,
        85–87, 90, 153
Rhodes, Randi, 15
Ricchetti, Steve, 193
Richard, Barry, 95–96, 105, 133, 204,
    205, 208, 209, 212, 217, 220, 228,
    229, 231–32, 240
Rizzo, Frank, 43
Roberts, Carol, 81, 82, 88–90, 92
Roberts, Clay, 62, 63, 64, 65–66, 67,
    70–71, 72, 73, 76, 77, 187, 188,
    189
Roberts, John G., 184, 273
Roberts, Julia, 54
Robinson, Jeffrey, 211, 256
Rogow, Bruce, 83, 84, 92–93, 122, 164
Roseborough, Teresa, 211, 251
Rosenberg, Robert, 163
Ros-Lehtinen, Ileana, 149, 153
Rove, Darby, 51
Rove, Karl, 42, 51, 54, 238, 267
Russell, Leon, 104
Russert, Tim, 131

Safire, William, 86
St. Petersburg Times, 68

Sandler, Joe, 31, 32, 98
Sasso, John, 84
Sauerbrey, Ellen, 28
Sauls, N. Sanders:
  ballots requested by, 211–13, 217,
    232, 243
  decision rendered by, 228–29
  Democratic appeal against, 212, 216,
    229, 235–36, 240
  Democratic "contest" heard by, 202–3,
    207, 208, 210–13, 216–23, 228–29,
    231, 235
  legal background of, 203–4, 209, 212
  media coverage of, 204
  Republican defense before, 204, 205,
    207, 210, 212–13, 220–23, 228,
    261
  witnesses before, 216–23
Sautter, Chris, 28, 34, 36, 38–39, 44
Scalia, Antonin, 215, 248, 250–51, 263,
  266–67, 275
Schwarzkopf, H. Norman, 41, 130
Seligman, Nicole, 106
Seminole County, Fla., 197–202, 207,
  208–10, 229, 234–35, 240, 276
Shakespeare, William, 12
Sharpton, Al, 266
Shaw, Leander, Jr., 128, 232, 235
Shrum, Robert, 17, 18, 27, 30, 54, 205,
  227, 239, 269, 276
Simpson, Alan, 201
Simpson, O. J., 213
60 Minutes, 224–25
Smith, Chesterfield, 32, 33
Smith, Craig, 257
Smith, Dorrance, 129–30, 225
Smith, Ralph "Bubba," 170–71, 175, 202
Socialist Worker Party, 38–39
Souter, David, 249, 250, 260, 261, 262,
  264, 266, 275
Spargo, Tom, 222
Specter, Arlen, 145, 201
Spencer, Tom, 151
Squier, Bob, 257
Stafford, John, 172–73
Stahl, Lesley, 224–25
states' rights, 48, 100, 183, 184, 215,
  257, 261–62
Steel, Hector & Davis, 33, 97, 114–15
Steinberg, Mark, 98
Steinbrenner, George, 112
Stengel, Casey, 11
Stevens, John Paul, 249, 250, 262, 264,
  266
Stipanovich, Heather, 189
Stipanovich, J. M. "Mac":
  Harris influenced by, 69–70, 73, 76,
    82, 102, 114, 118, 185–86, 187,
    188, 189, 260–61
  political background of, 68–69

recounts as viewed by, 71–72, 73, 76,
    91
Stipanovich, Mary, 189
Stoessel, Mary Ann, 249
Stone, Nydia, 145, 147
Stone, Robert, 179
Stone, Roger, 144–45, 147, 153
Stowe, Matt, 184
Strauss, David, 106
Streett, Graham, 23
Strip Tease (Hiaasen), 140
Suarez, Xavier, 141, 148
Sukhia, Ken, 68
Sullivan, Brendan V., Jr., 207
Sullivan, David, 165
Summers, Glen, 184
Supreme Court, Florida:
  Democratic appointees to, 46–47,
    112–13, 176, 234
  draft opinions of, 133–34
  election-law rulings of, 112, 113–14,
    181, 183–84, 215–16, 227–28,
    230–31, 235, 237, 241–42, 243
  Florida legislature vs., 137–38, 181,
    215–16, 230–31, 259, 264
  Harris enjoined by, 124, 126–29, 130,
    132–38, 151, 185–86
  Klock's request to, 117, 122, 126
  legal preparations by, 125–26
  Lewis's rulings appealed to, 106–7,
    110, 136–37
  media coverage of, 132–33
  recount allowed by, 152, 154, 164,
    166, 176, 182, 186, 188, 211, 212,
    230–57, 264
  reputation of, 112–13, 125, 275
  Rogow's lawsuit before, 92–93, 122,
    126, 164
  Sauls's decision appealed to, 212, 216,
    229, 235–36, 240
  U.S. Supreme Court's oversight of,
    181, 215–16, 227–28, 230–31, 235,
    237, 246, 249, 259, 260, 261–62,
    263
Supreme Court, U.S.:
  audiotaped proceedings of, 214–15
  Bush's writs of certiorari recognized by,
    181–85, 213–16, 227–28
  Clinton's appointees to, 5
  conservative vs. liberal factions of,
    182–83, 216, 260
  dissenting opinions in, 250–51,
    263–67
  Florida Supreme Court's decisions
    examined by, 181, 215–16, 227–28,
    230–31, 235, 237, 246, 249, 259,
    260, 261–62, 263
  law clerks of, 181, 184, 241, 263–64
  opinions rendered by, ix, 227–28,
    263–67

oral arguments before, 182, 215–16, 248, 258–63
per curiam decisions of, 227–28, 263–67
presidential election of 2000 decided by, 6, 42, 48, 92, 176, 181–85, 206, 249, 258, 263, 265, 266, 275, 281
recount stay issued by, 246, 247, 248–55, 258–69, 278, 281
Republican appointees to, 113, 182–83
Sweeney, John, 153, 156

Tabuteau, Jean-Claude, 3
Tallahassee Democrat, 233
Taylor, Kristin Clark, 208
Terrell, Irv, 210, 222
Terwilliger, George, 50, 95, 97
Texas, 135, 168, 271
Thanksgiving Day (2000), 158–59, 166–67, 180–81
"Thanksgiving stuffing," 176, 185, 196, 197, 200–201
This Week, 130
Thomas, Clarence, 10, 201, 214, 215, 248, 261, 263
Tilden, Samuel J., 6, 195
Today, 42–43, 45
Tompkins, Warren, 96
Tribe, Laurence, 92, 100, 106, 184, 215, 229, 257–58, 260
Trump, Donald, 145
Tutwiler, Margaret, 95, 145, 273

Unger, Jason, 171
United States v. Nixon, 216
USA Today, 173, 278–79

Vlasto, Chris, 129
Vogel, Robert L., 113–14
Volusia County, Fla.:
canvassing board of, 147
recount for, 39, 71–72, 83, 102, 104, 105, 115, 116, 236
sheriff elections of (1996), 113–14
undervotes in, 236
vote margin in, 19–22, 38–39, 63, 165–66
voters:
African-American, 39, 168–72, 173, 175, 194, 201, 266–67, 281
complaints by, 3–5, 9, 12–13, 15, 31, 80–81
identification numbers for, 198
incompetent, 15, 175
intent of, 85–86, 87, 113–14, 161–62, 167–68, 200, 211, 231, 237, 241, 243, 280–81

lists of, 169
logic and accuracy tests for, 78–79
military personnel as, 96, 129–32, 197, 200–201, 224
votes:
equality of, ix, 50–51, 53, 100–101, 185
illegal, 169
statistical reallocation of, 35, 55
uncounted, 38, 223, 231
see also ballots
voting machines:
complaints about, 4
examinations of, 29
optical scanners in, 64, 65, 66, 218–19, 262
punch-card system for, 14, 77, 87, 154–55, 178, 216, 217–22, 262
vote tabulations by, 72–76, 90, 113–14, 121, 161–62, 168, 217–22
Votomatic machines, 14

Walker, Helgi, 184
Wallace, Mark, 83, 85, 186
Washington Post, 98, 178, 194
Waters, Craig, 125–26, 127, 136, 237
Weldon, Curt, 98
Wells, Charles, 125, 128, 134, 230, 232, 234, 235, 246
Westmoreland, William, 111
Wexler, Robert, 15
White, Byron, 10, 214
Whitewater investigation, 193
Whitman, Christine Todd, 225
Whouley, Michael:
in Democratic recount effort, 11, 12, 54, 83, 84, 165, 180, 199, 201, 254–55
election-day activities of, 16–18, 21–24, 27, 29
Gore's first concession speech stopped by, 21–24
political background of, 11–12
Wilder, Douglas, 27, 29
Will, George F., 214

Yarbo, Jeff, 22–23
Young, John Hardin, as recount specialist, 27–29, 31, 34, 36, 38–39, 42, 44, 66, 83, 154, 156, 157, 161–62, 163, 165, 166, 173, 243–44, 245, 279

Zack, Stephen, 210, 217, 221–22, 234
Zellner, Natalie, 12–13
Zoellick, Robert, 52, 94–95, 273

ABOUT THE AUTHOR

JEFFREY TOOBIN is a staff writer at *The New Yorker,* the legal analyst for ABC News, and the author of the critically acclaimed bestsellers *A Vast Conspiracy: The Real Story of the Sex Scandal That Nearly Brought Down a President* and *The Run of His Life: The People v. O. J. Simpson.* He served as an assistant United States attorney in Brooklyn and as an associate counsel in the office of independent counsel Lawrence E. Walsh—which provided the basis for his first book, *Opening Arguments: A Young Lawyer's First Case—United States v. Oliver North.* He is a magna cum laude graduate of Harvard Law School. Toobin lives in New York City with his wife and two children.